Leading Systemic School Improvement Series
...helping change leaders transform entire school systems

This Rowman & Littlefield Education series provides change leaders in school districts with a collection of books written by prominent authors with an interest in creating and sustaining whole-district school improvement. It features young, relatively unpublished authors with brilliant ideas, as well as authors who are cross-disciplinary thinkers.

Whether an author is prominent or relatively unpublished, the key criterion for a book's inclusion in this series is that it must address an aspect of creating and sustaining systemic school improvement. For example, books from members of the business world, developmental psychology, and organizational development are good candidates as long as they focus on creating and sustaining whole-system change in school district settings; books about building-level curriculum reform, instructional methodologies, and team communication, although interesting and helpful, are not appropriate for the series unless they discuss how these ideas can be used to create whole-district improvement.

Since the series is for practitioners, highly theoretical or research-reporting books aren't included. Instead, the series provides an artful blend of theory and practice—in other words, books based on theory and research but written in plain, easy-to-read language. Ideally, theory and research are artfully woven into practical descriptions of how to create and sustain systemic school improvement. The series is subdivided into three categories:

Why Systemic School Improvement Is Needed and Why It's Important. This is the *why*. Possible topics within this category include the history of systemic school improvement; the underlying philosophy of systemic school improvement; how systemic school improvement is different from school-based improvement; and the driving forces of standards, assessments, and accountability and why systemic improvement can respond effectively to these forces.

The Desirable Outcomes of Systemic School Improvement. This is the *what*. Possible topics within this category include comprehensive school reform models scaled up to create whole-district improvement; strategic alignment; creating a high-performance school system; redesigning a school system as a learning organization; unlearning and learning mental models; and creating an organization design flexible and agile enough to respond quickly to unanticipated events in the outside world.

How to Create and Sustain Systemic School Improvement. This is the *how*. Possible topics within this category include methods for redesigning entire school systems; tools for navigating complex change; ideas from the "new sciences" for creating systemic change; leadership methods for creating systemic change; evaluating the process and outcomes of systemic school improvement; and financing systemic school improvement.

The series editor, Dr. Francis M. Duffy, can be reached at 301-854-9800 or fmduffy@earthlink.net.

Leading Systemic School Improvement Series
Edited by Francis M. Duffy

1. Francis M. Duffy. *Moving Upward Together: Creating Strategic Alignment to Sustain Systemic School Improvement.* 2004.
2. Agnes Gilman Case. *How to Get the Most Reform for Your Reform Money.* 2004.
3. Linda Darling-Hammond et al. *Instructional Leadership for Systemic Change: The Story of San Diego's Reform.* 2005.
4. Rita Schweitz and Kim Martens. *Future Search in School District Change: Connection, Community, and Results.* 2005.
5. Scott Thompson. *Spirituality and Public School Improvement.* 2005.
6. Francis M. Duffy. *Power, Politics, and Ethics in School Districts: Dynamic Leadership for Systemic Change.* 2005.
7. Merrelyn Emery. *The Future of Schools: How Communities and Staff Can Transform Their School Districts.* 2006.
8. Robert T. Hess and James W. Robinson. *Priority Leadership: Generating School and District Improvement through Systemic Change.* 2006.
9. Francis M. Duffy and Patti L. Chance. *Strategic Communication During Whole System Change: Advice and Guidance for School District Leaders and PR Specialists.* 2006.

Strategic Communication During Whole-System Change

Advice and Guidance for School District Leaders and PR Specialists

Francis M. Duffy
Patti L. Chance

Leading Systemic School Improvement, No. 9

Rowman & Littlefield Education
Lanham, Maryland • Toronto • Plymouth, UK
2007

Published in the United States of America
by Rowman & Littlefield Education
A Division of Rowman & Littlefield Publishers, Inc.
A wholly owned subsidiary of The Rowman & Littlefield Publishing Group, Inc.
4501 Forbes Boulevard, Suite 200, Lanham, Maryland 20706
www.rowmaneducation.com

Estover Road
Plymouth PL6 7PY
United Kingdom

Copyright © 2007 by Francis M. Duffy and Patti L. Chance

All rights reserved. No part of this publication may be reproduced, stored in a retrieval system, or transmitted in any form or by any means, electronic, mechanical, photocopying, recording, or otherwise, without the prior permission of the publisher.

British Library Cataloguing in Publication Information Available

Library of Congress Cataloging-in-Publication Data

Duffy, Francis M. (Francis Martin), 1949–
  Strategic communication during whole system change : advice and guidance for school district leaders and PR specialists / Francis M. Duffy, Patti L. Chance.
    p. cm.— (Leading systemic school improvement)
  Includes bibliographical references.
  ISBN-13: 978-1-57886-530-7 (cloth : alk. paper)
  ISBN-10: 1-57886-530-1 (cloth : alk. paper)
  ISBN-13: 978-1-57886-531-4 (pbk. : alk. paper)
  ISBN-10: 1-57886-531-X (pbk. : alk. paper)
    1. Educational change—United States. 2. Communication in education—United States. I. Chance, Patti L., 1955– II. Title.
  LB2817.3.D843 2007
  371.2–dc22   2006021860

∞ ™ The paper used in this publication meets the minimum requirements of American National Standard for Information Sciences—Permanence of Paper for Printed Library Materials, ANSI/NISO Z39.48-1992. Manufactured in the United States of America.

To my first grandson, Logan Paul Duffy—I loved you since the day I found out you were on the way, and I love you even more now that you've arrived.

FMD

To Ed, whose work on visionary leadership has continued to inspire me!

PLC

Contents

Acknowledgments	ix
Prologue	xi

Section 1: Navigating Whole-System Change in School Districts: What Change Leaders and School PR Specialists Need to Know to Support the Journey ... 1

1	Strategic Communication	3
2	Why Whole-System Change Is Needed: The Topography of Whole-System Change and a Compass to Navigate It	17
3	A Change Leader's Guide to Shaping a School District's Future	37
4	How to Transform an Entire School District: A Change Navigation Protocol for School Systems	57

Section 2: How Strategic Communication and School Public Relations Can Support Whole-System Change in School Districts ... 93

5	Public Relations in Times of Great Change: A Systems Perspective	95
6	Establishing Relationships and Building Trust to Facilitate School District Improvement	113
7	Creating School District Renewal Through a Shared Vision	129
8	Changing Minds and Hearts: A Challenge for Strategic Communication	139
9	Power, Politics, and Ethics: Dynamic Leadership for Systemic Change in School Districts	157

Section 3: Voices From the Field 169

Essay 1: Communicating with Key Stakeholders to Enable Strategic Change 171
Marilyn Saltzman

Essay 2: Finding and Engaging the "Influentials": Effective School Public Relations During Times of Great Change 183
Barbara M. Hunter

Essay 3: The Role of a School Board in Communicating Change in Front of and Behind the Camera 193
Anne L. Bryant

Essay 4: The Role of School Public Relations: Bringing Order Out of Chaos 203
Sylvia Soholt

Essay 5: Community Involvement in Decatur's Journey Toward Excellence 213
Sunni Lee and Charles M. Reigeluth

Epilogue: Communicating in Times of Great Change 233

About the Authors 247

Acknowledgments

Those of you who have written books understand what I'm about to say. Books don't get written without help, and this help comes in an assortment of forms.

First, I would like to thank Dr. Patti Chance for her willingness to collaborate with me in writing this book. The book could not have been completed without her knowledge and expertise.

Books also don't get written without publishing contracts, and publishing contracts don't get offered unless the editorial director has confidence in a book. I'd like to thank Dr. Thomas Koerner, vice president and editorial director of Rowman & Littlefield Education, for his confidence in this book.

Section 3 of this book contains five essays written by six busy professionals (one essay was coauthored). Thanks to Marilyn Saltzman, Barbara Hunter, Anne Bryant, Sylvia Soholt, Sunni Lee, and Charles Reigeluth for their essays. Their essays added the voice of experience to the book that enriched and deepened the content that Dr. Chance and I provided in sections 1 and 2 of the book.

Prologue

Whole-system change in school districts does not focus soley on individual school buildings, instructional programs, or supporting services; that kind of change is called piecemeal change. Whole-system change does not focus solely on making small improvements over time; that kind of change is called incremental change or continuous improvement. Whole-system change, instead, focuses on making simultaneous fundamental changes in three key sets of organizational variables that affect a school system's overall performance. We call these sets of variables "change-paths": Path 1—improve a district's relationship with stakeholders in the external environment; Path 2—improve a district's core and supporting work processes; and Path 3—improve a district's internal social infrastructure. This kind of change is called transformational whole-system change and it creates great change in a school district and its community.

Times of great change in school districts require strategic communication with internal and external stakeholders, including using school public relations tools and techniques. Strategic communication is needed to build the political support required to launch a systemwide change process in a school district and carry that process through to completion. Strategic communication is also required to keep a systemwide change effort on the course marked by a district's strategic framework (which includes its mission, vision, and strategic goals). This book provides theoretical and practical advice and guidance to district-based change leaders and school public relations (PR) specialists on how they can lead and support their district's transformation journey by engaging in strategic communication.

Readers should not expect a description of strategic communication and school public relations tools and techniques. Instead, they will find information about what change leaders and school public relations specialists need to know about why whole-district change is needed and about how they can support that process through strategic communication.

The information presented in section 1 creates the context for the remainder of the book. This information answers two important questions your colleagues and community members will have when they are faced with the prospect of creating and sustaining whole-system change in your school district: "Why do we need to do this?" followed quickly by "How do we do this?"

In chapter 1, you will learn about strategic communication—what it is and how you can incorporate strategic communication in your change process. Chapter 2 provides you with an in-depth exposition of a contemporary rationale for why whole-system change is needed in school districts. Chapter 3 expands on the rationale found in chapter 2 by providing advice and guidance on shaping the future of school systems. Then, in chapter 4, you will find a summary of a special change navigation protocol designed specifically to help change leaders create and sustain whole-system change in their school districts.

The context provided in section 1 creates a foundation for describing specific ways in which strategic communication concepts and tools can be used during times of great change. Examples of specific applications of strategic communication are found in section 2.

Chapter 5 embeds school public relations within the concept of school districts as systems. Chapter 6 focuses on using school public relations and strategic communication to build relationships and trust, two dynamics that are critical for the success of a school district's transformation journey. Chapter 7 explores another important principle: the importance of a clear and powerful vision for the future of a school system.

Chapter 8 begins with the premise that whole-system change is complex but not impossible. Because of its complexity, it is important for change leaders to gain political support for this kind of fundamental change. Gaining support often requires getting people to change their minds and hearts about the meaning of whole-system improvement, about what it takes to create and sustain whole-system change, and about what they can do to support this kind of fundamental change. This chapter focuses on what it takes to influence and attempt to change people's minds and hearts—their mental models.

Chapter 9 introduces readers to the dynamic trio of power, politics, and ethics. Effective change leaders and school public relations experts must use power and political skills in ethical ways to create and sustain whole-system change in their districts. This requirement raises issues that can be resolved or managed using effective strategic communication and public relations tools. The interplay among the variables (power, politics, and ethics) is examined, as well as the implications for strategic communication.

In section 3, we introduce essays written by several public relations experts and change leaders who have experienced or are currently engaged in whole-system change in school districts. Their essays represent the voice of experience. The rationale for this section is that we believe it is important to share with readers the views of school public relations practitioners and experienced change leaders regarding their role during times of great change.

Essay 1 is written by Marilyn Saltzman. Her essay focuses on communicating with key stakeholders to enable strategic change. Ms. Saltzman is the retired manager of Communications Services for the Jefferson County Public Schools in Colorado. In essay 2, Barbara Hunter writes about finding and engaging influential stakeholders to support whole-district change. Ms. Hunter is the director of communications for the National School Boards Association.

Dr. Anne Bryant wrote essay 3. Her essay is about the role of a school board in communicating change. Dr. Bryant is the executive director of the National School Boards Association. Essay 4 is by Sylvia Soholt. Her essay describes her views about bringing order out of chaos by using school public relations processes and tools. Ms. Soholt is a school public relations consultant in Washington State.

Ms. Sunni Lee and Dr. Charles Reigeluth wrote essay 5, which is about how change leaders in the Metropolitan School District of Decatur Township, Indiana, are engaging community members in their district's current transformation journey. Dr. Reigeluth is facilitating that district's transformation in collaboration with several of his doctoral students, including Ms. Lee. Dr. Reigeluth is a professor in the Instructional Systems Technology Department at Indiana University, Bloomington. Ms. Lee is a doctoral student in the Instructional Systems Technology Department.

SECTION 1

Navigating Whole-System Change in School Districts: What Change Leaders and School PR Specialists Need to Know to Support the Journey

When complex and rapid change is required, people have an extraordinary need for information. The information presented in this section responds to this need.

Strategic communication is a methodology used to develop and communicate important messages to various publics. The tools and techniques of school public relations are subsumed by the concept of strategic communication. Chapter 1 presents a summary of what strategic communication is and how it can support your district's transformation journey.

Not all information provided during times of great change is of equal value and importance. Of paramount importance to your stakeholders and your colleagues is their need to know why transformational change is needed and how that change can be created and sustained. Therefore, two key strategic communication messages must be developed and communicated consistently to all of a school system's stakeholders in response to the questions "Why do we need to transform our entire school system?" and, "How do we transform our entire school system?" Chapters 2 and 3 answer the "why" question, and chapter 4 answers the "how" question.

Strategic communication about why whole-system change is needed and about how to create and sustain whole-system change must be communicated consistently and repeatedly. The messages also have to be believable and understandable. To meet these criteria for effective strategic communication, change leaders and school public relations specialists must have a solid general understanding of 1) the nature of systems and how they function; and 2) how to improve them. This understanding will help them develop consistent, believable, and understandable messages for their district's internal and external stakeholders.

Although this section provides you with information to explain why whole-system change is needed and about how to create and sustain it, you will not find information about why your district needs to improve. You will need to create that message early in your transformation journey by assessing your district's performance and then identifying improvement opportunities you can seize and performance needs to which you must respond. Unless you make a well-documented and convincing case for why your district needs to improve, you will not get the internal and external political support you need to launch a transformation journey. Advice and guidance about how to build a case for transforming your district can be found in the literature on data-based decision-making (for example, see information developed by Edvantia, formerly called Appalachian Regional Education Laboratory—AEL, and the Council of Chief State School Officers at http://www.ael.org/dbdm/overview.cfm).

CHAPTER 1

Strategic Communication

Few would argue with the observation that many school systems throughout America are faced with a compelling need to change if they are to respond effectively to the increasing demands of their external environments: demands such as those from parents who expect a quality education for their children no matter where they live, demands to respond to the educational needs of children from minority groups, and demands to respond to the requirements of federal and state legislation, among others. Even though the need to change is recognized by educators in many school systems, the level of apprehension about when and how to change remains high in these systems. There is a heavy cloak of uncertainty about the future and how to shape it.

The level of uncertainty that educators have about the future of their school systems can be made worse as they question their emotional and intellectual readiness to do what it takes to make the journey to that future. These doubts about change often take the form of four questions:

1. Is this change really necessary?
2. Does our school system have the emotional, physical, and financial capacity to make these changes?
3. What's in this for me?
4. How do I need to respond to these changes if I am to continue working in this district?

Helping educators in your school district answer these questions and engaging your faculty and staff in a discussion of the answers is one of the important challenges you will face as change leaders and school public relations (PR) specialists. The tools and processes of strategic communication can be useful for managing this challenge as you prepare your school system for its transformation journey.

STRATEGIC COMMUNICATION

Strategic communication, according to D'Aprix (1996), "is an effort to connect the organization's vision, mission, and business goals to the forces and opportunities that exist in the marketplace and that give purpose to the work that people perform" (p. 51). We can change this definition to fit school systems: Strategic communication connects a school district's vision, mission, and strategic goals to the needs and aspirations of a community and its children, and this kind of communication gives purpose to the work that educators do in their school districts.

Strategic communication helps school systems and the people who work in those systems negotiate their role in society. Strategic communication relies on responsible behavior on the part of change leaders and PR specialists in school districts who establish two-way communication so that the district can influence the opinions and behavior of key publics (employees, consumers, government, community, media), as well as to respond and adapt to the needs and aspirations of those publics.

D'Aprix (1996, p. 3) wrote about the role of strategic communication during times of change in organizations. He said,

- Communication is an essential tool for accomplishing change.
- Communication is a tool that is often used poorly or thoughtlessly.
- To the degree that communication is used poorly in organizations, it confuses people. It makes them angry, and it feeds whatever skepticism or cynicism they feel about the motives of the people who lead them—in the process, worsening their fears and making them more resistant to change.
- There is a far better way.

And what is the "far better way" to which D'Aprix alluded? It's strategic communication that is organized and implemented as a system rather than as a collection of fragmented communication programs and public relations messages that compete for attention and leave your faculty and staff struggling to make sense of it all. In response to this kind of fragmented, nonsystemic communication, D'Aprix observed that "Life in a work organization is too confusing and too complex to permit such a simplistic and . . . irresponsible solution" (p. xii).

D'Aprix (1996, pp. 80–99) offered a strategic communications model to help managers align individual effort with organizational goals. This model can also be adapted to help change leaders create strategic alignment in their school system, which is Step 2 in the Step-Up-To-Excellence (SUTE) protocol that is presented in chapter 4. D'Aprix's model requires change leaders and PR specialists to help their colleagues answer six questions. The questions are:

1. What is my job? You answer this question by:
    a. providing clear descriptions of people's responsibilities and roles and talking about expectations.
    b. setting agreed-upon priorities and deadlines.
    c. supplying the information needed to do the job.
    d. involving employees at appropriate times in planning, decision making, and implementing changes (which is at the heart of the SUTE protocol).
2. How am I doing? This question is answered by:
    a. providing feedback—positive and negative—on performance.
    b. telling employees what they have done right as well as what they have done wrong.
    c. discussing mutual actions for performance improvement.
    d. making feedback a frequent and timely activity.
    e. learning how to listen effectively and how to coach people so they can improve their performance.
3. Does anyone care? This question is answered by:
    a. taking time to listen and talk honestly with employees and value them as people.
    b. practicing management by wandering around.
    c. holding staff meetings in which people have the opportunity to express their ideas and concerns.
    d. soliciting feedback about your own leadership style.

e. recognizing and acting on people's ideas.
   f. practicing common day-to-day courtesies and civilities.
4. How is my unit doing? Behaviors that support this question are:
   a. sharing general business (in the case of school systems, district performance) information on a timely basis.
   b. discussing work-group objectives and how they match overall organizational objectives.
   c. recognizing work-group accomplishments.
   d. discussing the need for work-group performance improvement.
   e. finding opportunities to assemble the group for dialogue or celebration.
5. Where are we headed? Behaviors that address this question are:
   a. gaining a personal appreciation and knowledge of the organization's vision, mission, and strategic direction.
   b. internalizing the company's (that is, the district's) value system and behaving accordingly.
   c. showing personal conviction and commitment to the district's vision, mission, and strategy.
   d. relating work-group experience to the vision, mission, and values and help keep people focused.
   e. being present to the workforce in ways that make them feel they are being led by someone who understands and cares.
6. How can I help? To help faculty and staff understand how they can help achieve the district's goals and enact its vision, you should demonstrate the following behaviors:
   a. providing genuine opportunities for involvement.
   b. empowering people to take the initiative and make decisions without second guessing them.
   c. supporting the risk takers even when they make a mistake.
   d. recognizing and reward true contributions.
   e. encouraging and supporting cross-functional collaboration (this is an example of horizontal alignment).
   f. promoting mutual trust.

Coffman (2004) offered additional insights to the meaning of strategic communication. She said,

Nonprofit organizations are now continuously being challenged to be more strategic in their communications efforts. Communications activities must add up to more than a series of isolated events such as the dissemination of an occasional publication or press release. Being strategic requires that nonprofits be more deliberate, innovative, savvy, and less reactive in their communications practice. Nonprofits are encouraged to regard communications as essential to their overall success and integrate it throughout their organizations. (p. 1)

Coffman (2004, p. 3) also identified sixteen essential strategic communications practices and grouped them into three categories: (1) strategy, (2) implementation, and (3) support and alignment. Each of the sixteen communications practices is linked to specific criteria for evaluating the practices. The criteria were adapted from the work of Bonk, Griggs, and Tynes (1999). The sixteen strategic communications practices and their associated criteria are

Category 1: Strategy
Identify the vision. The communications vision is aligned with, but distinct from, the organization's overall mission.
Choose goals and outcomes. Goals and outcomes are well defined and measurable, and help guide a defined plan of action.
Select target audiences. Audiences are specific (not the general public) and include key decision makers or individuals with influence on the issue.
Develop messages. Messages are specific, clear, and persuasive, reflect audience values, and include a solution or course of action.
Identify credible messengers. Messengers are seen as credible by the target audiences, and can be recruited and available to the cause.
Choose communications mechanisms/outlets. Outlets (for example, air media and on-the-ground media) are chosen for their access and availability to target audiences.
Scan the context and competition. Risks and contextual variables that can affect communications success are identified and factored into planning when possible.

Category 2: Implementation
Develop effective materials. Materials are developed in attractive,

accessible, and varied formats for maximum exposure and visibility.

Build valuable partnerships. Linkages exist with internal and external stakeholders who can help align with and carry the message.

Train messengers. Internal and external messengers are trained in key messages and are consistent in their delivery.

Conduct steady outreach. Outreach and dissemination to audiences through multiple outlets is regular and sustained.

Monitor and evaluate. Activities and outcomes are regularly monitored and evaluated for purposes of accountability and continuous improvement.

Category 3: Support and Integration

Support communications at the leadership level. Management understands and supports communications as an integral part of organizational viability and success.

Earmark sufficient resources. Fund-raising regularly includes dedicated resources for communications practice.

Integrate communications throughout the organization. Communications is seen as an integral part of every organizational project or strategy.

Involve staff at all levels. Communications is not seen as an isolated function; most, if not all, staff members have some knowledge and/or participation in communications efforts.

DESIGNING EFFECTIVE STRATEGIC COMMUNICATION

Effective strategic communication aims to garner support for whole-system change.[1] If you want your faculty and staff to support your district's transformation journey, you have to convince them that the changes you are trying to achieve are worthwhile. Put another way, school systems do not exist to employ teachers, administrators, and other staff. School systems exist to educate a community's children. Therefore, if you want educators and external stakeholders to support your district's transformation journey, the changes you propose and the change process you want to use must be rooted in the core societal purpose of your school system—a noble and necessary purpose simply stated as "Our district exists to educate our community's children."

Gaining support for whole-system change also requires you to convince your colleagues and external stakeholders that the changes you envision for your district are within their grasp rather than beyond their reach. This is an important psychological principle for gaining support for change, because if people believe that what you are proposing is impossible, they won't join you on the journey.

Effective strategic communication in support of your district's transformation journey will have five characteristics. These characteristics were adapted from D'Aprix (1996, pp. 23–24). They are:

1. Create and communicate a clear and simple case for your transformation journey that is based on the core purpose of your school system (that is, educating students).
2. Clearly identify and communicate what the students in your system need to know and be able to do prior to graduating at the end of 12th grade. This information connects your system to the needs and aspirations of your community and its children—which is its core purpose.
3. Formulate and communicate a plan to meet the needs and aspirations of your community and its children by transforming your system (this happens during the pre-launch phase of the change navigation protocol presented in chapter 4).
4. Outline the consequences of success and failure.
5. Repeatedly and consistently communicate the above messages.

Effective strategic communication can only be achieved if it is organized and systematic. The following advice can help you design an effective strategic communication program in support of your district's transformation journey.

Assess you communication needs. Effective strategic communication connects your school system's mission, vision, and strategic goals to your community's needs and aspirations for educating children. Given this purpose, you need to identify the audience for your strategic communication, construct and clarify your message, and choose appropriate media for communicating the messages. Coffman's (2004) 16 essential strategic communication practices, described above, are particularly helpful for conducting this kind of audit.

Plan your strategic communication. Strategic communication is not simply a matter of sending out a letter or an e-mail. You need to plan your strategic communication program carefully so that all external and internal stakeholders are repeatedly and consistently getting the messages that you want them to get about whole-system change. Your planning should also focus on the timing for releasing messages. To have an impact, messages need to be communicated to the right people, at the right time, in the right place, and in the right way.

Identify your audiences. Different audiences have different communication needs. Who are the audiences for your strategic communication? What are their communication needs? What is the best way to ensure that the right message is delivered *and* understood by these audiences?

Shape your messages. The messages you create should be consistent and they should communicate accurate information. The information should also be understandable and not filled with "education-ese" or technical jargon. The messages also have to be shaped to conform to the communication needs of your audiences and to the requirements of the media you are using to deliver the messages; that is, your message has to be appropriate for your various audiences and media platforms.

Identify your communicators (see Marilyn Saltzman and Barbara Hunter's essays in section 3 for more about this). Some people are natural communicators. They have a way with people and a way with words. Some people do not have these traits, but when they stand to deliver a message people pay attention because these people are influential and respected. Some people can communicate effectively with one audience but fail in their communication with another audience. An effective strategic communication plan must consider who in your system must deliver the important strategic communication messages and to which audiences.

Choose appropriate media. In today's society there are many media through which you can communicate important messages about your district's transformation journey. The selection of media must be made in response to the communication needs of your various audiences. The selection of media is also driven by the cost of the media. Further, it is important to use a multimedia approach to delivering your message; that is, to get your messages about your district's transformation journey into the heads and hearts of the people working in your district and the stakeholders in your district's external environment, you should use as many different media as you can afford.

Evaluate your communication program. Things worth doing must be frequently evaluated to ensure that they are effective. This principle also applies to your strategic communication program. Your evaluation should focus on the communication process and its outcomes and should include summative and formative evaluation. The On-Track Seminars that are part of the transformation methodology described in chapter 4 can be used for this purpose.

Acquire adequate funding. Effective strategic communication requires financial resources. If you do not fund your communication program with adequate financial resources, you will not be able to communicate effectively. And if you cannot communicate effectively, your transformation journey will be in jeopardy of failing. So, when you are seeking funds to support your transformation journey, it will be important to include a budget line item for your strategic communication program.

STRATEGIC COMMUNICATION AND THE EMOTIONAL CYCLES OF CHANGE

Strategic communication should also be designed to help people through the emotional cycles of change. Transforming an entire school district requires broad and deep systemwide change. The changes will create stress for external stakeholders and for people working inside your school system. The stress will cause people to move through either of two emotional cycles of change. Supporters of your transformation journey will move through an emotional cycle described by Kelly and Conner (1979), while people who are responding to the transformation will move through a second, but different, emotional cycle that was described by Leibowitz and Lea (1985). The emotional phases in each cycle are highlighted below.

The Emotional Cycle for Those Supporting the Transformation

It can be predicted that the people leading the transformation journey for your school system will experience strong emotions as they move forward on that journey. It is important to develop strategic communication about this emotional cycle. Knowing about these emotions will help your change leaders increase their personal effectiveness as they anticipate and respond to the emotions they will predictably experience. The cycle proceeds as follows:

Uninformed optimism. When change leaders first take on the leadership tasks for a transformation journey, they will be filled with unbridled optimism. They will believe in their hearts that they can lead the transformation and that the entire district will be transformed as planned. This emotion is called uninformed optimism. But then they start leading the transformation and their emotions plummet precipitously into the next stage as they face the realities of leading complex, systemwide change: ambiguity, complexity, chaos, and human resistance.

Informed pessimism. The realities of large-scale change can be brutal. People who were thought to be supportive show their true colors as obstructionists. Resistance to the transformation process emerges from all corners, nooks, and crannies of the system. Anger and fear escalate into interpersonal and intergroup conflict. The "pedestrians" in the system sit and watch with the heartfelt belief that "this too shall pass." But, if the change leaders have great courage, passion, and vision, and if they persevere toward the district's vision, then changes will begin to emerge. As they perceive these early successes and begin to see glimmers of hope, they will move into the next phase of the emotional cycle.

Hopeful realism. Although the change leaders believed at the beginning of the transformation journey that they could create and sustain all kinds of changes, they now realize that they have to focus on a few important changes. Their energy and effort focus on bringing these few important changes to the forefront of their change leadership. They work hard to build internal and external political support for these few important changes and their efforts start to succeed. With this success, they move into the next phase of the emotional cycle.

Informed optimism. With the identification of a few important changes and with growing political support for these changes, the change leaders now become increasingly optimistic that their school system will be transformed, even though they may not achieve everything that they had hoped for at the beginning of the journey. So, with this informed optimism, they lead effectively. Their district is transformed to create and sustain several important changes in their district's environmental relationships, core and supporting work processes, and in the internal social infrastructure. Their success brings them to the end of the transformation journey and to the last phase of the emotional cycle.

Rewarding completion. Celebrating success is often set aside as unimportant or frivolous. It is, however, a critical phase of the emotional cycle of change for those leading your district's transformation for the life of a school system. In the Step-Up-To-Excellence transformation protocol described in chapter 4, a spiral of improvement is created that will move your school system through periodic cycles of transformation. At the completion of each cycle, it will be important for the change leaders to celebrate their success. This celebration will bring important psychological and emotional closure to the transformation journey the change leaders just completed and, just as important, it will recharge their motivation to lead change in the future.

The Emotional Cycle for People Responding to Change

The people planning and leading your transformation journey are not the only ones moving through an emotional cycle. The others, who are responding to the change process and the outcomes of those changes, are also going through an emotional cycle that proceeds as follows.

Immobilization. When the reality sets in that the change leaders are unequivocally committed to transforming your school system, and as they begin the Pre-Launch Preparation phase of the change navigation protocol described in chapter 4, many of the faculty and staff in your system will freeze in their tracks with disbelief and distrust. This is especially true if your system has been through failed change efforts in the past.

Denial. Despite the initial resistance to change that the change leaders are experiencing early in your district's transformation journey, they push forward. As faculty and staff see the change leaders moving forward, they will move into a period of denial as expressed in comments like "This too shall pass" or "We've been through this before and nothing happened then."

Self-doubt. But the transformation journey continues, and faculty and staff begin to wonder about how they will fit into the new school system that is being created; they begin to fear the loss of friends, prestige, and favored programs, and they wonder what the future will hold for them in their transforming school system.

Letting go. The transformation journey starts to create important changes in the district's relationships with external stakeholders, in the core and supporting work processes, and in the internal social infrastructure. As the change proposals are implemented and new programs, policies, working relationships, and so on begin to emerge, faculty and staff start letting go of their old ways, their old beliefs, and their old mental models about how to succeed in their district.

Testing options. As people let go of their old ways, old beliefs, and old mental models, they start to test new ideas and behaviors (see chapter 8 for more information about unlearning and learning mental models). They learn what works and what doesn't work for them. They learn what they know and don't know.

Searching for meaning. As people test new expectations and as they learn what they need to unlearn and learn, they start to search for meaning. They start to ask themselves, "What does all this mean for me and for this district?" They also start to reflect on what they need to do to succeed in their transforming school system.

Integration. As they reflect on what they need to do to succeed in the "new" system, faculty and staff start to integrate all of the personal changes they made in response to the requirements of the transformation journey into their personal mental models—the ones that guide their thinking and influence their feelings about their work.

Renewal. The faculty and staff who successfully moved through this emotional cycle now find themselves experiencing a sense of personal renewal and see their system being renewed through the transformation journey. This perception of personal and systemwide renewal provides them with emotional energy and increases their motivation to do what it takes to ensure that their school system succeeds.

Both of these emotional cycles are difficult to move through, especially if people are not aware of the different phases. Developing strategic communication to explain these cycles will help your colleagues and external stakeholders move through the cycles more effectively.

CONCLUSION

Change leaders must create an environment supporting their district's transformation journey. The success of the transformation journey relies significantly on the quality of the strategic communication early in the transformation journey and especially during the journey as your school system makes a transition from what it is to what you want it to become.

Strategic communication is also particularly important for anticipating and managing resistance to change and the negative emotional components of transformational change. To be effective at doing this, your strategic communication program must present a fair and balanced assessment of the challenges of transformational change and then design communications that describe those challenges in a positive and accurate way. Strategic communication designed in this way can make the difference between the way people perceive and ultimately support the change process and its outcomes.

Further, the deeper and broader the changes you are proposing, the more comprehensive and persistent your strategic communications program must be. The messages you develop and communicate must also be simple and understandable. If the messages are intended to be acted upon, they shouldn't be too technical. If the messages are intended for administrators in your district, they need to be actionable; that is, they need to be structured so administrators can internalize the messages and then take action. If the messages are meant to motivate and influence, they must be laden with powerful emotional multisensory images (Laborde, 1987). Determining the appropriate content of the messages and the appropriate method for delivering the messages to the appropriate audiences is one key to effective strategic communication.

REFERENCES

Bonk, K., Griggs, H., & Tynes, E. (1999). *Strategic communications for nonprofits.* San Francisco: Jossey-Bass.

Coffman, J. (2004). *Strategic communications audits.* Washington, DC: Communications Consortium Media Center. Retrieved on March 26, 2006, from www.mediaevaluationproject.org/WorkingPaper1.pdf

D'Aprix, R. (1996). *Communicating for change: Connecting the workplace and the marketplace.* San Francisco: Jossey-Bass.

Kelly, D., & Conner, D. (1979). The emotional cycle of change. In *Annual handbook for group facilitators.* Tucson, AZ: University Associates.

Laborde, G. Z. (1987). *Influencing with integrity.* Palo Alto, CA: Syntony.

Leibowitz, Z. B., & Lea, H. D. (Eds.) (1985). *Adult career development.* Alexandria, VA: National Career Development Association. (ERIC Document Reproduction Service No. ED325749)

ENDNOTES

1. Examples of real-life strategic communication plans for school districts from the Dysart Unified School District No. 89 in El Mirage, Arizona, can be viewed at: http://www.dysart.org/news/other_docs/Strategic_Communications_Plan_2005.pdf; and from the Grant Joint Union High School District in Sacramento, California, at: http://www.grant.k12.ca.us/OfficeServices/SuperintendentOfficesJurisdiction/communicationsPublicRelations/Assets/PDF/OfficeOfCommunicationsPlan.pdf

CHAPTER 2

Why Whole-System Change Is Needed: The Topography of Whole-System Change and a Compass to Navigate It

To navigate whole-district change, you need to be familiar with the topography of whole-system change and you need a compass and map to navigate that terrain. The topography and compass are described in this chapter and in the next chapter. This information will help you answer the question, "Why do we need to transform our entire school system?"

First, you'll read about the nature of organizations as open systems. The information about open systems represents the topography of change that you will need to navigate to transform your district. A set of conditions that needs to exist in a school district before you can begin whole-system change in your district is presented next. Following that information, you'll read about nine principles to guide your district's transformation journey. These conditions and principles are your compass for navigating whole-system change in your school district.

Having an overview of the change topography and a compass in hand, however, is not enough to make a transformation journey. You also need a detailed map that can show you *how* to get to where you want to go. The map for your transformation journey is a special change protocol called Step-Up-To-Excellence. This protocol is described in chapter 4.

Before examining the compass needed to navigate whole-system change, let's orient ourselves to the change topography.

THE CHANGE TOPOGRAPHY: WHAT A SYSTEM IS AND HOW IT FUNCTIONS

Before presenting information on the nature of organizations as systems, we want to be clear that this chapter is not an in-depth exploration and discussion of all existing systems concepts and principles. Instead, we touch in a general way on a few of the concepts that we think will provide you with an overview of the change topography that your system must traverse during a transformation journey.

To transform an entire school system from what it was and what it is into what it ought to be, change leaders and school PR specialists must have a good basic understanding of how their school districts function as systems. Open systems theory provides a useful framework for developing this understanding.

Open Systems Theory

A simple figure depicting a school system is shown in Figure 2.1, which has the following components: an external environment, inputs, a work process (core work and supporting work), an internal social infrastructure that supports the work process, outputs, and a feedback loop. Burke (2002) commented on the relationship of these parts when he said, "All of these parts compose a whole, a total organization that represents an entity different from the simple sum of its elements and dimensions, which is a basic tenet of Gestalt psychology" (p. 44). In Figure 2.1, the system to be improved is everything inside the dotted line.

An open system depends on its external environment for its "life energy." In the case of school systems, life energy is composed of human, technical, and financial resources. Not only do resources come into a school system, but the system must continually interact with its environment to resupply its resources. It is this relationship with an environment that makes a school district an open system.

A school system, as depicted in Figure 2.1, takes in required resources from its environment and converts those resources into a valued service for its community; that is, it uses the resources to educate a community's children. The quality of that education is then evaluated by parents and other stakeholders, and the evaluation results create a feedback loop that influences the availability of future resources for a school system.

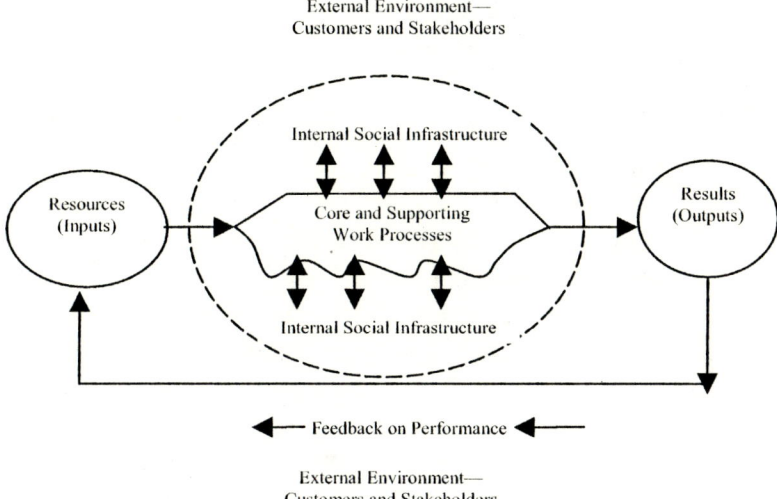

Figure 2.1. A simple picture of a school district as an open system

Characteristics of Open Systems

Von Bertalanffy (1950) and Katz and Kahn (1978) described characteristics that define an open system. Ten of these that we think are relevant to school systems are summarized below.

1. *Importation of energy.* All school systems need energy from their external environments. This energy is provided in the form of the human, technical, and financial resources that districts need to educate children. Declining resources threaten the performance of a school system; therefore, system leaders invest a lot of their personal energy in identifying and securing the resources their school systems need to perform.
2. *Throughput.* For a school system, throughputs are processes by which resources are converted into a valued service; that is, human, technical, and financial resources are converted into educational services provided to children and into supporting services such as administration, supervision, busing, cafeteria services, custodial services, and other pupil personnel services.

The conversion process (the core and supporting work processes) is shored up by an internal social "infrastructure" that creates an internal "work life" for the people working in the system. This internal infrastructure includes organization design, power and political dynamics, organization culture, communication processes, evaluation processes, reward systems, and so on. The work processes and the internal social infrastructure are significantly intertwined and inseparable; therefore, both must be improved simultaneously.

3. *Output.* School districts provide educational services to students. Teachers organize the best information they can learn about their subject area and they present that information to students using a teaching method. Students take that information and transform it into personal knowledge. Although teachers facilitate this knowledge-construction process, it is ultimately a student's responsibility to learn because teachers cannot *make* students learn. This teaching-learning process frequently occurs across 14+ years (prekindergarten through 12th grade); therefore, a student's education is not what he or she learns in the third grade or in a middle school. His or her learning is the cumulative effect of his or her "learning career" in a school district (in the case of highly mobile students who go in and out of school districts, this learning is still a function of their "learning career" and not what they learn in a particular grade).

4. *Systems are cycles of events.* For every graduating class of high school seniors, there is a beginning class of preschoolers or kindergarteners. For every sixth-grade class moving into seventh grade, there is a class of fifth graders replacing that graduating sixth-grade class. School district performance is driven by cycles of learning. In this way, this "cycle of events" is a key identity-marking feature of a school system.

Further, these learning cycles create boundaries for a school system. These boundaries are invisible but real. There is a boundary between each grade in a school system. There is a boundary between each level of schooling in a district. These boundaries are often referred to as the "cracks" that kids fall through.

5. *Negative entropy.* Katz and Kahn (1978) defined entropy as a process that " is a universal law of nature in which all forms of organization move toward disorganization or death . . . [but] by importing more energy from its environment than it expends, the open system can store energy and acquire negative entropy" (p. 25).

If a school district is not getting the resources it needs to perform well, district leaders do not ask, "What can we do about this entropy?" They do, however, realize that if they don't take positive steps to increase the quality and quantity of needed resources, their district will suffer terribly. For school districts, resources include not only money and top-notch teachers but also the goodwill of their community, good relations with stakeholder groups, and a reputation for being an excellent school system. These intangible resources also have to be replenished and "stored" for future use. Negative entropy is the replenishment of needed resources that replace and exceed consumed resources (Duffy, 2003).

6. *Information input, negative feedback, and the coding process.* School districts as systems need information from their customers and stakeholders about how their services are perceived and valued. This information often takes the form of positive and negative feedback. Negative feedback, in particular, has a way of helping school districts improve their services because it creates pressure for change.

School districts cannot possibly respond to all the feedback they receive—positive or negative, so leaders in the district "select" which feedback to pay attention to and which feedback to ignore. This selection process results in feedback being sorted into broad categories that leaders think are relevant to their particular system. This sorting process is called coding.

7. *Steady-state and dynamic homeostasis.* Homeostasis can be "steady" or "dynamic." Homeostasis is also called equilibrium. There are three broad categories of equilibrium: balancing equilibrium (that is, the forces in a school district that keep it in a steady or stable state); neutral equilibrium (for example, this is like having a car running but in neutral . . . the driver steps on

the gas, the engine revolutions increase, but the car doesn't move; when a change is introduced to a system, if activity increases and nothing changes, the organization is in a state of neutral equilibrium); and reinforcing equilibrium (that is, where a school district breaks out of its steady-state equilibrium and permanently moves to a new level of equilibrium, which can be a turn for the worse as well as a turn for the better).

8. *Differentiation.* Entropy is a natural process of energy depletion. Negative entropy is when energy is replenished. As a school district replenishes and stores energy (that is, by employing negative entropy), it often grows in size. As it grows in size, bureaucracy often emerges in the guise of hierarchical levels and departmentalization. Hierarchy and departmentalization is a managerial attempt to divide up the work of a district to make it easier to be effective. Dividing up the work is called differentiation (Lawrence & Lorsch, 1967). Uncontrolled differentiation creates what we frequently refer to as "organization silos"—that is, discrete, relatively autonomous departments, programs, or divisions that do not communicate with each other.

Not only does differentiation occur as school districts grow in size, but a fascinating process called "internal elaboration" (Haines, 1999) emerges. Internal elaboration is organization complexity in full bloom and in rapid propagation. With internal elaboration, there is an explosion of policies and procedures to control human behavior. Avenues of approach to solving problems that were once simple become twisting and turning urban back alleys. That which was once a simple request by a teacher to attend a national conference becomes a bureaucratic exercise in getting multiple "permission" signatures. Human beings have an annoying capacity to transform appropriate simplicity into unfathomable complexity, and this is what happens when internal elaboration runs unchecked.

9. *Integration and coordination.* To counterbalance unchecked differentiation and internal elaboration, managers use integration and coordination. Integration is when units or organization levels that must collaborate to produce a service or product are nat-

urally clustered so they can do that. In a school district, integration occurs when a high school and all the middle and elementary schools that feed into it are organized as a cluster because the schools must collaborate to provide students with a "total" education.

The internal social "infrastructure" of a school district (which includes organization culture, power and political dynamics, organization design, policies, procedures, reward systems, and so on) is the primary vehicle for achieving integration and coordination. This is true because while differentiation can be created on paper by redrawing the organization chart and can be facilitated by reassigning people or by rewriting job descriptions, integration and coordination are quintessential interpersonal activities requiring trust, commitment, and collaboration. To achieve effective integration and coordination, school districts need an internal social infrastructure marked by the three features delineated in the previous sentence.

10. *Equifinality.* Von Bertalanffy (1950) first espoused this principle. He said an organization can achieve a single goal from different starting points and by following a variety of paths. This principle seems to have escaped "School District Management 101" courses for some school district administrators. Frequently, district administrators "require" everyone in a school district to pursue district goals in *exactly* the same way, on *exactly* the same time line, and with *exactly* the same resources. This brand of forced "uniformity of means" is assumed to result in "uniformly high quality ends." Experience, however, suggests that this assumption is often false.

Unity of purpose does not require uniformity of action. Unity of purpose does not preclude equifinality. People in a school district can walk arm-in-arm without seeing eye-to-eye. People in a district can pursue districtwide goals in a variety of different yet acceptable ways. However, all this interaction must be aligned with a district's grand strategy and future vision, and must be done "for the good of the whole."

Ackoff's Principles for Understanding Organizations as Systems

Ackoff (1999, pp. 6–8) added to our understanding of organizations as systems. He said a system is a whole entity consisting of several parts with the following properties (which we modified to fit school systems):

1. The whole (for example, a whole school system) has one or more defining properties or functions; for example, a defining function (that is, a system's main purpose) of a school district is to educate children and teenagers.
2. Each part in the system (for example, each school in a district) can affect the behavior or properties of the whole; for example, a couple of low-performing schools in a district can drag a whole district down.
3. There are subsets of system parts that are essential for carrying out the main purpose of the whole but they cannot, by themselves, fulfill the main purpose of the system; for example, teachers and classrooms in a single school building are essential parts of a school system and they are necessary for helping a school system fulfill its purpose, but these "parts" cannot and never will be able to do what the whole system does.
4. There are also subsets of parts that are not part of the core work process but are needed to support the core work process (for example, administration, supervision, and pupil personnel services).
5. Because a system interacts with its external environment, it is said to be an "open system." A school district, therefore, is an open system. Its external environment consists of its community, individuals and groups, the state and federal governments, and society in general. That part of a school district's environment that it can influence but not control is called its "transactional" or "task" environment. The part of the environment that a school district is affected by but cannot influence or control is called its "contextual" or "general" environment. To succeed, a system needs to improve the relationship it has with its transactional environment and work to anticipate pressure from its contextual environment.

6. The way in which an essential part of a system affects the whole system depends on its interaction with at least one other essential part; for example, the effect a single school has on the whole district depends on the interaction that school has with other schools in the district.
7. The effect that a particular subset of essential parts has on the whole system depends on the behavior of at least one other subset of parts. For example, let's say that a school district is organized prekindergarten to 12th grade. This means the core work process for that district is 14 steps long (preK–12th grade). Now, let's say that district leaders are concerned about the performance of their high school (which represents a subset of the system). This high school contains grades 9–12. Then, let's say that the performance of that high school is dragging down the overall performance of the district on state assessments. It would be a mistake to focus improvement efforts only on the high school because its performance is affected by at least two other subsets of schools (that is, the elementary and middle schools that "feed" kids into those high schools). Since all essential parts of a school system interact either indirectly or directly, it would be reasonable and "systemic" to examine and determine how these other parts are affecting the performance of the high school. Focusing improvement only on the high school would be a nonsystemic and, therefore, piecemeal approach to improvement.
8. A system is a whole entity that cannot be divided into individual parts without loss of its essential properties or functions. For example, the dominant approach to school district improvement is called school-based management or site-based improvement. This approach has had the consequence of dividing school systems into their aggregate parts—individual schools. These individual schools are then assumed to have the ability to fulfill the essential purpose of a school system—that is, providing children with a total education. But individual schools do not and never will provide children with a total education; they only provide children with a partial education represented by the curriculum for the grades embedded in a particular school. When a school

system is managed in this way—by disaggregating it into its individual parts—its effectiveness as a system deteriorates rapidly.

Because a system derives its effectiveness from the synergistic interaction of its parts rather than from what the parts do independent of the system, when efforts are taken to improve the individual parts separate from the system (as in school-based improvement), the performance of the whole system deteriorates and the system may be significantly weakened. This is one reason why school-based improvement has generally failed to improve schooling throughout a district.

Lumsden and Lumsden (2004, pp. 18–19) offered additional insights to the nature of organizations as systems. Their insights are interpreted below.

Systems are powered by interrelationships and interdependency. Changes made in one part of a system ripple through the system and affect other parts. Sometimes the effects are minimal, sometimes they are moderate, and sometimes they are devastating. This concept requires you to anticipate the impact of the change decisions you make during your transformation journey.

Communication flow is necessary to link subsystems (chapter 5 provides additional information about the concept of communication flow). Within a system, communication must flow between and among individuals, teams, schools, clusters of schools, and the central service center (a/k/a the central administration). By linking these people through vertical and horizontal communication flows, you are creating strategic alignment. Strategic alignment is absolutely necessary for creating a high-performing school system. Creating strategic alignment happens during step 3 in the change navigation protocol presented in chapter 4.

Systems have a symbiotic relationship with an external environment. As described in this chapter and in chapter 3, school districts are open systems. An open system has a symbiotic relationship with its environment. Information, resources, ideas, and so on flow into and out of school systems. Improving the relationship between a system and its environment is one of three important goals of transforming a school system. The other two goals are to improve the district's core and supporting work processes and to improve its internal social infrastructure.

A change protocol for making these kinds of changes is presented in chapter 4.

Norms govern behavior in systems. Norms are unspoken rules governing behavior in systems. Norms can be functional or dysfunctional. There are norms for almost every human behavior in a system, including communication. Dysfunctional norms are identified and modified or eliminated when you take steps to improve your system's internal social infrastructure.

Roles are ways of behaving that affect relationships. A role defines the way a person behaves in a school system. Some roles are formal such as "teacher," "superintendent," or "secretary." Other roles are informal; for example, some people become "connectors"—people who are good at bringing people together; some are "comedians"—people who are good at bringing humor into relationships. Formal roles are examined and refined when you examine your system's internal social infrastructure.

Cybernetic processes facilitate the growth and development of systems. A cybernetic process provides feedback and assessment data to people in systems. Cybernetic processes include performance appraisal processes, program evaluation processes, and feedback mechanisms. These processes are part of your system's internal social infrastructure.

A COMPASS FOR NAVIGATING WHOLE-SYSTEM CHANGE

Conditions for Effective Whole-System Change in School Districts

Any methodology created to support a school district's effort to engage in whole system change will probably *not* work in low-performing districts because these districts do not possess the conditions necessary to engage in whole-system change. This conclusion is based on research focusing on large-scale change in organizations that suggests that the best time to introduce large-scale change in an organization is when that system is performing well (see, for example, Burke, 2002; Cummings & Worley, 2001). The conditions for effective whole-district change that we believe are important are:

- senior leaders who act on the basis of personal courage, passion, and vision—not on the basis of fear, self-survival, or self-interest;
- leaders and followers who are willing and able to break or circumvent rules to create powerful innovations—not those who are rule bound;
- senior leaders who conceive of their districts as whole systems—not as a confederation of individual schools and programs;
- leaders and followers who have a clear view of the opportunities that system transformation offers them—not a view of "We can't do this because . . .";
- leaders and followers who possess the professional intellect, change-minded attitudes, and change navigation skills to move their districts toward higher levels of performance—not people without an inkling about the requirements of navigating whole-system change; and,
- human, technical, and financial resources to sustain a large-scale improvement process over 5 to 7 years (large-scale change can take this long)—not resources "stolen" from successful programs to pay for systemic change.

If the above conditions begin to emerge within a low-performing district prior to engaging in systemic change, then a whole-district change methodology may have a chance of producing desirable improvements in those districts. Therefore, instead of depriving low-performing districts of opportunities to engage in whole-system change, change leaders should first focus on developing the conditions listed above as part of their efforts to prepare their district for whole-system change.

Nine Principles for Navigating Whole-District Change

There are nine principles that we think should be considered when creating a framework for any protocol to transform entire school systems (Duffy, 2004). These principles are:

Principle #1

A school district's external environment is complex and unstable. The environments school districts find themselves in are increasingly complex and unstable. This complexity and instability is being driven by the triple engines of standards, assessments, and accountability (Duffy, 2002). In complex and unstable environments, school districts need to be able to plan for the future while also being able to respond quickly to unanticipated events.

Principle #2

The capacity to anticipate the future and respond quickly to unanticipated events is partially a function of an organization's internal social "infrastructure." A school district's social infrastructure includes its organization culture, communication patterns, power and political dynamics, the reward system, policies and procedures, and organization design. Social infrastructure has a significant influence on educators' capacity and willingness to plan for the future and respond to unexpected events. A new social infrastructure for school systems that would increase capacity and willingness would have the following distinguishing characteristics. It would:

- favor skill-based work, professional knowledge, and networked relationships;
- be anchored to a network of teams with their collective knowledge, talent, and resources;
- support and encourage flux (discussed below under Principle #7) rather than linear, sequential change;
- create broad and easy opportunities for horizontal and vertical participation and collaboration; and,
- connect people to each other and to resources in ways that help a school district as much as possible to take charge of its own destiny (as opposed to being externally forced to improve).

Principle #3

Biological metaphors most accurately describe how social networks function. The biological metaphor that seems to work best for organizations with a networked internal social infrastructure is "ecosystem." In nature, some ecosystems offer scarce opportunities for life (polar ice caps), while others offer overflowing opportunities (equatorial jungles). If we think of a school system as an ecosystem, it too can offer scarce or abundant opportunities for success. Scarcity or abundance of opportunities in school districts depends on a district's collective vision for its current and future capacities and competencies and on the design of its internal social infrastructure. The district's grand vision and its internal social infrastructure significantly influence people's thoughts, feelings, and actions. If most people in a district choose to think, feel, and act as if their district can never improve, they won't improve. If most people in a district choose to think, feel, and act as if they have the creative potential to move their district toward breathtakingly higher levels of performance, they can and will make that journey toward higher levels of performance. The power of choice, either individually or collectively, has been repeatedly proven to have an extraordinary effect on human performance; or, as Jean-Paul Sartre (1934) once said, "We are our choices."

Principle #4

Creating a web of accountabilities using networked teams doesn't mean that authority and control are surrendered to the networked "mob." In all school districts, the voice of leadership must always be present and heard even though significant steps are taken to redesign leadership positions so incumbents can practice effective transformational leadership instead of being micromanagers of the status quo. Without the voice of leadership from the top of a school district, people freeze in place when there are too many change options to be considered. Without some element of leadership at the top, the many at the bottom are often paralyzed by an overabundance of choices. The creation of an internal social infrastructure that honors and uses formal leadership roles while simultaneously creating and sustaining networked teams will provide powerful moments for creating innovative ideas to improve student, faculty and staff, and whole-system learning.

Principle #5

A networked social infrastructure stimulates creativity and innovation. Creativity and innovation present breathtaking opportunities for improvement. As opportunities for improving schooling emerge and are taken, still newer opportunities will begin to emerge at a faster rate. This is somewhat like the financial principle of compound interest. Therefore, change leaders need to find ways to help educators seize opportunities, succeed at using them, and then help others build their success upon those earlier successes. This creates compound organizational learning.

Principle #6

Peak performance is an illusion. In the 21st-century environment for a school district, there are multiple performance peaks that evoke images of the Rocky Mountains where some peaks are lower than others. What if the peak a district sits atop is a low compared to others, but educators inside the district don't realize it? Wouldn't the perception of being at peak performance be an illusion?

Another problem for school districts is not too much success but too little perspective. Great success creates a perceptual wall that obstructs the view of opportunities to move toward higher levels of performance. If educators in a district cannot see the next higher performance peak, how can they go there? They cannot go to what they cannot see.

A third problem for school districts is that successful districts become remarkably creative in defending their status quo. They argue against the need to improve because they see themselves already at their peak. But sitting too long on any performance peak when there are higher peaks to climb will not be tolerated by our 21st-century society.

All school districts sit atop a performance peak, no matter what that level of performance might be. The path to the next higher performance peak is not a straight "as the crow flies" line. A clear view of the next higher level of performance is not a straight shot forward and upward. There is only one way to get to the next higher peak: A district has to go downhill before it can go back up. It has to become temporarily less effective, less skilled, and less successful as people learn new knowledge and skills.

The "first down, then up" principle is a plain English way of describing Seyle's (1956) general adaptation syndrome theory. This theory suggests that when an organization is stressed (for example, by the requirements of change), that system's performance will first decline before it ascends to a new level of performance. The problem for school districts is, however, that the more successful a school district is, the less inclined it is to let go of what it does and move down the performance curve toward the edge of chaos (a phrase coined by Roger Lewin, 1992). This capacity to let go has to be built into a school system.

The "first down, then up" journey happens when educators start questioning their district's success. Not everything they do has to be abandoned completely, but everything they do needs to be questioned completely. During this questioning, they must be open to stunning opportunities for innovative ideas to improve student, teacher, and whole-system learning. They must also be ready to discard those programs and activities that are proven to be ineffective or are effective but clearly not aligned with the district's grand vision and strategic direction. By getting rid of failing or nonaligned programs and activities, space is created for new programs and activities.

Principle #7

School district improvement methodologies must move from the concept of change to concept of flux. The field of organization improvement is moving away from the concept of change to the concept of flux (Kelly, 1998). While change focuses on creating new programs, ideas, and so on, flux is about managing creative destruction followed by rebirth. Flux breaks down the status quo and creates a temporary foundation for innovation and the rebirth of a school district. Innovation, in turn, continues to disrupt the status quo, especially if it introduces breakthrough improvements into a system. Because innovation is a core requirement for transforming a district, the quest for innovation must be unending; and robust innovation can only be sustained by a school district hovering at the edge of chaos but never falling over the edge.

Innovative systemic flux brings educators and school systems to the edge of chaos. Despite the gut-wrenching prospect of teetering at the edge of chaos, there is a need to sustain innovative flux so school districts can move unwaveringly toward higher performance peaks. By teetering at the edge of chaos, school systems can find stunningly creative solutions to the puzzles they are trying to solve—puzzles such as "How do we establish and sustain positive and productive relationships with our community?" "How do we provide children with world-class instruction?" and "How do we provide our teachers and support staff with a motivating and satisfying work life?"

Sustaining innovation is particularly tricky because it requires the nerve-wracking condition of a school system being out of balance and at the edge of chaos (that is, in a state of controlled yet creative disequilibrium). Thus, a school district wanting to sustain innovative thinking and puzzle solving must create for itself a state of controlled disequilibrium in much the same way that people skillfully dancing on ice remain on the verge of tumbling but continually catch themselves and never fall down. To be innovative, to move to the next higher peak of performance, a school system cannot anchor itself to its past or current performance peak. Change leaders in school districts must build into their districts the capacity to exploit flux, not outlaw it.

Principle #8

Don't solve problems, seek opportunities. When change leaders seek to find opportunities instead of seeking problems to be solved, this shift in perspective builds and sustains creative and emotional energy for school district renewal and embeds a positive approach to innovation into the internal social infrastructure of a school system. Lippitt (1980) validated this perspective through research that confirmed that people tend to perform more productively and develop better long-term plans when working on positive goals and visions rather than focusing on solving problems. Focusing on exciting opportunities releases creative energy and keeps people engaged over a longer period of time. Thus, instead of asking "What's wrong?" educators should seek opportunities to improve their school systems by asking and answering four questions: (1) "What future do we want for our system?" (2) "Where are we now?" (3) "What do we need to do in order to create that desirable future?" and (4) "How do we simultaneously navigate three winding change-paths leading to that future"?

Principle #9

There are three paths leading to a transformed school system. The literature on whole-system change (for example, Emery & Purser, 1995; Pasmore, 1988; Pasmore, Frank, & Rehm, 1992) tells us that there are three riverlike paths that must be followed to transform an organization: Path 1—improve the organization's relationships with its external environment; Path 2—improve the organization's core and supporting work processes; and Path 3—improve the organization's internal social "infrastructure." Additional information about these three paths is found in chapters 3 and 4.

CONCLUSION

To transform your district by simultaneously moving along three winding change-paths from the present to the future, you need a methodology that is simultaneously mechanistic (that is, structured and systematic) and organic (that is, flexible, agile, and adaptable to changing circumstances and unexpected opportunities). You also need a methodology that is appropriately simple, given the complexity of transformational change (this is the lesson of Ockham's Razor—the most elegant solution to a problem is the one that is appropriately simple in relation to the complexity of the problem—not overly simple, and definitely not overly complex).

Creating and sustaining fundamental change in a school system is also a complex endeavor. Complex, however, doesn't mean impossible. It means there is a lot to do, and a lot of that has to be done simultaneously. Transformation is not a quick fix for your district's performance. It's not about tinkering at the edges of your system. Fundamental change is about drilling down to the core of your system, uncovering unhealthy or failing system dynamics, envisioning a desirable future for your district, and then creating change along three riverlike paths toward that future.

The information provided in this chapter gives you an overview of the change topography you must traverse if you want your district to make a transformation journey. We also provided some information that can serve as a compass to help orient you to the nature of district as a system. The next chapter enriches the above information by adding more depth to your understanding of what it takes to shape the future of your school system.

REFERENCES

Ackoff, R. L. (1999). *Re-creating the corporation: A design of organizations for the 21st Century.* New York: Oxford University Press.

Burke, W. W. (2002). *Organization change: Theory and practice.* Thousand Oaks, CA: Sage.

Cummings, T. G., & Worley, C. G. (2001). *Organization development and change* (7th ed.). Cincinnati, OH: South-Western College.

Duffy, F. M. (2002). *Step-Up-To-Excellence: An innovative approach to managing and rewarding performance in school systems.* Lanham, MD: ScarecrowEducation.

Duffy, F. M. (2003). *Courage, passion, and vision: A guide to leading systemic school improvement.* Lanham, MD: ScarecrowEducation/American Association of School Administrators.

Duffy, F. M. (2004, summer). The destination of three paths: Improved student, faculty and staff, and system learning. *The Forum, 68*(4), 313–324.

Emery, M. & Purser, R. E. (1995). *The search conference: A comprehensive guide to theory and practice.* San Francisco: Jossey-Bass.

Haines, S. G. (1999). *The manager's pocket guide to systems thinking and learning.* Amherst, MA: HRD Press.

Katz, D., & Kahn, R. L. (1978). *The social psychology of organizations* (2nd ed.). New York: John Wiley & Sons.

Kelly, K. (1998). *New rules for the new economy: 10 radical strategies for a connected world.* New York: Penguin Books.

Lawrence, P. R., & Lorsch, J. W. (1967). *Organization and environment: Managing differentiation and integration.* Cambridge, MA: Harvard Business School.

Lewin, R. (1992). *Complexity: Life on the edge of chaos.* New York: Macmillan.

Lippitt, R. (1980). *Choosing the future you prefer.* Washington, DC: Development Publishers.

Lumsden, G., & Lumsden, D. (2004). *Communicating in groups and teams* (4th ed.). Belmont, CA: Wadsworth.

Pasmore, W. A. (1988). *Designing effective organizations: The sociotechnical systems perspective.* New York: Wiley & Sons.

Pasmore, W., Frank, G., & Rehm, R. (1992). *Preparing people to participate in organizational change: Developing citizenship for the active organization.* Cleveland, OH: Pasmore & Associates.

Sartre, J. P. (1934). *Theory and practice of psychotherapy.* New York: Brooks/Cole.

Seyle, H. (1956). *The stress of life.* New York: McGraw-Hill.

von Bertalanffy, L. (1950). An outline of general systems theory. *British Journal of the Philosophy of Science, 1,* 139–164.

CHAPTER 3

A Change Leader's Guide to Shaping a School District's Future

This chapter provides additional insights into why whole-school systems need to be transformed rather than improving pieces of them. It begins with an explanation of what it takes to transform entire systems, including a discussion of transformational leadership. The chapter concludes by offering guidance on how to shape the future of your school district.

ORGANIZATION TRANSFORMATION

Organization transformation is a change strategy that aims to create significant and simultaneous changes in three sets of organizational variables, which Duffy (2003a; Duffy & Dale, 2001; Duffy, Rogerson, & Blick, 2000) calls change-paths: Path 1—improve a district's relationship with its external environment; Path 2—improve a district's core and supporting work processes; and Path 3—improve a district's internal social "infrastructure." This section of the chapter explores the concept of organization transformation that follows these three paths.

The VUCA Environment

Not too long ago, the environment for school systems was rather simple and stable. Not any more. Federal legislation such as No Child Left Behind and the triple societal engines of standards, assessments, and accountability have increased the instability and complexity of school districts' environments to extraordinary levels. Add to this frenetic mix our mobile society with its transient families who expect that their children's education in their next hometown will be at least as good as the education they receive in their current hometown, even if the new school district is 3,000 miles away. This complexity and instability puts significant demands on senior leaders in school systems with responsibility for determining the future of their districts.

Many contemporary authors writing about organization transformation (for example, Hock, 1995; Wheatley, 1999, 2001) rightly point out that those who manage organizations and try to improve them are locked inside an outdated and unhelpful mental model—a mental model often characterized as Newtonian or mechanistic. Yesterday's organizations were able to use and benefit from the mechanistic metaphor because the environments they existed within were relatively stable and simple. Today's organizations, including many school systems, find themselves in environments that are *v*olatile, *u*ncertain, *c*omplex, and *a*mbiguous (VUCA) (Murphy, 2002). Organization designs best suited for VUCA environments are those using contemporary metaphors often characterized as organic (Daft, 2001).

Some authors characterize a VUCA environment as chaotic. Dee Hock (1995) is one of these people. He coined a new term to describe this kind of environment: *chaordic*—the combination of chaos and order. If change leaders want to provide strategic leadership to transform their school systems using a conceptual framework like Hock's notion of chaordic organizations and Murphy's (2002) VUCA model, these transformation-minded change leaders must accept the premise that their school systems are self-organizing, adaptive, nonlinear, complex systems that exhibit characteristics of both chaos and order.

Change leadership within a chaordic, VUCA environment occurs within a strategic arena. The strategic arena for transforming school systems extends over at least three levels—local, state, and federal. Strategic leadership to shape the future of a school system through transformational change must focus on anticipating, identifying, and coordinating hopes, aspirations, policies, and legislation at all three levels. At the local level, strategic leadership focuses on a school district's community's hopes and aspirations for its youth. At the state level, strategic leadership to transform a school system focuses on the policies and requirements of state departments of education. At the federal level, strategic leadership to transform a school system focuses on interpreting and responding to the requirements of federal legislation affecting education (for example, No Child Left Behind). If change leaders are "blind" to this three-level strategic arena, then they will probably fail to transform their school systems.

The turbulent environments within which many school districts exist also create metaphorical "white water" (Vaill, 1991). To navigate this white water, some change leaders are awakening to the need to transform their school systems in fundamental ways by creating simultaneous changes along the three change-paths identified above. These fundamental changes also result in an examination and a reshaping of a district's basic purpose; its identity as an agency of its community; and its relationship with parents, community members, and other external stakeholders.

Fundamental, transformational change is required to navigate the white water. Incremental change—or as it is sometimes called, continuous improvement—is grossly ineffective for functioning effectively within a white-water environment. It is ineffective because of the focus of continuous improvement. The focus is on tweaking the status quo to make it incrementally better. There is, however, a role for continuous improvement in a transformation process: It must follow, not precede, transformation.

Organization transformation is often required in response to complex and unstable environments. This kind of fundamental change is often associated with significant modifications in an organization's grand strategy, which, in turn, requires changes in an organization's relationships with its external environment, in its core and supporting work processes, and in its internal social infrastructure. Deep and broad fundamental change of this sort requires a new mental model for organizing and managing organizations that leads to qualitatively different ways of perceiving, thinking, and behaving in organizations (Cummings & Worley, 2001).

Approaches to Fundamental (Transformational) Change

All approaches to creating fundamental change have five common features (Cummings & Worley, 2001, pp. 499–501). These features are described below. We added two features (6 and 7) to this list that we think are needed to shape the future of a school system. Transformation . . .

1. is triggered by disruptions in an organization's environment or within itself,
2. is systemic and revolutionary,
3. requires a new organizing paradigm,
4. is driven by senior executives and line management,
5. requires continuous innovation and learning,
6. requires a reshaping of a school district's organization culture, and
7. requires courageous, passionate, and visionary leadership.

Let's take a closer look at each of these features.

Transformation Is Triggered by Disruptions

Tushman, Newman, and Romanelli (1986, pp. 29–44) suggested that transformational change is stimulated by disruptions in an organization's external and internal environments. These discontinuities, interpreted for school systems, are summarized below.

1. *Industry discontinuities:* In education, these discontinuities are found in legal, political, economic, and technological conditions that affect how a district operates. The federal legislation called *No Child Left Behind* is an example of an "industry" discontinuity in the field of education.
2. *Product life-cycle shifts:* In education, teachers are knowledge workers and school districts are knowledge-creating organizations (Duffy, 2002). One first-level outcome of their work—their "product"—is the information they learn, organize, and present to students. The second-level and primary "product" of their work is educated students. Product "life-cycle" discontinuities significantly affect first-level outcomes (the information that is learned, organized, and presented to students) and they ultimately affect the second-level outcome; for example, teachers are inundated with the latest "flavor of the month" teaching method, they

are swarmed by the latest developments in how to tap into students' learning styles, and what they thought was state of the art quickly becomes passé. If these discontinuities are perceived as valid and significant, they can trigger transformation.
3. *Internal company dynamics:* In education, these discontinuities include changes in a school district's culture, changing student demographics, changing teacher demographics, or frequent superintendent turnover.

Disruptions like the ones described above can severely shake up a school district and push it to alter dramatically its grand strategy and, in turn, its mission, values, organization design, systems, and procedures. Of course, this is not always a bad thing. Sometimes these kinds of disruptions are required to break a system's status quo and start it moving toward transformation.

Transformation Is Systemic and Revolutionary

Transformation requires fundamental and deep changes in a school district's relationship with its external environment, in its core and supporting work processes, and in its internal social infrastructure (which includes organization design, organization culture, job descriptions, and the reward system). Changes of this kind and of this magnitude are often characterized as systemic and transformational.

Transformation also requires different tools and techniques for making a successful transformation (Burke, 2002), which include total system events such as the Community Engagement Conference and System Engagement Conference that are part of the Step-Up-To-Excellence methodology (Duffy, 2002, 2003a, 2004), which is presented in the next chapter. Transformation also should occur rapidly so that it doesn't get bogged down in organizational politics, individual resistance, or other forms of organizational inertia (Tushman, Newman, & Romanelli, 1986). In making the same point, Cummings and Worley (2001) said, "The faster an organization can respond to disruptions, the quicker it can attain the benefits of operating in a new way" (p. 500).

Because school districts are systems, all of their features and components tend to connect to each other by complex cause and effect loops and tend to reinforce each other through a system phenomenon known as balancing equilibrium (or the status quo). These complex and mutually reinforcing system dynamics make it difficult to improve a system in a piecemeal manner (Cummings & Worley, 2001, p. 500). All of these dynamics fall into three broad categories (environmental relationships, core and supporting work processes, and internal social infrastructure) and must be improved simultaneously and in a coordinated fashion (Duffy, Rogerson, & Blick, 2000; Miller, Friesen, & Mintzberg, 1984).

Transformation Is Driven by Senior and Line Managers

Real-world experience is clear that senior executives and other line managers must drive transformation (Kotter, 1996; Waldersee, 1997). In school districts, the senior executives are the superintendent and his or her immediate assistants. Line managers include building principals. Without the unequivocal and highly visible commitment and substantial participation of these leaders, transformational change in school districts will fail.

Tushman, Newman, and Nadler (1988) described three key roles for executive leaders during times of transformational change:

1. *Envisioning:* articulating a clear and credible description of a new strategic orientation for the organization, setting new and challenging performance standards to move toward, and appreciating the organization's past accomplishments.
2. *Energizing:* demonstrating personal excitement for and unequivocal commitment to the new strategic direction and its related goals, and communicating early success to build energy to support the transformation.
3. *Enabling:* providing resources needed to complete the transformation, rewarding performance that supports the transformation, building a new management team to lead the transformed organization, and developing management systems to support the transformation process.

Transformation Requires Innovation and Learning

Transforming a school system means that the way the district is organized and how it operates in the future must be significantly different than in the present or the past. To create this kind of transformation, significant innovation and learning is required. Two of the most insidious obstacles blocking this kind of innovation and learning are personal and organizational mental models (see chapter 8 for additional information about unlearning and learning mental models).

In organizations, there are generally two broad categories of mental models—personal and organizational (Duffy, 2003a, 2003b). Changing personal mental models is greatly facilitated by using a knowledge-creation process (Duffy, 2002). Knowledge creation in school districts surfaces personal knowledge and mental models, makes that knowledge and those models explicit, and then converts the best of these into organization-wide knowledge and mental models while simultaneously helping people unlearn ineffective or inappropriate mental models.

Your school district's organizational mental model is found in the way people in your district think about it as an entity. To shape a new future for your district, educators in your district, including you, have to change the way you think about it. Every behavior in your district is shaped by its mental model. Every key action taken is prompted and reinforced by that model. Your district will not be transformed unless the controlling mental model is changed.

In many ways, your district's controlling mental model is like the autopilot on an airplane. Imagine that a plane you are piloting is stuck on autopilot and you want to change direction. You and your copilot can wrestle the steering yoke toward the direction you want to go, but eventually you will both tire and release your grip. The autopilot will then retake control of the plane and move it back to its original flight path—the one that was internally programmed into the autopilot computer.

This is what happens when you try to transform your school district without changing your district's controlling mental model. The mental model is the district's autopilot. You can wrestle with change until you tire and when you surrender to your fatigue, the district will move back to its original flight path—the one internally programmed into your district's culture. This is the experience behind the French folk wisdom expressed by French novelist Jean-Baptiste Alphonse Karr, who wrote *"Plus ça change, plus c'est la même chose"* (The more things change, the more they stay the same).

There is a more effective way to transform a district: Reset your district's autopilot—its mental model. This is an important principle because transformational change always starts first in peoples' minds. The way they think determines how they feel, the way they feel determines how they act, and the way they act determines whether or not transformation is successful.

Thoughts influence feelings and feelings influence behavior. These cause-and-effect relationships imply choice. People choose to think a certain way, choose to feel a certain way, and choose to behave in a certain way. What people often fail to realize, however, is that all choices have consequences. Many difficulties in shaping the future of a school system occur because people make choices on the basis of several frequently unreliable sources, all of which have predictable consequences.

- *Organization culture* (everyone is doing it). Just because "everyone" (which usually isn't really everyone) is doing it is not the basis of a good choice.
- *Tradition* (we've always done it this way). Tradition is a manifestation of balancing equilibrium, otherwise known as status quo. It often is expressed in the question, "What's the precedent for this?" If you want to transform your district in new and innovative ways, there is no precedent.
- *Reason* (it seemed like the logical thing to do). Human thinking processes are notoriously flawed. Many people (perhaps most) do not consistently use well-structured reasoning processes and prefer to use mental heuristics for making decisions—heuristics that are frequently linked to emotion.
- *Emotion* (it just felt right). Some folks rely on how they "feel" about something when making decisions. These feelings are often rationalized as intuitive insights or common sense.

Instead of choices being made on the basis of the above sources, what school districts need are shared standards of organizational, team, and individual performance that are developed through a highly participative process that engages community members, faculty, and staff in structured interactions to create those standards. Then choices are made against the standards of performance. Therefore, one of the most important steps you will take to shape the future of your district is to settle the issue of what the standards of performance will be (districtwide, cluster, school, team, and individual standards of performance).

Transformation Requires a New Organizing Paradigm

Organization transformation, by definition, is an example of second-order change, also known as gamma change (Cummings & Worley, 2001). Gamma change creates stunning shifts in individual and organizational mental models or paradigms. Metaphors are often created to help people understand the new paradigms (Duffy, 2003a). Examples of metaphors that help educators think differently about their school systems include "learning communities" and "system of excellence."

A powerful new paradigm (or mental model) for shaping the future of a school system is defined by features such as high participation of faculty and staff in determining the future of their district; a central office that functions as a central service center; leadership roles that are less complex, less stressful, and more focused on true leadership behaviors; and an organization design that is more democratic, more agile, and more flexible, thereby creating a school district that has the capacity to seize opportunities at the intersection of anticipatory planning and unanticipated events (Duffy, 2003a).

Transformation Requires a Reshaping of a School District's Culture

Changes in a school district's culture should support changes in that district's strategic direction, mission, and vision. Cultural change focuses on the "people" part of a school system—the part called the internal social "infrastructure." The internal social infrastructure supports (or constrains) people doing their work. It is composed of organization design, policies, power and political dynamics, procedures, job descriptions, and, most important of all, the district's culture.

Duck (2001) calls organization culture "The Change Monster"—that collection of human forces that either facilitate or prevent transformation. Culture is most often captured in the phrase, "This is the way we do things around here." Culture is a complex, interwoven fabric composed of people's collective assumptions, beliefs, and values. A direct, head-on approach to changing culture will meet with difficulty, resistance, and strong human emotion (Burke, 2002).

If a district's culture is an obstacle to reshaping its future, then initiating changes to that culture is a very important early transformation activity. In fact, it can be predicted that if you cannot change your school district's culture (which is part of its internal social infrastructure), your transformation effort will fail—no culture change, no transformation. One of the reasons that organization culture is so powerful is that it is driven by your faculty and staff's collective basic assumptions (that is, the controlling mental model) about the purpose of your district, the norms that govern behavior in the district, and the values you all have for educating children and for how you treat the adults who work in the system. These basic assumptions, beliefs, and values, when enacted individually and collectively, produce cultural artifacts. These artifacts include observable behavior, management systems, policies, procedures, organization design, and the physical design of your buildings.

School districts do their work within increasingly complex and changing environments. To adapt effectively to this complexity and rate of change, school districts need to redefine their strategic direction through organization transformation. However, implementing a new strategy aimed at transformation can meet serious resistance from a school district's existing culture. In this way, an organization culture that was once a source of strength for a district becomes a major liability. Restyling a district's internal social infrastructure, which includes its culture, is therefore an important part of your school system's transformation.

Transformational Change Requires Courageous, Passionate, and Visionary Leadership

Courageous, passionate, and visionary leadership must begin at the highest level of a school system and then spread throughout a school district (Duffy, 2003a). Courage helps leaders stand their ground in the face of adversity. Passion gives them the psychological and emotional energy they need to persevere toward the goal of transformation. A vision describes a desirable future for a school system to move toward.

Courage, passion, and vision are useless in isolation. They must be simultaneously present in a district's change leaders. A leader can have courage, but not have passion or vision. A passionate leader might lack the courage of his or her convictions and cave in to political pressure to give up the dream. A visionary leader without courage and passion is a person with a dream but who doesn't have the strength of character or emotional energy to make that dream real. Courage, passion, and vision are powerful when they exist as a triad.

Courageous, passionate, and visionary leadership must also be transformational. Burns (1978) distinguished between traditional managers (transactional leaders) and leaders who work to transform their organizations (transformational leaders). Tichy and Devanna (1986) expanded on Burns's ideas, asserting that managers engage in very little change but manage what is present and leave things much as they found them when they depart; that is, they become masters of the status quo. Transformational leadership, they observed, is marked by leadership for change and innovation that is provided in the spirit of entrepreneurship. These transformational leaders transform organizations by moving them toward a vision of a desirable future for the organization.

It is important to note, however, that transformational leaders do not abandon transactional management tasks. Instead, their transactional skills serve as a foundation for providing transformational leadership. Their transactional management practices are required to complete daily routines (Leithwood, 1992). Leithwood, however, maintained that these transactional practices "do not stimulate improvement . . . [rather] transformational leadership provides the incentive" (p. 9).

Who are the transformational leaders who stimulate fundamental change in their school districts? These leaders must exist first at the superintendent's level and then they must be distributed throughout a school district. If change leaders' courageous, passionate, and visionary leadership is like a leadership "tree," to shape the future of their district they need a "forest" of courageous, passionate, and visionary leaders. Therefore, transformational leadership is not restricted to a single person. Anyone can provide this kind of leadership. Leadership of this class can emerge from the ranks of building principals, teachers, cafeteria workers, bus drivers, janitors, central office staff, school board members, and students. Anyone who is proactive in the process of translating visions into reality can and should be identified and then developed into a transformational leader (Block, 1987).

WHAT IT TAKES TO TRANSFORM SCHOOL SYSTEMS

Organization transformation requires fundamental and radical changes in how educators in school systems perceive, think, and behave. Evolutionary change such as continuous improvement isn't a transformation strategy. Tweaking the organization and continuously improving the status quo won't work if you are trying to create fundamental, transformational change. To achieve transformation, you and your colleagues need to alter extensively your collective assumptions, beliefs, and values about what your district stands for, how it functions, how it is designed, how it treats people, how it relates to stakeholders, what its management philosophy is, and the numerous processes, procedures, policies, and so forth that shape people's behavior at the individual, school, cluster, and district levels; in other words, you have to reshape your district's controlling mental model.

The reality of transforming your school system is also never a sum of the visible changes you create. The reality of transformation is found in a compelling idea that is first sown and grown inside the minds and hearts of your colleagues; that is, to transform your district, you and your colleagues must be liberated from the constraints of the past and present by the power of an idea—a vision of a desirable and exciting future for your district. Once liberated from the cognitive and emotional shackles of the past and present, you and your colleagues will have the capacity and creativity to fashion unparalleled future opportunities for improving student, faculty and staff, and whole-system learning.

For the promise of school district transformation to become powerful enough to unleash emotional and psychological energy and collective imagination, your change leadership must aim to (1) crystallize the hopes and dreams of your people around a strategic vision that creates unity of purpose for your district; (2) provide the means and resources to achieve that vision; and (3) help your colleagues and stakeholders see that the changes you are proposing are within their grasp, not beyond their reach. Your people must see, understand, and embrace the vision and then believe that there are ways and resources to achieve it (see chapter 7 for more information about shared visions).

It is also important to know that establishing unity of purpose does not require uniformity of thought and action. You can have a shared vision and still encourage and support divergent points of view about how to arrive there. In the field of organization development, encouraging divergent paths toward a single, unifying vision is called the principle of equifinality (Cummings & Worley, 2001).

Transforming an entire school district is a "mass movement" of people, structures, and programs toward a new future. The desire for change is, at best, a superficial motive for making this kind of transformation. Hoffer (1951) explored the nature of mass movements. He spoke of the art of "religiofication"—that is, the art of turning practical purposes into holy causes. If you want to transform an entire school system, the practical purpose for doing that (improving student, faculty and staff, and whole-system learning) must be turned into a holy cause for your faculty, staff, and community.

Of course, a holy cause is just a metaphor for the kind of motivation you and your colleagues need to possess if you want to transform your school system. This kind of motivation will be necessary if you want to "unfreeze" your district and start it moving in the direction of the vision that you and your colleagues have for the district. Helping your colleagues to experience the motivation associated with a holy cause will require you to use effective strategic communication skills.

GUIDANCE FOR SHAPING YOUR DISTRICT'S FUTURE

The following advice builds upon the information presented above and in the previous chapter. The advice is connected to the real-world experience of real people working to transform real school systems (for example, Togneri & Anderson, 2003; also see Lee and Reigeluth's essay in section 3 of this book).

Shaping your district's future must be guided by the knowledge that good school districts must move toward higher levels of performance. There are many good school systems in the United States and throughout the world. At the dawn of the 21st century, however, good is not good enough to bring our children to the knowledge they have a right to and with which they will bring us and themselves to the future. Not only is good not good enough, but as Collins (2001) says,

> Good is the enemy of great. And that is one of the reasons why we have so little that becomes great. We don't have great schools, principally because we have good schools. We don't have great government, principally because we have good government. Few people attain great lives, in large part because it is just so easy to settle for a good life. The vast majority of companies never become great, precisely because the vast majority become quite good—and that is their main problem. (p. 1)

Shaping your district's future also entails identifying and exploring the controlling mental model that influences all aspects of work life in your district. That mental model is often reflected in your district's current vision statement and strategic plan. It is always embedded in your district's internal social "infrastructure"—that collection of system features that support (or inhibit) people doing their work, which includes organization design, organization culture, policies, procedures, communication patterns, and so on.

Shaping your district's future necessitates the direct and meaningful involvement of your district's customers (parents and students) and key external stakeholders (community groups, influential individuals in the community, and state department of education people, for example). Your district's faculty and staff must also be directly and meaningfully involved in shaping your district's future.

Shaping your district's future means you must know, understand, and apply effective approaches to strategic planning so you can get to the future you envision. When engaging your district in strategic planning, you must aim to create a district significantly different from the one you have now. If you don't, the planning will not be strategic (Cook, 2000).

Shaping your district's future requires you and your colleagues to learn and become skillful at using an organizational transformation methodology that is systemic, systematic, comprehensive, and organic—for example, Step-Up-To-Excellence (Duffy, 2002), which is described in the next chapter. The reason you need an appropriate methodology is because organization transformation is complex and messy. A methodology with the aforementioned characteristics can help you sort out the complexity and work through the mess. A methodology to create and sustain systemic change also has to be embedded into your district's organization design so that it becomes a permanent part of how your district operates. Even when your current superintendent leaves, the next superintendent and all after him or her should be required by school board policy to use that same methodology to create desirable and valued improvements in your district.

Shaping your district's future takes you on a fascinating and sometimes confusing journey. Along the way you will be surprised by unplanned opportunities and unanticipated threats. You need to reshape your district's organization design to create flexibility and agility so your faculty and staff can respond quickly and effectively to these surprises.

Shaping your district's future means you improve not only the academic side of your district but also the nonacademic supporting units. Children are in school to learn, but their experiences on the bus going to school, on the athletic playing fields, or in the cafeteria can add value to their educational experience, or those experiences can make their lives in school miserable.

Shaping your district's future demands attention to aligning all parts of your school system to support a superordinate goal—the unifying goal, the big dream, the grand vision for your district. This alignment must be vertical up through your system and horizontal across teams, departments, schools, and clusters of schools.

Shaping your district's future compels you to counter the illusion of peak performance. In nature, successful organisms adapt to their environments by evolving to peaks of success. Successful school districts are like this too because they evolve to their current performance peaks. For school districts, however, there are multiple peaks that evoke images of the Rocky Mountains, where some peaks are lower than others. What if the peak your district sits atop is low compared to others but folks inside the district don't realize it? Wouldn't that lack of perspective create a false sense of success?

Shaping your district's future requires a new mental model for the meaning of "organizational change." The new mental model transports you from the world of "change" to the world of "flux" (Kelly, 1998). While change focuses on creating differences, flux is about managing creative destruction followed by nascence. Flux breaks down the status quo while creating a temporary foundation for innovative puzzle solving and rebirth. Innovation destroys the status quo by introducing creative improvements to a system. The quest for innovation is amaranthine. Robust innovation sustains itself by poising on the edge of constant chaos.

Shaping your district's future requires all people working in your district to take deliberate actions to sustain the improvements you create. Sustaining innovation is particularly tricky since it emanates from a system being out of balance (in a state of creative disequilibrium). Thus, a school district wanting to sustain innovative thinking and puzzle solving must create for itself a state of controlled disequilibrium whereby it remains suspended in an almost-falling state—inclined to fall but continually catching itself and never quite toppling. To be innovative, to move to the next higher peak of performance, a school system cannot anchor itself to its past or current performance peak.

Shaping your district's future requires you to give up trying to solve problems and focus instead on seeking opportunities. The power of compounded results (for example, compound interest) is one of the most potent physical forces on Earth. Each opportunity seized in a school district can be compounded if it becomes a platform for launching yet other innovations. Like a chain reaction, one well-placed innovation can trigger dozens of innovation progeny. New opportunities are created in a combinatorial fashion just as people combine and recombine the same twenty-six letters of the English alphabet to write an infinite number of books.

Shaping your district's future demands strategic alignment. Strategic alignment has two dimensions: vertical and horizontal. Vertical alignment ensures that the work of individuals supports the goals of their teams, the work of the teams support the goals of their schools (or supporting work units), the work of the schools supports the goals of their clusters, and the work of the clusters supports the grand vision and strategic direction of the district. Horizontal alignment connects individuals, teams, schools, and clusters with your district's customers and external stakeholders.

CONCLUSION

You and your colleagues can shape the future of your school district by engaging in transformational change. Your district's future, however, is not sitting out there in time and space waiting for your arrival. You must be proactive in shaping that future by influencing events, making strategic decisions, and taking strategic action that moves you ever closer to the future you and your colleagues envision for your school district. Along the way, your district has to be flexible and agile enough to respond quickly to unanticipated opportunities and threats.

As you anticipate and respond to unexpected events, the original vision you had for your district will be reshaped. This reshaping is normal and it is to be expected because your district's future is not a static location sitting out there in the future. Your district's future is something you have to envision and shape by moving along a timeline that leads you through the near future into the distant future. As you make that journey through time, the circumstances, assumptions, and beliefs you used to frame your original vision may change, thus requiring you to reshape your district's envisioned future. This is a normal and predictable experience and nothing to fret about because organizations of all kinds never perfectly achieve the future they initially envision for themselves.

To make a transformation journey like the one you've been reading about in chapters 2 and 3, you need more than a view of the change topography and a compass to orient you to the terrain. You also need a detailed map to show you *how* to navigate a complex transformation journey. The map is provided in the next chapter in the guise of a change navigation protocol especially designed to help you navigate whole-system change by simultaneously following the three change-paths described earlier. The protocol is called Step-Up-To-Excellence (Duffy, 2002, 2003a, 2004).

Because each school district is unique, however, the way that Step-Up-To-Excellence is used will vary depending on the unique circumstances of each district using the methodology. Therefore, as you read the description of the protocol and its various activities in the next chapter, please keep in mind that you will need to adapt the protocol to fit your particular circumstances.

REFERENCES

Block, P. (1987). *The empowered manager: Positive political skills at work.* San Francisco: Jossey-Bass.

Burke, W. W. (2002). *Organization change: Theory and practice.* Thousand Oaks, CA: Sage.

Burns, J. M. (1978). *Leadership.* New York: Harper & Row.

Collins, J. (2001). *Good to great: Why some companies make the leap . . . and others don't.* New York: HarperCollins.

Cook, W. J., Jr. (2000). *Strategics: The art and science of holistic strategy.* Westport, CT: Quorum Books.

Cummings, T. G., & Worley, C. G. (2001). *Organization development and change* (7th ed.). Cincinnati, OH: South-Western College.

Daft, R. L. (2001). *Organization theory and design* (7th ed.). Cincinnati, OH: South-Western College.

Duck, J. D. (2001). *The change monster: The human forces that fuel or foil corporate transformation & change.* New York: Random House.

Duffy, F. M. (2002). *Step-Up-To-Excellence: An innovative approach to managing and rewarding performance in school systems.* Lanham, MD: Scarecrow Education.

Duffy, F. M. (2003a). *Courage, passion and vision: A guide to leading systemic school improvement.* Lanham, MD: Scarecrow Education/American Association of School Administrators.

Duffy, F. M. (2003b). I think, therefore I am resistant to change. *Journal of Staff Development, 24*(1), 30–36.

Duffy, F. M. (2004). *Moving upward together: Creating strategic alignment to sustain systemic school improvement.* No. 1, Leading Systemic School Improvement Series. Lanham, MD: Rowman & Littlefield Education.

Duffy, F. M., & Dale, J. D. (Eds.) (2001). *Creating successful school systems:*

Voices from the university, the field and the community. Norwood, MA: Christopher-Gordon.

Duffy, F. M., Rogerson, L. G., & Blick, C. (2000). *Redesigning America's schools: A systems approach to improvement.* Norwood, MA: Christopher-Gordon.

Hock, D. W. (1995). The chaordic organization: Out of control and into order. *World Business Academy Perspectives, 9*(1), 5–18.

Hoffer, E. (1951). *The true believer: Thoughts on the nature of mass movements.* New York: Harper & Row.

Karr, J.-B. A. (n.d.). Jean-Baptiste Alphonse Karr. Retrieved on March 17, 2006, from http://www.reference.com/browse/wiki/Jean-Baptiste_Alphonse_Karr

Kelly, K. (1998). *New rules for the new economy: 10 radical strategies for a connected world.* New York: Penguin Books.

Kotter, J. P. (1996). *Leading change.* Boston, MA: Harvard Business School Press.

Leithwood, K. (1992). The move toward transformational leadership. *Educational Leadership, 49*(5), 8–12.

Miller, D. L., Friesen, P. H. & Mintzberg, H. (1984). *Organizations: A quantum view.* Englewood Cliffs, NJ: Prentice-Hall.

Murphy, R. (2002). Managing strategic change: An executive overview. Retrieved on June 15, 2005, from http://www.carlisle.army.mil/usawc/dclm/pdf/MurphyMgtText03.pdf

Tichy, N. M., & Devanna, M. A. (1986). The transformational leader. *Training and Development Journal, 41*(7), 27–32.

Togneri, W., & Anderson, S. E. (2003). *Beyond islands of excellence: What districts can do to improve instruction and achievement in all schools—A leadership brief.* Washington, DC: Learning First Alliance.

Tushman, M. L., Newman, W. H., & Nadler, D. A. (1988). Executive leadership and organizational evolution: Managing incremental and discontinuous change. In R. H. Kilmann & T. J. Covin (Eds.). *Corporate transformation: Revitalising organisations for a competitive world* (pp. 102–130). San Francisco: Jossey-Bass.

Tushman, M. L., Newman, W. H., & Romanelli, E. (1986). Convergence and upheaval: Managing the unsteady pace of organizational evolution. *California Management Review, 29*(1), 29–44.

Vaill, P. (1991). *Managing as a performing art: New ideas for a world of chaotic change.* San Francisco: Jossey-Bass.

Waldersee, R. (1997). Becoming a learning organization: The transformation of the workforce. *Journal of Management Development, 16*(4), 262–274.

Wheatley, M. J. (1999). *Leadership and the new science.* San Francisco: Berrett-Kohler.

Wheatley, M. J. (2001). Bringing schools back to life: Schools as living systems. In F. M. Duffy & J. D. Dale (Eds.), *Creating successful school systems: Voices from the university, the field and the community* (pp. 3–19). Norwood, MA: Christopher-Gordon.

CHAPTER 4

How to Transform an Entire School District: A Change Navigation Protocol for School Systems

In the previous two chapters, you found a description of the topography of whole-system change and a compass to navigate the terrain, including advice about what it takes to shape the future of your school system. That information will help school PR specialists and change leaders answer the question, "Why do we need to transform our entire school system?" But knowledge of the topography and a compass in hand is not enough to navigate whole-system change. You also need a detailed map—a method that shows you *how* to arrive at your destination.

This chapter provides you with a "map" in the form of a change navigation protocol specially designed to help you create and sustain whole-system change in your school district. The information describing the protocol will help you answer the question, "How do we transform our entire school system?" The protocol is called Step-Up-To-Excellence (SUTE) (Duffy, 2002, 2003, 2004a, 2004b, 2004c).

Every time SUTE is presented to an audience, there is at least one person who calls out some "yes, but" statements questioning whether the protocol is practical, doable, or valid. Three "yes, buts" that are frequently heard and responses to them are found near the end of this chapter.

THE NEED FOR A WHOLE-DISTRICT TRANSFORMATION PROTOCOL

Rolling across America is a long train called "The School Improvement Express." The triple societal engines of standards, assessment, and accountability are pulling it. The lead engine goes by the name "The No Child Left Behind Engine That Could." The rolling stock is composed of school systems and a myriad of contemporary school improvement models, processes, and desirable outcomes. The train has once again come to a stop at a broad and deep abyss that goes by the name "The Canyon of Systemic School Improvement." On the far side of the abyss lies the "Land of High Performance." The train and some of its riders want to go there. In fact, they have wanted to go there for years but have failed to make the crossing, and so they keep returning here to the edge of the abyss to stare across with longing in their hearts, wondering how they will ever traverse the canyon.

Standing at the edge of this great abyss, some educators see a threat while others see an opportunity. Some see an impossible crossing, while others see just another puzzle to be solved. Meanwhile, the pressure in the three great "engines" for setting standards, assessing student learning, and holding educators accountable for results continues to build and shows no sign of dissipating. The "engineers" have their hands on the train's brakes but they can feel the pressure trying to edge the train forward, which feels like having one foot on the brake of a car while stepping on the gas with the other foot.

Even though the train has rolled across a lot of ground and although its passengers have done good things along the way, there they stand one more time looking out over the abyss, wondering how in the world they will get to the other side. Some of those standing at the edge say, "Impossible, can't be done." Others say, "We've tried this before and failed then." Still others stand there and theorize about the complexity of crossing such a canyon. "It's so hard to define the boundaries of the canyon. Just what is a system, what does it mean, is it this or is it that? We need this, this, this, and that or we'll never cross," they suggest, but then they take no action to do what's needed. Still others, looking backward at the terrain covered by the long train say, "What's behind us is the future. What we've done in the past is what we should continue to do." But there it is in the distance—beckoning from across the canyon—the land of high performance with the promise of incomparable student, faculty and staff, and whole-system learning.

There is a significant and pressing need to cross the "Canyon of Systemic School Improvement" (for example, see Houlihan & Houlihan,

2005). Responding to this need requires a methodology specially designed to create and sustain whole-system change in school districts. One way is found in the Step-Up-To-Excellence (SUTE) protocol described below. Before examining the protocol, let's consider the traditional approach to managing change.

THE TRADITIONAL APPROACH TO MANAGING CHANGE

The traditional approach to managing change was developed by Kurt Lewin (1951). It is illustrated in Figure 4.1. What Lewin said is that to change a system, people first envision a desired future. Then, they assess their current situation and compare the present to the future, looking for gaps between what is and what's desired. Next, they develop a transition plan composed of long-range goals and short-term objectives that will move their system straight forward toward its desired future. Along the way there will be some unanticipated events that emerge, but it is assumed that the "strength" of anticipatory intentions (goals, objectives, strategic plans) will keep those unexpected events under control and thereby keep the system on a relatively

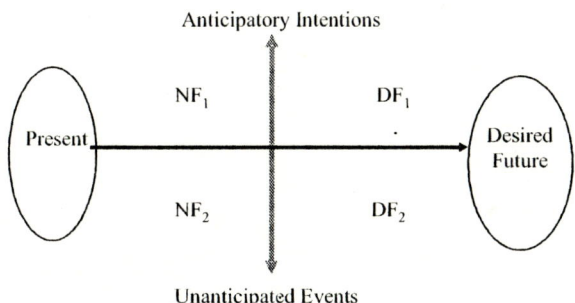

NF_1 = near future, planned
DF_1 = distant future, planned
NF_2 = near future, unplanned
DF_2 = distant future, unplanned

Copyright 2001 by Francis M. Duffy, Ph.D. All rights reserved.
www.thefmduffygroup.com

Figure 4.1. The traditional change-path—straight forward to the future

straight change-path toward the future. The problem with this approach is that it doesn't work in contemporary organizations.

Instead of the "straightforward-to-the-future" assumption represented in Figure 4.1, the complexities of contemporary society and the pressures for rapid change, combined with an increasing number of unanticipated events and unintended consequences during change, have created three winding change-paths: Path 1—an organization's relationships with its environment; Path 2—its core and supporting work processes; and Path 3—its internal social infrastructure. These winding change-paths are illustrated in Figure 4.2.

If you assume that there is a single strategic path from the present to

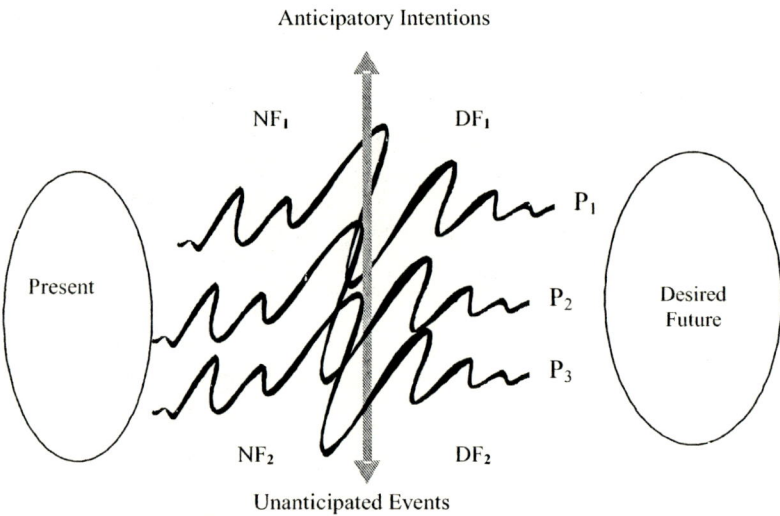

NF_1 = near future, planned
DF_1 = distant future, planned
NF_2 = near future, unplanned
DF_2 = distant future, unplanned

P_1 = Path 1: Environmental relationships
P_2 = Path 2: Core and supporting work
P_3 = Path 3: Internal social infrastructure

Copyright 2001 by Francis M. Duffy, Ph.D. All rights reserved.
www.thefmduffygroup.com

Figure 4.2. Today's nonlinear change-paths in complex organizations

the future that is relatively straightforward when there are actually three winding paths, then as you try to transform your system you will soon be off the true paths and lost. To see how you would be off the true paths (the three winding paths), trace your finger along the assumed straight change-path in Figure 4.3. Wherever the straight path leaves the winding paths, you will be off course and lost. When off course and lost, people often revert back to their old ways

To move an entire school system along the three paths identified above, you need a whole-system transformation protocol that will serve as a map to locate and navigate the three nonlinear paths to higher student, teacher and staff, and whole-district learning. Further, this kind of

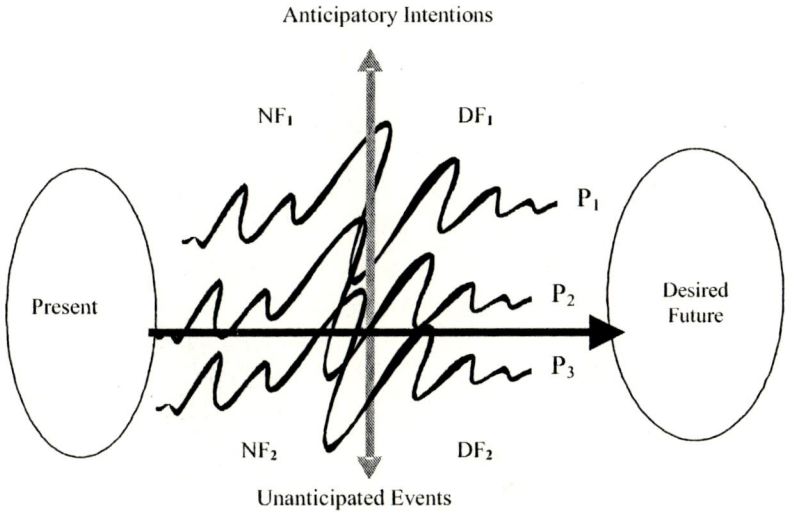

NF_1 = near future, planned
DF_1 = distant future, planned
NF_2 = near future, unplanned
DF_2 = distant future, unplanned

P_1 = Path 1: Environmental relationships
P_2 = Path 2: Core and supporting work
P_3 = Path 3: Internal social infrastructure

Copyright 2001 by Francis M. Duffy, Ph.D. All rights reserved.
www.thefmduffygroup.com

Figure 4.3. *Assuming a straight change-path means you're off the true paths and lost*

change protocol will only work if certain conditions exist within school systems and if the protocol is based on key principles for navigating whole-system change, all of which were presented in chapters 2 and 3. Let's examine the three change-paths before exploring the change protocol.

THREE PATHS TO IMPROVEMENT

Over the past 50 years, a lot has been learned about how to improve entire systems (see chapters 2 and 3). One of the core principles of whole-system change is that three sets of key organizational variables must be improved simultaneously (for example, see Pasmore, 1988). These three sets of variables are characterized as change-paths in the protocol presented below.

Path 1: Improve a District's Relationship with Its External Environment

A school district is an open system (see chapter 2). An open system is one that interacts with its environment by exchanging a valued product or service in return for needed resources. If you want your district to become a high-performing school system, you need to have a positive and supporting relationship with stakeholders in your district's external environment. But you can't wait until you transform your district to start working on these relationships. You need positive and supporting relationships shortly before you begin making important changes within your district. So, you have to improve your district's relationships with key external stakeholders as you prepare your school system to begin its transformation journey.

Path 2: Improve a District's Core and Supporting Work Processes

Core work is the most important work of any organization. In school districts, the core work is a sequenced instructional program (for example, often a preK–12th grade instructional program) conjoined with classroom teaching and learning (Duffy, 2002, 2003). Core work is maintained and enriched by supporting work. In school districts, supporting work roles include administrators, supervisors, education specialists, librarians, cafeteria workers, janitors, bus drivers, and others. Supporting work is important to the success of a school district, but it is not the most important work. Classroom teaching and learning is the most important work and must be elevated to that status if a school system wants to increase its overall effectiveness.

When trying to improve a school system, both the core and supporting work processes must be improved. Further, the entire work process (for example, preK–12th grade) must be examined and improved, not just parts of it (for example, not just the middle school, not just the language arts curriculum, or not just the high school). One of the reasons the entire work process must be improved is because of a systems improvement principle expressed as "upstream errors flow downstream" (Pasmore, 1988). This principle reflects the fact that mistakes made early in a work process flow downstream, are compounded, and create more problems later on in the process; for example, consider a comment made by a high school principal when he first heard a description of this principle. He said, "Yes, I understand. And I see that happening in our district. Our middle school program is being 'dumbed-down' and those students are entering our high school program unprepared for our more rigorous curriculum. And there is nothing we can do about it." Upstream errors always flow downstream.

Improving student learning is an important goal of improving the core and supporting work processes of a school district. But focusing only on improving student learning is a piecemeal approach to improvement. A teacher's knowledge and skill are probably two of the most important factors influencing student learning (Learning Point Associates, n.d.). So, taking steps to improve teacher learning must also be part of any school district's improvement efforts to improve student learning.

Improving student and teacher learning is an important goal of improving work in a school district—but this is *still* a piecemeal approach to improving a school district. A school district is a knowledge-creating organization and it is, or should be, a learning organization. Professional knowledge must be created and embedded in a school district's operational structures, and organizational learning must occur if a school district wants to develop and maintain the capacity to provide children with a quality education. So, school system learning (that is, organizational learning) must also be part of a district's improvement strategy to improve its core and supporting work.

Path 3: Improve a District's Internal "Social Infrastructure"

Improving work processes to improve learning for students, teachers and staff, and the whole-school system is an important goal but it is still a piecemeal approach to change. It is possible for a school district to have a fabulous curriculum with extraordinarily effective instructional methods but still have an internal social "infrastructure" (which includes organization culture, organization design, communication patterns, power and political dynamics, reward systems, and so on) that is demotivating, dissatisfying, and demoralizing for teachers. Demotivated, dissatisfied, and demoralized teachers cannot and will not use a fabulous curriculum in remarkable ways. So, in addition to improving how the work of a district is done, improvement efforts must focus simultaneously on improving a district's internal social "infrastructure."

The social infrastructure of a school system needs to be redesigned at the same time the core and supporting work processes are redesigned. Why? Because it is important to ensure that the new social infrastructure and the new work processes complement each other. The best way to ensure this complementarity is to make simultaneous improvements to both elements of a school system.

Hopefully, this three-path metaphor makes sense because the principle of simultaneous improvement is absolutely essential for effective whole-system improvement (for example, see Emery, 1977; Pasmore, 1988; Trist, Higgin, Murray, & Pollack, 1963). In the literature on systems improvement, this principle is called joint optimization (Cummings & Worley, 2001, p. 353).

THE CHANGE MAP: STEP-UP-TO-EXCELLENCE

Step-Up-To-Excellence (SUTE) is a whole-system transformation protocol especially constructed to help educators navigate three change-

HOW TO TRANSFORM AN ENTIRE SCHOOL DISTRICT   65

paths toward whole-district transformation. This protocol combines proven and effective tools for whole-system improvement. These tools have been used singly and effectively for more than 40 years; and when combined they provide educators with a comprehensive, unified, systematic, and systemic protocol for redesigning their entire school system. The protocol is illustrated in Figure 4.4.

SUTE is an innovative approach to creating and sustaining whole-system change in school districts. The change navigation protocol for implementing SUTE is highlighted below. The protocol also links the theory of systemwide organization improvement to proven tools for improving whole systems and innovative methods for improving knowledge work. The phrase "proven tools" is not used frivolously.

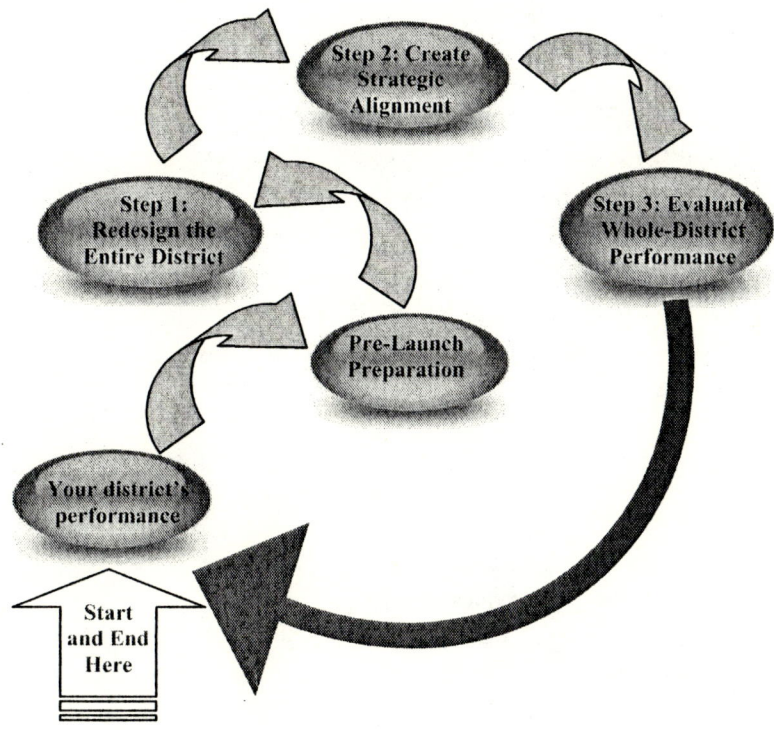

SM 2002 by Francis M. Duffy. All rights reserved. www.thefmduffygroup.com

Figure 4.4. Step-Up-To-Excellence^{SM}

Tools integrated into SUTE have years of research and successful experience supporting their effectiveness. Two of these tools are Merrelyn Emery's *Search Conference* and *Participative Design Workshop* (Emery, 2006; Emery & Purser, 1996). A third tool that can be used instead of Emery's Search Conference is Weisbord and Janoff's Future Search (Schweitz & Martens with Aronson, 2005). A fourth tool is Harrison Owen's (1991, 1993) Open Space Technology. Elements of Dannemiller's Real Time Strategic Change (Dannemiller & Jacobs, 1992; Dannemiller-Tyson Associates, 1994) also have been blended into SUTE. Another set of tools incorporated into SUTE is from field of sociotechnical systems (STS) design (for example, van Eijnatten, Eggermont, de Goffau, & Mankoe, 1994; Pava, 1983a, 1983b).

Concepts and Principles Underpinning the SUTE Change Protocol

The unit of change for SUTE is an entire school system. This is an essential principle that forms the foundation of the SUTE protocol. The rationale for this principle can be drawn from teachings as old as the Bible where it was said, "As a body is one though it has many parts, and all the parts of the body, though many, are one body . . . If one part suffers, all the parts suffer with it; if one part is honored, all the parts share the joy" (1 Corinthians 12:12, 12:26). In much the same way, a school district is one system even though it is composed of many parts.

Although a school district is a system, the dominant approach to improving school districts is not systemic; rather, it has been based on the principles of school-based management, which aims to improve schooling on a one-school-at-a-time or one-program-at-a-time basis. Many of the best current and past education reform programs are limited in their scope of impact because they focus almost exclusively on changing what happens inside single schools and classrooms. This focus is not misguided. Schools and classrooms are where changes need to happen. School-based reform must continue, but it needs to evolve to a different level because this focus is insufficient for producing widespread, long-lasting districtwide improvements.

The one-school or one-program-at-a-time approach is insufficient because it creates piecemeal change. Piecemeal change inside a school district is an approach that at its worst does more harm than good and at its best is limited to creating pockets of "good" within school districts. When it comes to improving schooling in a district, however, creating pockets of good isn't good enough. Whole-school systems need to be improved.

If history offers any guidance for the future, one consequence of piecemeal change is that good education change programs that attempt to improve student learning will come and go, largely with mediocre results. When there is success, it will be isolated in "pockets of excellence." Regarding this phenomenon, Michael Fullan (in Duffy, 2002) said,

> What are the "big problems" facing educational reform? They can be summed up in one sentence: School systems are overloaded with fragmented, ad hoc, episodic initiatives—[with] lots of activity and confusion. Put another way, change even when successful in pockets, fails to go to scale. It fails to become systemic. And, of course, it has no chance of becoming sustained. (p. ix)

Jack Dale, Maryland's Superintendent of the Year for 2000 and the current superintendent of the Fairfax County Public Schools in Virginia, commented on the problem of incremental, piecemeal change. He said piecemeal change occurs as educators respond to demands from a school system's environment. He asked (in Duffy, 2002),

> How have we responded? Typically, we design a new program to meet each emerging need as it is identified and validated. . . . The continual addition of discrete educational programs does not work. . . . Each of the specialty programs developed have, in fact, shifted the responsibility (burden) from the whole system to expecting a specific program to solve the problem. (p. 34)

Another person who commented on the ineffectiveness of piecemeal change was Scott Thompson, assistant executive director of the Panasonic Foundation, which is a sponsor of districtwide change. In talking about piecemeal change, Thompson (2001) said, "The challenge [of school improvement], however, cannot be met through isolated programs; it requires a systemic response. Tackling it will require fundamental changes in the policies, roles, practices, finances, culture, and structure of the school system" (p. 2).

Regarding the inadequacies of the one-school-at-a-time approach, Lew Rhodes (1997), a retired assistant executive director for the American Association of School Administrators, said,

> It was a lot easier 30 years ago when John Goodlad popularized the idea of the school building as the fundamental unit of change.... But now it is time to question that assumption—not because it is wrong—but because it is insufficient. Otherwise, how can we answer the question: "If the building is the primary unit at which to focus change efforts, why after 30 years has so little really changed?" (p. 19)

Focusing school improvement only on individual school buildings and classrooms within a district also leaves some teachers and children behind in average and low-performing schools. Leaving teachers and students behind in average or low-performing schools is a subtle but powerful form of discrimination. School-aged children and their teachers, families, and communities deserve better. It is morally unconscionable to allow some schools in a district to excel while others celebrate their mediocrity or languish in their desperation. Entire school districts must improve, not just parts of them.

There are two additional consequences of piecemeal change within school systems. First, piecemeal improvements are not and never will be widespread; second, piecemeal improvements are not and cannot be long-lasting. Widespread and long-lasting improvements require districtwide change led by courageous, passionate, and visionary leaders who recognize the inherent limitations of piecemeal change and who recognize that a child's educational experience is the cumulative effect of his or her "education career" in a school district.

The SUTE Change Protocol

SUTE is a three-step process preceded by a Pre-Launch Preparation phase and it is cyclical.[1] The SUTE journey proceeds as follows:

- Pre-Launch Preparation
- Step 1: Redesign the entire school district

- Step 2: Create strategic alignment
- Step 3: Evaluate the performance of the entire school district
- Recycle to Pre-Launch Preparation

Pre-Launch Preparation

One of the most common reasons for the failed transformation efforts is the lack of good preparation and planning (Kotter, 1996). What happens during the preparation phase will significantly influence the success (or failure) of your district's transformation journey. So you have to take the time to do these activities in a carefully considered manner. Quick fixes almost always eventually fail, even though they may produce an immediate illusion of improvement.

The early Pre-Launch Preparation activities are conducted by the superintendent of schools and several hand-picked subordinates. At least one member of this small team must be a skillful and highly regarded school PR specialist. All of these people comprise a "pre-launch team." The superintendent may also wish to include one or two trusted school board members on this small starter team. It is also important to know that this small team is temporary and it will not lead the transformation journey that will be launched later in the preparation phase. This team only has one purpose—to complete early activities to prepare the district for whole-system change.

There are many pre-launch preparation activities (see Duffy 2003, 2004c). They are all important. Some of the tasks should be initiated simultaneously (for example, building political support among internal and external stakeholders while simultaneously scouting-out "best-practices" and funding sources to support the change process). Others need to be sequenced (for example, assess and document the need for the district to change; followed by the development of clear and powerful public relations messages about that need; followed by a Community Engagement Conference; followed by a System Engagement Conference).

Sirkin, Keenan, and Jackson (2005) identified four key factors that affect the success or failure of a transformation effort. These factors should be addressed during the Pre-Launch Preparation phase. Sirkin,

Keenan, and Jackson called these the "hard factors of change." They are:

- *Duration:* the amount of time needed to complete the transformation initiative;
- *Integrity:* the ability of the change leadership teams to complete the transformation activities as planned and on time; which is directly affected by the team members' knowledge and skills for leading a transformation journey;
- *Commitment:* the level of unequivocal support for the transformation demonstrated by senior leadership, as well as by employees;
- *Effort:* the amount of effort above and beyond normal work activities that is needed to complete the transformation.

Let's look at each of these factors more closely as they relate to school system improvement.

Hard Factor #1: Duration. There is a common assumption that transformation efforts that require longer timelines are more likely to fail. Contrary to this common assumption, Sirkin, Keenan, and Jackson's (2005) research suggested that long-term transformation efforts that are evaluated frequently are more likely to succeed than short-term projects that are not evaluated. It seems that the frequent use of formative evaluation during a transformation journey has a significant positive effect on the success of that journey.

Hard Factor #2: Integrity. The question this factor addresses is "Can we rely on the change leadership teams that we create to facilitate the transformation journey effectively and successfully?" The importance of the answer to this question cannot be understated. The success of your district's transformation journey will be directly affected by the attitudes, knowledge, and skills of the people who staff the various teams that must be chartered and trained to provide change leadership. You need to get your best people on these teams, where "best" means smart, articulate, influential, and unequivocally committed to the transformation goals.

Hard Factor #3: Commitment. Transformational change must be led from the top of your school district. The superintendent must not only provide verbal support for the transformation, but he or she must also demonstrate behavioral support by participating in transformation activities.

Initial commitment to the transformation journey must also be present among approximately 25% of your faculty and staff. This cadre of supporters is called a "critical mass" (Being First, 2006). Block's (1986) discussion of political groups in organizations offered an effective way to identify who does and does not support leadership in organizations. His model can be modified to identify members of the critical mass needed to support your district's transformation journey.

Block used two dimensions (vertical and horizontal) to identify five political groups in organizations. When adapted to support your district's transformation journey, the vertical axis of his model represents the level of agreement about your district's transformation goals. The horizontal axis represents the level of trust between and among people in your district. The intersection of these two axes creates four political groups, with a fifth group straddling the well-known and often lamented "fence":

1. *Allies:* these are people with whom you have high goal agreement and high trust;
2. *Opponents:* these are people with whom you have low goal agreement, but high trust—it may be possible to convert these people into allies;
3. *Bedfellows:* these are people with whom you have high goal agreement, but low to moderate levels of trust;
4. *Adversaries:* these are people with whom you have low agreement on goals and low trust—you will probably never be able to convert these people to allies or bedfellows;
5. *Fence-sitters:* these people cannot decide where they stand on the goal of transforming your school district. They usually have a wait-and-see attitude toward the changes that are being proposed.

Block offered political strategies for working with each group. These strategies can be used during the Pre-Launch Preparation phase to build internal and external political support for your district's transformation journey.

Hard Factor #4: Effort. When planning the transformation of a school district, change leaders sometimes don't realize or don't know how to deal with the fact that faculty and staff are already busy with their day-to-day responsibilities (see objection #3 at the end of this chapter). If, in addition to these existing responsibilities, faculty and staff are asked to join the change leadership teams that are required to transform their district, their level of resistance toward the transformation journey will increase.

Sirkin, Keenan, and Jackson (2005, p. 6) suggested that ideally the workload of key employees (that is, those who have direct change leadership responsibilities) should not increase more than 10% during a transformation effort. Beyond the 10% limit, resources for change will be overstretched, employee morale will plummet, and interpersonal and intergroup conflict will increase. Therefore, decisions must be made about how to manage the workload of the people who are invited to join the teams that are formed to lead the SUTE journey.

Making a launch/don't launch decision. At some point during this phase, the pre-launch team will decide if their school system is ready or not ready to launch a full-scale transformation journey; that is, they will make a "launch/don't launch" decision. If a launch decision is made, then a new leadership team is chartered and trained to provide strategic leadership for the duration of the transformation journey. This team, because of its purpose, is called a Strategic Leadership Team. It is composed of the superintendent and several others, including teachers and building administrators appointed to the team by their peers (not by the superintendent). This team also appoints and trains a Change Navigation Coordinator who provides daily, tactical leadership for the SUTE journey.

Near the end of the Pre-Launch Preparation phase, the Strategic Leadership Team and Change Navigation Coordinator organize and conduct a 1- to 3-day Community Engagement Conference that can bring into a single room hundreds of people from the community who then self-organize into smaller discussion groups around topics related to the district's transformation effort. This conference is designed using Harrison Owen's (1991, 1993) Open Space Technology design principles. The results of this conference are used as front-end data for another large-group event for the district's faculty and staff that follows soon after the Community Engagement Conference. This event is called a System Engagement Conference.

The System Engagement Conference is a strategic planning conference that brings the whole district into one room. Bringing the whole district into the room, however, doesn't mean that every single person who works in the district participates in the conference. Instead, the Strategic Leadership Team and Change Navigation Coordinator ask each department, team, and unit within the district to send at least one person to participate in the conference. In this way, the whole system is represented in the conference room. This conference uses the design principles of Weisbord and Janoff's Future Search (in Schweitz & Martens with Aronson, 2005) or Emery's (2006) Search Conference (either set of design principles will work for this conference). The outcome of the conference is a new strategic framework for the district that includes a new mission, vision, and strategic goals, as well as parameters for guiding the transformation journey. This framework is developed using data collected from external stakeholders who participated in the earlier Community Engagement Conference.

At the completion of the System Engagement Conference, the Strategic Leadership Team and Change Navigation Coordinator organize the district into academic clusters (for example, an academic cluster can be one high school and all the middle and elementary schools that feed into it), a cluster for the central administration staff, and a cluster for all other supporting work units. They also charter and train a Cluster Design Team for each cluster.

As stated earlier, the unit of change for SUTE is an entire school system rather than individual schools or work units within a system. Although the entire system is the unit of change, the SUTE journey is navigated by organizing the system into academic clusters, a cluster for the central administration, and a cluster for all nonacademic supporting work units. The design team for the academic clusters must include at least one school-based administrator and one teacher from each level of schooling within the cluster (for example, in a preK–12th grade cluster, there should be one administrator and one teacher from each of the elementary, middle, and secondary levels of schooling). This membership formula ensures that the entire instructional program within an academic cluster is represented.

One cluster is also formed for the central office staff. This cluster includes all the functions housed in the central administration unit. Finally, there is cluster formed for the nonacademic supporting work units (for example, cafeteria, building and grounds maintenance, and transportation).

All of these clusters are formed to facilitate the district's transformation journey. Each cluster has a Cluster Design Team that is trained in the principles of whole-system change. Each team guides the SUTE transformation journey within its respective cluster. The daily work of all the Cluster Design Teams is coordinated by the Change Navigation Coordinator. The Strategic Leadership Team provides broad strategic oversight of the teams and supervises the Change Navigation Coordinator.

Step 1: Redesign the Entire School District

Navigating whole-system change requires simultaneous improvements along the three paths, as listed above and in chapters 2 and 3. Making simultaneous changes along these three paths is a core principle from the field of organization development (for example, see Emery, 1977; Pasmore, 1988; Trist, Higgin, Murray, & Pollack, 1963). This principle is often called joint optimization (Cummings & Worley, 2001).

Near the beginning of Step 1, the Cluster Design Teams collaborate with the Change Navigation Coordinator to organize their respective clusters to begin the transformation journey. They do this by chartering Site Design Teams within each school building inside the academic clusters, each department within the central office cluster, and each unit within the supporting work cluster. These Site Design Teams are staffed by highly regarded faculty and staff who do the daily work of teaching children, operating their administrative units, or providing support services. The people on these teams will be the ones who create innovative and powerful ideas for improving their building or work unit's (1) relationships with the external environment, (2) work processes, and (3) internal social infrastructure. Involving people in this way is an important principle because the field of systemic change believes that the people who actually do the work are the people best qualified to improve it (Emery, 1977, 2006; Emery & Purser, 1996; Weisbord, 2004). The Site Design Teams are formed early in Step 1 and they receive training on principles of whole-system change. This training is provided by the Change Navigation Coordinator and the Cluster Design Teams in collaboration with an external consultant.

At the completion of the training on whole-system change, each of the academic Cluster Design Teams organizes a Cluster Engagement Conference. These conferences are designed in the same way as the earlier System Engagement Conference by using Weisbord and Janoff's (in Schweitz & Martens with Aronson, 2005) Future Search principles or Emery's (2006) Search Conference principles. The central office and supporting work unit clusters will have a similar conference later in the transformation journey.

The Cluster Engagement Conferences are 1- to 3-day events. Each Cluster Design Team invites all of the Site Design Teams within its cluster to participate in the conference. The purpose of the conference is to create a "fuzzy" idealized design (Ackoff, 2001; Banathy, 1991, 1992; Lee & Woll, 1996; Reigeluth, 1995) for each cluster. The idealized design must be aligned with the district's new strategic framework (mission, vision, and strategic goals) that was created during the earlier System Engagement Conference. This idealized design must also frame in broad terms how each cluster will make simultaneous improvements along the three change-paths: Path 1—its relationships with external stakeholders, Path 2—its work processes, and Path 3—its internal social infrastructure.

The Cluster Design Conferences are quickly followed by a Redesign Workshop for each cluster. Each Cluster Design Team organizes this event for all of the Site Design Teams within its cluster. All members of the Site Design Teams participate in these workshops. The Redesign Workshops are organized using Emery's (2006) principles for designing Participative Design Workshops. The outcome of these events is a proposal for transforming each academic cluster and every school within each cluster. These proposals contain specific, actionable ideas for making simultaneous improvements along the three change-paths identified earlier (that is, each cluster's environmental relationships, work processes, and internal social infrastructure).

The number of change proposals will vary depending on the number of academic clusters within a district. It is appropriate and acceptable for each cluster to have different ideas for making improvements within their clusters as long as the ideas are clearly aligned with the district's grand vision and strategic framework. Allowing faculty and staff within each cluster to create innovative but different ideas for making improvements within their cluster is an example of applying the principle of equifinality (Cummings & Worley, 2001) to empower and enable the people who actually do the work of the district to make changes that make sense to them.

Although each cluster is encouraged to create innovative ideas for making simultaneous improvements along the three change-paths for their cluster, all of these improvements must be unequivocally aligned with the district's grand vision and strategic framework. To ensure this strategic alignment, the Strategic Leadership Team reviews all of the redesign proposals. Items marked for rejection or put on hold for a later implementation date must be negotiated with the Cluster Design Teams that proposed them before those decisions are finalized. Items accepted for implementation will become part of the final redesign proposal developed later in the transfiguration journey.

Now it's time for the central office and supporting work units to join the transformation journey. The core work of the district is classroom teaching and learning. The core work process is embedded in the academic clusters that just completed their redesign activities (Cluster Engagement Conferences followed by Redesign Workshops). To be an effective district, all other work in the school system must be aligned with and supportive of the district's core work processes (that is, classroom teaching and learning); therefore, the central office and supporting work units must be redesigned to clearly and unequivocally support the changes that were proposed for the academic clusters.

The central office and supporting work units participate in the same redesign process that the academic clusters just completed; that is, they participate in Cluster Engagement Conferences and Redesign Workshops. The major outcome of the Cluster Engagement Conference and Redesign Workshops for the central office is to transform that unit into a central service center that acts in support of the academic clusters and the schools within those clusters while simultaneously supporting the district's grand vision and strategic framework. The major outcome of the Cluster Engagement Conference and Redesign Workshops for the supporting work units is to devise ways in which the work of these units can best support the academic clusters and the individual schools within them while also supporting the district's grand vision and strategic framework.

The Strategic Leadership Team now has redesign proposals from each of the academic clusters, the central office cluster, and the supporting work unit cluster. These proposals are consolidated into a master redesign proposal for the entire school system, which is then submitted to the district's school board for review and approval.

Next, the Strategic Leadership Team and Change Navigation Coordinator have the challenging task of finding the money to implement the master change proposal. Earlier during the Pre-Launch Preparation phase, the Strategic Leadership Team scouted out funding opportunities by identifying some state and federal agencies or philanthropic organizations that could be sources of money to support their district's transformation journey. Now, they approach these agencies and organizations by submitting grant proposals requesting financial support. While waiting to secure outside money to support their transformation journey, they can kick-start the journey by reallocating money found within their district's current budget.

Money from outside agencies is often characterized as "extra" money because it is above and beyond the money in a district's normal operating budget. Even though extra money may be needed to sustain the first cycle of a transformation journey, money to kick-start a transformation journey can be found in district's current operating budget using budget reallocation strategies. Further, future cycles of SUTE should also be funded by permanent dollars in a district's budget. Additional information about how to pay for systemic change is found near the end of this chapter and in Duffy (2003).

Once the district has "seed" money to kick-start the transformation journey, the Strategic Leadership Team distributes the financial, human, and technical resources to the Cluster Design Teams so they can implement their sections of the master redesign proposal. The Cluster Design Teams delegate implementation responsibilities to the Site Design Teams within their domain. The implementation activities are managed on a daily basis by the Site Design Teams in each building and work unit and coordinated by the respective Cluster Design Teams in collaboration with the Change Navigation Coordinator. The Strategic Leadership Team provides broad strategic oversight of the entire implementation phase.

Implementation of new ideas and practices will require the school system, all the clusters, all of the individual schools and work units, and all individual faculty and staff to move through a learning curve, which always starts with a downhill slide in individual and organizational performance followed by an upward climb toward excellence (this learning curve is characterized as the "first down, then up" principle). Organizational Learning Networks (OLN) can facilitate and support the "first down, then up" experience. OLNs are informal communities of practice that focus learning on issues, problems, or opportunities related to the implementation of a district's master redesign proposal. They can be designed using DuFour and Eaker's (1998) principles for organizing learning communities. To facilitate the development and dissemination of professional knowledge throughout the school system, the OLNs are required to share their learning with everyone in the district.

Most large-scale change efforts fail during the implementation period, especially if the change timeline is long and if the transformation activities and outcomes are not periodically evaluated (Sirkin, Keenan, & Jackson, 2005). Because of the possibility of failure, it is important for the various change leadership teams to design and facilitate On-Track Seminars. On-Track Seminars are designed using Preskill and Torres's (1998) principles of evaluative inquiry. The formative evaluation data from these seminars are used to keep the transformation journey on course toward the district's grand vision and strategic goals. These seminars also:

- Facilitate individual, team, and districtwide learning;
- Educate and train faculty and staff to use inquiry skills;
- Create opportunities to model collaboration, cooperation, and participation behaviors;
- Establish linkages between learning and performance;
- Facilitate the search for ways to create greater understanding of what affects the district's success and failure; and,

- Rely on diverse perspectives to develop understanding of the district's performance.

During the period of formative evaluation, it is important to assess the quality of discontent among people working in the school system and among key external stakeholders. The quality of discontent is a diagnostic clue about the relative success of a school system's transformation journey. In less healthy organizations, people complain about little things—low-order grumbles. These gripes are manifestations of what Abraham Maslow (in Farson, 1996, p. 93) called deficiency needs. In successful organizations, people have high-order gripes that focus on more altruistic concerns. In very successful organizations, people engage in meta-gripes—complaints about matters of beauty ("look at the condition of our building"), of truth ("I should have received all of the facts") of justice ("the way he was treated is just not right"), and of a need for self-actualization ("I am starving for professional growth opportunities"). When you hear these meta-gripes, you know your system is stepping up to excellence.

Step 2: Create Strategic Alignment

After redesigning the district, Step 2 invites change leaders and their colleagues to align the work of individuals with the goals of their teams, the work of teams with the goals of their schools and work units, the work of schools and work units with the goals of their clusters, and the work of clusters with the goals of the district. Combined, these steps are referred to as "creating strategic alignment."

Creating strategic alignment accomplishes three things (Duffy, 2004c). First, it ensures that everyone is working toward the same broad strategic goals and vision for the district. Second, it weaves a web of accountabilities that makes everyone who touches the educational experience of a child accountable for his or her part in shaping that experience. And third, it has the potential to form a social infrastructure that is free of bureaucratic hassles, dysfunctional policies, and obstructionist procedures that limit individual and team effectiveness. It is these dysfunctional hassles, policies, and procedures that cause at least 80% of the performance problems that are usually blamed on individuals and teams (Deming, 1986).

Step 3: Evaluate Whole-District Performance

Finally, in Step 3, the performance of the entire transformed district is evaluated using principles of summative evaluation (for example, Stufflebeam, 2002, 2003). The purpose of this level of evaluation is to measure the success of everyone's efforts to educate children and to support the education process. Evaluation data are also reported to stakeholders in the environment to demonstrate the district's overall effectiveness.

After change leaders and their colleagues work through all three steps of Step-Up-To-Excellence, they then focus on sustaining school district improvement by practicing continuous improvement at the district, cluster, school, team, and individual levels of performance. Then, after a predetermined period of stability and incremental improvements, they "step-up" again by cycling back to the Pre-launch Preparation phase. Achieving high performance is a lifelong journey for a school district.

IN ANTICIPATION OF "YES, BUTS"

Whenever Step-Up-To-Excellence is presented to an audience, predictably three key objections are voiced. These common objections and responses to them are presented below. It is very important for change leaders and school PR specialists to anticipate objections to whole-system change and then prepare well-crafted messages that preempt the objections. By anticipating and preempting the objections, initial resistance to change can be significantly reduced. Further, the best time to anticipate and preempt objections is during the Pre-Launch Preparation phase of SUTE.

Objection #1: "Yes, This Is an Interesting Idea, but Where Is It Being Used?"

One of the greatest "innovation killers" in the history of mankind is captured in the question, "Where is this being used?" or its corollary,

"Who else is doing this?" Can you imagine Peter Senge (1990) being asked this question when he first proposed his Fifth Discipline ideas; or perhaps Morris Cogan (1973) when he first described the principles of Clinical Supervision?

New ideas, by definition, are not being used anywhere, but they *want* to be used. However, being the first at doing anything, especially doing something that requires change with broad scope and deep scale, demands a high degree of leadership courage, passion, and vision. Many change leaders in education do indeed have the requisite courage, passion, and vision to be the first to try innovative ideas for creating and sustaining systemic school improvement, but they don't know how to lead whole-system change. These heroic leaders need a protocol especially designed to create and sustain whole-district change.

The most direct answer to the above objection is that Step-Up-To-Excellence is being used in the Metropolitan School District of Decatur Township in Indianapolis, Indiana. The protocol has been blended with a protocol created by Dr. Charles Reigeluth called the Guidance System for Transforming Education (GSTE). Dr. Reigeluth is also facilitating that systemic change effort.[2] Essay 5 in section 3 of this book has more information about this district's transformation journey. Although this is the direct answer to the objection, more needs to be said.

New methodologies to create and sustain districtwide change are not perfect and they never will be. Educators should not even try to find a perfect protocol. Instead, they need to examine new methods for navigating whole-district change, study how they work, find glitches in the processes, and search for logical flaws in the reasoning behind the methods. Then, assuming that a method is based on sound principles for improving whole systems, educators should then think about how they might modify the methodology to make it work for their districts.

Some people read about whole-district change and exclaim, "Impossible!" Impossible is what some people think can't be done until someone proves them wrong by doing it. Whole-district change not only "is possible," but it has been done successfully in school systems throughout the United States; for example, in the Baldrige award-winning Chugach Public Schools in Anchorage, Alaska, and the Pearl River School District in New York. Other districts engaged in districtwide change were described in a research study by Togneri and Anderson (2003). The districts in that study were:

- Aldine Independent School District, Texas
- Chula Vista Elementary School District, California
- Kent County Public Schools, Maryland
- Minneapolis Public Schools, Minnesota
- Providence Public Schools, Rhode Island

The improvements these districts experienced were guided by many of the principles that underpin SUTE. So, if educators read about a protocol that seems impossible, they should ask, "If other school districts are using ideas and principles like these, why can't we?"

Some of your colleagues will read about whole-district change and say, "Impractical!" Not only are the core principles and change-tools based on these principles practical, many of them are proven to work in school districts and other organizations throughout the United States. So, if and when your colleagues think that trying to improve an entire school system is impractical, you should ask them, "If other school districts have used these principles effectively, why can't we?"

Some people will read this chapter and proclaim, "Wow, these ideas are really far out. They are *way* outside the box." It is our hope that readers *will* say this. If they do, this means we have succeeded in offering them some innovative ideas to think about and apply. And, if and when they see something that seems "way outside the box," they should ask, "If this idea is outside the box, what box are we in?" and "Do we want to stay inside this box of ours?"

Objection #2: "Yes, This Is a Nice Idea, but How Do We Pay for This?"

The second biggest innovation killer in the world is found in the question, "How do we pay for this"? Unlike traditional reform efforts, whole-district change cannot be sustained solely through small increases in operating budgets, nor can it be sustained with "extra" money from outside the district. Because systemic reform touches all aspects of a school district's core operations, it imposes significant resource requirements on a district and demands a rethinking of the way current resources are allocated, as well as some creative thinking about how to use "extra" money (that is, money from external sources) that will be needed to jump-start systemic reform.

Because there seems to be a scarce amount of literature on financing whole-district change, innovative, ground-level tactics, methods, and sources are needed to help educators find the financial resources they need to transform their school systems into high-performing organizations of learners. What follows are some insights about how to do this; these insights are explored more deeply in Duffy (2003).

Here you will find a brief presentation of some fundamental principles that are important for financing whole-district change.[3] Many of these principles are advocated by school finance experts (for example, Cascarino, 2000; Clune, 1994a, 1994b; Keltner, 1998; Odden, 1998). The fundamental principles are:

- Think creatively about securing resources. Instead of saying "We can't do this, because . . . ," say "We can do this. Let's be creative in figuring out how!"
- Develop a new mental model for financing school system improvement that helps you think outside the box for creating innovative solutions to your resource allocation challenges.
- Embed the resources to support a whole-district improvement protocol in your district's organization design and its normal operational budget.
- Develop a new mental model for financing school system improvement that helps you create innovative solutions to resource allocation challenges (Odden, 1998).
- Fund systemic improvement as you would fund a core program or activity with real dollars that are a permanent part of your budget.
- Reallocate current operating money to support whole-district improvement (Keltner, 1998).
- Over time, reduce "extra" resources for whole-district improvement to near zero while increasing internal resources to support systemic improvement.
- As needed, combine federal funds in innovative ways to directly

support districtwide improvements in teaching and learning (see Cascarino, 2000, p. 1).
- Focus your thinking on financing for adequacy rather than on financing for equity (see Clune, 1994a, 1994b).
- When seeking outside money, make sure that the requirements and goals of the funding agency do not conflict or constrain the vision and strategic direction of your redesign effort.
- Employ superior communication skills so all stakeholders recognize the true purpose of your budget reallocation strategy, how it will work, and what the benefits will be.

Objection #3: "Yes, Nice Idea, but We Can't Stop Doing What We're Doing."

Another important and significant obstacle to gaining support for whole-system change is that school districts have a core mission—that is, they must provide children with approximately 180 days of classroom teaching and learning. Given the complexity of whole-system change and given the time required to plan and implement systemwide change, some of your colleagues will object by saying, "Nice idea, but we can't stop doing what we're doing to participate in this kind of change process. We have to show up every day and teach kids."

Of course, this objection is based on the realities of life in school systems. That's why it is so difficult to respond to this objection. But there is a response and it is derived from the experiences of real people making real changes in complex organizations with core missions that cannot be ignored. The response to this objection is that the Strategic Leadership Team and Change Navigation Coordinator must create a parallel organization after the launch decision is made during the Pre-Launch Preparation phase.

The concept of parallel organization is from the fields of organization theory and design and systemic change (for example, Stein & Kanter, 2002). A parallel organization, which is sometimes called a "parallel learning structure" (Human Resource Development Council, n.d.) is a change management structure. The parallel organization is that collection of change navigation teams and change processes that is temporarily established to change an entire organization. It is created during the Pre-Launch Preparation phase of SUTE. A simple illustration of this concept is found in Figure 4.5.

The parallel organization is created by temporarily "transferring" carefully selected and trained educators into the parallel organization, which is constructed using the various change leadership teams and the SUTE protocol. These people then create the new system by following the protocol.

Educators not transferred into the parallel organization continue to operate the current school system, thereby helping the district to achieve its core mission—that is, educating children. Even though they are performing within the boundaries of the current system, these educators are participating in Organization Learning Networks to help

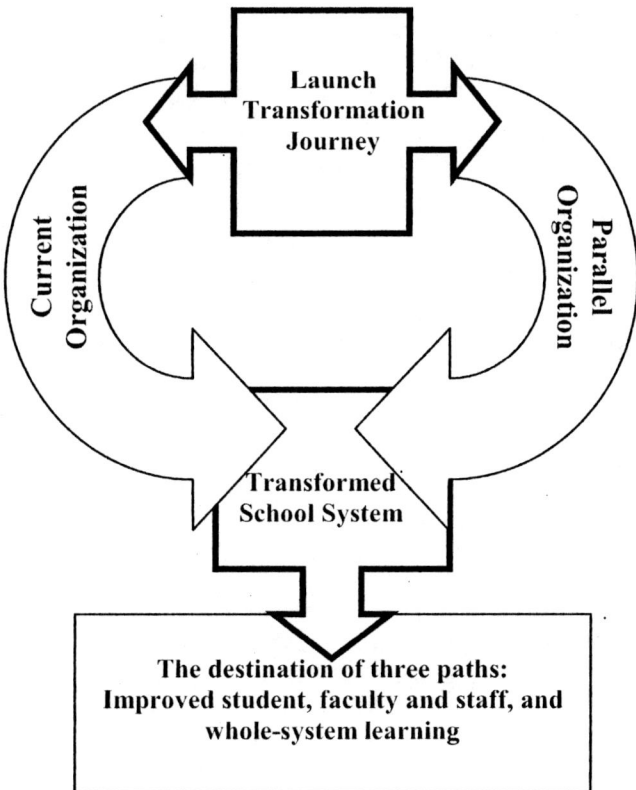

Figure 4.5. The parallel organization

them learn the new knowledge and skills they will need to perform successfully in the transformed school system.

In Step 1 of the SUTE protocol, a master redesign proposal is created. At some point during Step 1, that proposal is implemented. As it is implemented, the "old" system and the parallel organization merge to create a transformed system whereby the district continues to achieve its core mission, but it does so within the framework of a "new" system.

The transition from the current organization to the "new" organization is not easy. The transition period is a time of ambiguity, confusion, chaos, complexity, and great change. Your district's covert insurgents will work to undermine your leadership. External stakeholders will question your vision and wonder about your change leadership knowledge and skills. The "pedestrians" in your system will sit on the sidelines and watch and offer no support. Given these challenges, your district's change leaders will need personal courage to stand their ground in the face of adversity. Their passion for the core mission of your district (educating your community's children) will give them the emotional energy they need to persist on the transformation journey. And their vision of an exciting, desirable future for the district will be the North Star guiding their district ever closer to that envisioned future.

CONCLUSION

New change theory is based on the concept of flux. It recognizes that change is nonlinear and requires school districts to function at the edge of chaos as educators seek controlled disequilibrium to create innovative opportunities for improvement. New change theory tells us that to improve the performance level of a school district, the system must first move downhill before it can move up to a higher level of performance. New change theory requires school districts to use a networked social infrastructure where innovations are grown from within and used to create whole-district change. New change theory requires a simultaneous ability to anticipate the future and respond quickly to unanticipated events. New change theory requires a change protocol specifically designed to enact the concepts and principles that are part of the theory. This chapter provides you with an example of a protocol that satisfies these requirements.

New change theory also requires change leadership that is distributed throughout a school district—change leaders who are courageous, passionate, and visionary and who use their power and political skills in ethical ways. Leaders like this are priceless and absolutely necessary. Leaders of this class work their magic by helping others to see the invisible, to do the seemingly impossible, and to create new realities heretofore only imagined. Creating world-class school districts that produce stunning opportunities for improving student, faculty and staff, and whole-system learning can only be done under the stewardship of these kinds of transformational leaders.

Leading whole-system change is not for the timid, the uninspired, or the perceptually nearsighted. It requires personal courage, passion, and vision. It is our hope that you will find in the pages of this chapter and the rest of the book the key that unlocks or reinforces your personal courage, passion, and vision to lead this kind of large-scale transformation journey in your school district. If you do step forward to accept that mission, please know that you step forward into a world that is not fully illuminated by research findings, a world that is a minefield of sociopolitical warfare and turf battles, and into a world where you will often suffer emotional pain and feelings of betrayal by those you thought loyal. You may even lose your job. But, with courage, passion, and vision, we believe you can create a coalition of like-minded change leaders within and outside your district. In collaboration with this coalition, you can endure the pain and betrayal, move forward toward your shared vision for your district, and ultimately succeed in creating and sustaining previously unimagined opportunities for improving student, faculty and staff, and whole-system learning in your school district.

REFERENCES

Ackoff, R. L. (2001). A brief guide to interactive planning and idealized design. Retrieved on March 19, 2006, from http://www.sociate.com/texts/AckoffGuidetoIdealizedRedesign.pdf

Banathy, B. H. (1991). *Systems design of education: A journey to create the future*. Englewood Cliffs, NJ: Educational Technology Publications.

Banathy, B. H. (1992). The prime imperative: Building a design culture. *Educational Technology, 32*(6), 33–35.

Being First. (2006). How to build a critical mass of support to accelerate your change. Retrieved on April 22, 2006, from http://www.beingfirst.com/resultsfromchange/pastissues/200212.php#3

Block, P. (1986). *The empowered manager: Positive political skills at work*. San Francisco: Jossey-Bass.

Cascarino, J. (2000, November). *District Issues Brief—Many programs, one investment: Combining federal funds to support comprehensive school reform*. Arlington, VA: New American Schools, Inc. Retrieved on October 12, 2003, from http://www.naschools.org/uploadedfiles/ManyPrograms.pdf

Clune, W. (1994a). The shift from equity to adequacy in school finance. *Educational Policy, 8*(4), 376–394.

Clune, W. (1994b). The cost and management of program adequacy: An emerging issue in education policy and finance. *Educational Policy, 8*(4), 365–375.

Cogan, M. L. (1973). *Clinical supervision*. Boston: Houghton Mifflin.

Cummings, T. G., & Worley, C. G. (2001). *Organization development and change* (7th ed.). Cincinnati, OH: South-Western College.

Dannemiller, K., & Jacobs, R. W. (1992). Changing the way organizations change: A revolution in common sense. *Journal of Applied Behavioral Science, 28*, 480–498.

Dannemiller-Tyson Associates (1994). *Real-time strategic change: A consultant's guide to large scale meetings*. Ann Arbor, MI: Author.

Deming, W. E. (1986). *Out of the crisis*. Cambridge, MA: Massachusetts Institute of Technology, Center for Advanced Engineering Study.

Duffy, F. M. (1995). Supervising knowledge-work. *NASSP Bulletin, 79*(573), 56–66.

Duffy, F. M. (1996). *Designing high performance schools: A practical guide to organizational reengineering*. Delray Beach, FL: St. Lucie Press.

Duffy, F. M. (2002). *Step-Up-To-Excellence: An innovative approach to managing and rewarding performance in school systems*. Lanham, MD: ScarecrowEducation.

Duffy, F. M. (2003). *Courage, passion and vision: A guide to leading systemic school improvement*. Lanham, MD: ScarecrowEducation/American Association of School Administrators.

Duffy, F. M. (2004a, summer). The destination of three paths: Improved student, faculty and staff, and system learning. *The Forum, 68*(4), 313–324.

Duffy, F. M. (2004b). Navigating whole-district change: Eight principles for moving an organization upward in times of unpredictability. *The School Administrator, 61*(1), 22–25.

Duffy, F. M. (2004c). *Moving upward together: Creating strategic alignment to sustain systemic school improvement.* No. 1, Leading Systemic School Improvement Series. Lanham, MD: ScarecrowEducation.

DuFour, R., & Eaker, R. (1998). *Professional learning communities at work: Best practices for enhancing student achievement.* Bloomington, IN: National Education Service.

Emery, F. E. (1977). *Two basic organization designs in futures we are in.* Leiden, Netherlands: Martinus Nijhoff.

Emery, M. (2006). *The future of schools: How communities and staff can transform their school districts.* Leading Systemic School Improvement Series. Lanham, MD: Rowman & Littlefield Education.

Emery, M., & Purser, R. E. (1996). *The Search conference: A powerful method for planning organizational change and community action.* San Francisco: Jossey-Bass.

Farson, R. (1996). *Management of the absurd.* New York: Simon & Schuster.

Houlihan, G. T., & Houlihan, A. G. (2005). *School performance: How to meet AYP and achieve long-term success.* Rexford, NY: International Center for Leadership in Education.

Human Resource Development Council. (n.d.). Parallel learning structures. Retrieved on March 26, 2006, from http://www.humtech.com/opm/grtl/ols/ols6.cfm

Keltner, B. R. (1998). Funding comprehensive school reform. Rand Corporation. Retrieved on January 15, 2004, from http://www.rand.org/publications/IP/IP175/

Kotter, J. P. (1996). *Leading change.* Boston: Harvard Business School Press.

Learning Point Associates. (n.d.). Teacher quality. Retrieved on April 9, 2006, from http://www.ncrel.org/policy/feature/tq.htm

Lee, T., & Woll, T. (1996, spring). Design and planning in organizations. *Center for Quality of Management Journal, 5*(1). Retrieved on March 19, 2006, from http://cqmextra.cqm.org/cqmjournal.nsf/reprints/rp06900

Lewin, K. (1951). *Field theory in social science.* New York: Harper & Row.

Odden, A. (1998, January). *District Issues Brief: How to rethink school budgets to support school transformation.* Arlington, VA: New American Schools. Retrieved on October 25, 2002, from http://www.naschools.org/uploadedfiles/oddenbud.pdf

Owen, H. (1991). *Riding the tiger: Doing business in a transforming world.* Potomac, MD: Abbott.

Owen, H. (1993). *Open Space Technology: A user's guide.* Potomac, MD: Abbott.

Pasmore, W. A. (1988). *Designing effective organizations: The socio-technical systems perspective.* New York: Wiley & Sons.

Pava, C. H. P. (1983a, Spring). Designing managerial and professional work for high performance: A sociotechnical approach. *National Productivity Review,* 126–135.

Pava, C. H. P. (1983b). *Managing new office technology: An organizational strategy.* New York: New Press.

Preskill, H., & Torres, R. T. (1998). *Evaluative inquiry for learning in organizations.* Thousand Oaks, CA: Sage.

Reigeluth, C. M. (1995). A conversation on guidelines for the process of facilitating systemic change in education. *Systems Practice, 8*(3), 315–328.

Rhodes, L. A. (1997, April). Connecting leadership and learning. Arlington, VA: American Association of School Administrators. Unpublished manuscript.

Schweitz, R., & Martens, K. with Aronson, N. (Eds.) (2005). *Future Search in school district change: Connection, community, and results.* No. 3, Leading Systemic School Improvement Series. Lanham, MD: Rowman & Littlefield Education

Senge, P. (1990). *The fifth discipline: The art & practice of the learning organization.* New York: Doubleday.

Sirkin, H. L., Keenan, P., & Jackson, A. (2005, October). The hard side of change management. *Harvard Business Review,* 1–10.

Stein, B. A., & Kanter, R. M. (2002). Building the parallel organization: Creating mechanisms for permanent quality of work life. Retrieved on March 25, 2006, from http://www.goodmeasure.com/site/parallel%200rg/index.htm

Stufflebeam, D. L. (2002). CIPP evaluation model checklist: A tool for applying the fifth installment of the CIPP model to assess long-term enterprises. Retrieved on March 30, 2006, from http://www.wmich.edu/evalctr/checklists/cippchecklist.htm

Stufflebeam, D. L. (2003). The CIPP model for evaluation. Retrieved on March 30, 2006, from http://www.wmich.edu/evalctr/pubs/CIPP-Model Oregon10-03.pdf

Thompson, S. (2001, November). Taking on the "all means all" challenge. *Strategies for School System Leaders on District-Level Change, 8*(2). Retrieved on March 1, 2005, from http://www.aasa.org/publications/strategies/Strategies_11-01.pdf

Togneri, W., & Anderson, S. E. (2003). *Beyond islands of excellence: What districts can do to improve instruction and achievement in all schools—a leadership brief.* Washington, DC: Learning First Alliance.

Trist, E. L., Higgin, G. W., Murray, H., & Pollack, A. B. (1963). *Organizational choice.* London: Tavistock.

van Eijnatten, F., Eggermont, S., de Goffau, G., & Mankoe, I. (1994). *The socio-technical systems design paradigm.* Eindhoven, Netherlands: Eindhoven University of Technology.

Weisbord, M. R. (2004). *Productive workplaces: Organizing and managing for dignity, meaning, and community.* San Francisco: Jossey-Bass.

ENDNOTES

1. The first version of Step-Up-To-Excellence was called *Knowledge Work Supervision* (KWS). It was first described in Duffy (1995, 1996). KWS evolved into Step-Up-To-Excellence in Duffy (2002) and it had five steps. Recently, using feedback from the field, the protocol was improved by reducing the protocol to three steps, as described in this chapter.

2. You may visit the website for that district's transformation journey at www.indiana.edu/~syschang/decatur/change_process.html.

3. These principles were developed in collaboration with Jason Cascarino and Chris Henson. Jason is director of marketing and new initiatives for Citizen Schools in Boston. Chris is the assistant superintendent for business and facility services for the Metro Nashville Public Schools in Tennessee. Chris is also the former assistant director for finance and administration for the Franklin Special School District in Tennessee, where he helped develop financial strategies to pay for whole-system change in that district.

SECTION 2

How Strategic Communication and School Public Relations Can Support Whole-System Change in School Districts

Section 2 contains four chapters that show how strategic communication can be used to support whole-system change in school districts. It is important to emphasize that these chapters do not include specific PR or strategic communication tools and processes; rather, insights into the role of school PR and strategic communication during times of great change in school districts are offered.

Chapter 5 embeds the practice of school PR and strategic communications within the context of systems theory. Chapter 6 discusses the nature of trust in organizations and why trusting relationships are so important to successful change efforts. Chapter 7 shares ideas about the importance of using strategic communication strategies to develop and achieve a shared vision for a school system. Chapter 8 presents information about using school PR and strategic communication tools to change minds and hearts—a necessary, but challenging precursor to effective system transformation. Finally, chapter 9 offers insights to how power, politics, and ethics in school systems influence strategic communication during times of great change.

CHAPTER 5

Public Relations in Times of Great Change: A Systems Perspective

Much of what is commonly thought of as public relations deals with a school district's formal communication with stakeholders through news releases, parent and community newsletters, and media interviews. In the face of increased scrutiny and demands for accountability placed upon public schools today, superintendents and other school leaders may find themselves *reacting* to public concerns, media queries, and governmental mandates rather than *leading* their schools toward needed reforms. Even well-meaning advice to school administrators regarding preparing public relations strategies are often reactionary, such as the advice that instructs administrators to assemble media packets, determine talking points for key issues, and schedule media interviews carefully (Allen, 2004). Such strategies are better characterized as media relations. The Public Relations Society of America (n.d.), however, offered a broader perspective on the role and purpose of public relations. They said, "Public relations helps our complex, pluralistic society to reach decisions and function more effectively by contributing to mutual understanding among groups and institutions. It serves to bring private and public policies into harmony."

Systems thinking helps us understand that such communications are only one part of a much more complex flow of information. Because school districts are open systems, there is constant flow of information into and out of the district's environment. Indeed, a school district is not separate from its external environment because it influences as well as responds to cultural change and disruptions in the external environment. Systems theory provides a metaphor for understanding the complexities of strategic communication between a school system and its external environment, as well as for understanding communication with stakeholders within a school system.

USING SYSTEMS THINKING TO COMMUNICATE STRATEGICALLY

Three major concepts from systems theory emerge as important notions for school district leaders who want to develop effective public relations to support whole-system change: (1) inputs, outputs, and feedback loops; (2) communication networks; and (3) organization culture. Each concept is briefly discussed below. Additional information about the nature of school districts as systems is found in chapters 2 and 3.

Inputs, Outputs, and Feedback Loops

Systems, as originally described in the biological sciences, have four basic components: inputs, conversion process, output, and feedback loops (von Bertalanffy, 1975). In terms of school districts as systems, inputs include information from the external environment such as laws, regulations, financial and human resources, and parent or community attitudes toward a school system. Conversion processes include dialogue, teaching and learning, and problem solving. Outputs are the result of the system processes. Feedback is provided by external stakeholders as they evaluate the value and quality of the outputs.

System processes also include the internal organizational structure, tools, people, and communication patterns, which are collectively known as the system's internal social infrastructure. People within a school system include teachers, administrators, staff, and students. As participants within the school system, individuals take on prescribed roles identified by the district, such as teacher or administrator. Outside the school district, these same individuals are part of a larger social and political system; they are parents, taxpayers, church members, and so forth. Thus, to view a school district as an isolated system is simplistic and does not take into consideration the complexities of the school district as a system nested within larger systems.

School districts are organizations that also include both formal and informal systems (Getzels & Guba, 1957). The formal system is defined by the district's structure, prescribed roles, and expectations. Individuals within the district contribute to the informal system based upon their unique needs, wants, and personalities. The informal social system (sometimes called the internal social infrastructure) within a school district is powerful and impacts the daily activities within the district. Informal groups impact organizational cohesiveness, organizational members' perceptions and motivation, and the district's response to external events. The interaction between district goals and the specific needs of individuals working in the system results in behaviors within the system that define the district's culture. The culture also reflects the culture of the external environment surrounding the system.

Furthermore, organizational systems are characterized by patterns of social interactions within the system. Patterns of social interaction are evident at both the formal and informal levels. Social interaction patterns may be observed by noting who is communicating with whom. What are the formal, prescribed roles of those who interact? In what ways do people communicate (for example, collaboratively or in a directing and controlling way)? Is there an aura of equality or do formal roles and status play into the communication? Collectively, these patterns are part of a system's internal social infrastructure.

We know that school districts are open systems, meaning that they are influenced by a constant exchange of information, resources, and events that enter from the external environment. In turn, districts have outputs that are used and evaluated by external stakeholders. The outputs are educated students. The quality of the students' education is evaluated by the external stakeholders and the evaluation data become feedback for the system. For example, student achievement (output) in a school district may be reported as not meeting state and national standards as defined by legislative mandates. Feedback from the external environment comes in the form of newspaper headlines declaring "Local School District Deemed in Need of Improvement." Parents call the superintendent's office expressing their concerns about the poor teaching in the system. This feedback, along with other input into the system in the form of state requirements for preparing new school improvement plans and filing accountability reports with the state, in turn, causes a reaction by the system. Such input and feedback from the external environment has the potential to cause imbalance in the system. Teachers may become discouraged and upset or, on the other hand, they may exhibit new resolve to improve their students' achievement. It is at this point of system disequilibrium that effective change leadership is essential. In particular, a leader's communication is critical for helping the system regain balance. However, leaders should remember that effective communication is not necessarily *reactive* communication.

Communication is a dynamic, ongoing process. Organizational communication involves not only communication between and among individuals, but it is also affected by the structure of the district itself. Additionally, because school districts are open systems, organizational communication involves the flow of information from the environment into a school system and from the system into the environment. As information is channeled into the environment, it is interpreted, acted upon, and fed back into the system. Information is processed the same way when it comes into the school system from the external environment.

Communication Networks

Communication has been described as "the very essence of a social system" (Katz & Kahn, 1966). The complexities of communication are evident when discussed in the context of open systems theory. Patterns of communication within school systems and between a school system and its surrounding environment become apparent as information is channeled through networks of individuals. Networks are part of both the formal organizational structure and the informal communication structure in a school district. Organizational networks help us understand communication in terms of interpersonal communications, formal communication structures, and cliques of individuals who communicate most with each other. These networks are also part of a district's internal social infrastructure.

Four key communication roles that individuals play within networks are (a) gatekeeper, (b) liaison, (c) opinion leader, and (d) cosmopolite (Rogers & Agarwala-Rogers, 1976). A gatekeeper is a person whose position in a communication network is such that he or she controls messages flowing through a communication channel; for example, a superintendent's secretary often plays the role of gatekeeper by screening calls and visitors. The purpose of a gatekeeper is to decrease information overload and to filter out messages of low importance. This is a critical role that influences the effectiveness of a school district and its leaders, because the gatekeeper determines to a great extent what information the leaders receive.

Individuals may use informal communication channels to bypass the gatekeeper. In many ways, these informal channels allow leaders to keep a check on the formal gatekeeping function. In large organizations, several layers of gatekeepers may develop throughout the hierarchy, resulting in greater omissions and distortions of information. For instance, a superintendent of a large urban school district may deliberately insulate herself from the day-to-day operations of individual schools within her system. She then relies on her cabinet or assistant superintendents to keep her informed about important issues. While this is a necessary mechanism to prevent information overload for the superintendent, she should remember that the information she receives has been filtered. Thus, there are many opportunities for information to be distorted and chances are greater that the superintendent is only being given information that others want her to hear.

A second role in communication networks is the liaison. A liaison is an individual who connects two or more cliques within a system but who does not belong to any clique. Liaisons play a crucial role in connecting subsystems within a school district and in creating connections between the system and outside stakeholder groups. When liaisons are removed, a system tends to disintegrate into isolated cliques. Liaisons play strategic roles in the district and can either expedite or inhibit the information flow. When no informal liaison emerges, it may be important for organizations to create formal liaison positions. For example, an active parent volunteer, such as the PTA president, may play the role of an informal liaison between the superintendent and community. Parents may feel more comfortable communicating sensitive information to the PTA president than directly calling the district or school administration. The PTA president may be used as a sounding board for information a parent wants the superintendent or a principal to know but who feels that direct communication may violate an issue of trust with another parent, child, or community member. This places the PTA president in a situation where he must decide whether or not to communicate the information to the superintendent or must determine how to filter the information before presenting it to the superintendent. It is vital that school district and school-based leaders develop trusting relationships with key parents, teachers, and community members who find themselves in this liaison role.

A third role that emerges in communication networks is that of the opinion leader. The opinion leader role is informal rather than formal. People in this role regularly influence others' attitudes or behaviors. Opinion leaders generally have greater access to external and expert sources of information and they connect the district to the external environment. They also tend to be individuals who conform to the norms of the organization, thus giving them credibility with members of the organization. A teacher who is an opinion leader in a school may be one who is active in outside professional development activities but who is viewed as committed to the values and beliefs of the school district. Other teachers rely on this person's opinion and the information she brings to the school. Teachers trust the opinion leader not to promote practices or programs that are incompatible with the school district's norms. The opinion leader plays a critical role in a school system's improvement efforts. A superintendent wishing to introduce change into his school district would be wise to first communicate and develop alliances with identified opinion leaders. If opinion leaders are convinced that a proposed change would benefit the district, they will influence others to accept the change.

A fourth communication network role is that of the cosmopolite. This is a person who has a great deal of communication with the system's external environment. In school districts, cosmopolites may be administrators, teachers, or support staff. Their communications with the outside environment differ in that they are connected to many different aspects of the environment; for example, an administrator's list of community contacts might include community leaders, religious leaders, executives in professional organizations, and leaders in other neighboring school districts. An administrator with this kind of contact list would be positioned to bring new ideas from those outside sources into his or her school district. Teachers and support staff are also in a position to have greater contact with a variety of parents and students. These sources of information are vital links for understanding the opinions and concerns of external stakeholders, as well as for disseminating information to the community.

Communication Is Contextually Based

The concept of networks as a framework for systems thinking is rooted in the mathematical and scientific principle of mapping. When mapped, relationships in a network are not linear, rather they involve cyclical paths that can generate feedback loops (Capra, 1996). Networks as described by physicists such as Capra (1996), Buchanan (2002), and Barabasi (2002) involve complex patterns of interaction that are self-organizing. That is, systems or organizations can evolve and create new structures through the processes of development and learning.

Mapping or graphing theory further contributes to the notion of connectedness and relationship networking. The concept of "small world phenomenon" (Milgram, 1967), popularly known as the phenomenon of "six degrees of separation," describes how people are connected through randomly linked social networks. Milgram, a sociologist seeking to map social connections, conducted a "lost letter" experiment in which he found that letters misdirected were received by the intended person within six steps.

A related networking theory is found in a branch of mathematics known as graph theory. This theory demonstrates that no matter how many points there are in a distribution, they all can be linked together—even if there are a few randomly scattered points in that distribution. Sociological research conducted by Granovetter (1973) added to this mathematical concept in his discovery of "weak links." Social bridges from one social group to another, which Granovetter described as weak links, can tie together a large network of people using the fewest connections.

It is also important to remember that communication is contextually based and that it is nonlinear. Communication is also a transformational process (Kreps, 1990, p. 26–27). Further, numerous components of a communication program—including the reactions of people to messages, the meanings people extract from messages, the time and place of communication, the relationship between communicators, past experiences, and purposes people have for communicating—interact simultaneously in a communication process.

School districts often restrict and direct communication. School district leaders should be aware of how their district's organizational structure may affect their receipt and transmission of information, both through the formal and informal subsystems within the district. This is important because the formal and informal subsystems of communication may act as a check-and-balance system for ensuring the intent of a message is accurately received. Leaders should utilize both formal and informal channels of communication to transmit important messages to stakeholders. In addition, educational leaders must be sensitive to the roles individuals play in restricting or enhancing the flow of information.

The Communication Flow

Organizational communication involves not only communication inside a school system, but also communication to external stakeholders about the system's outputs and feedback from the stakeholders about the quality and quantity of those outputs. This kind of communication exchange creates a communication flow, no matter where the communication originates. In addition, leaders must keep in mind that messages received are filtered through channels of other people and through the experiences and perceptions of the receiver. There is no such thing as a simple, clear message.

To illustrate reciprocal flow of communication, consider the example of a superintendent who simply asks his secretary to hold all calls and visitors for 10 minutes while he conferences with a high school principal. During that 10-minute conference, the secretary receives a call from the Chamber of Commerce president asking to speak to the superintendent. The secretary replies that the superintendent is in a conference and offers to take a message. After leaving his name and number, the caller hangs up and tells his wife, who is leaving for work, that the superintendent is unavailable. When his wife arrives at her office, a co-worker greets her with a "Good morning" to which she replies,

"What's good about it?" When the co-worker asks what's wrong, she explains that she is worried about some trouble her high school son is having and that she and her husband have been unable to get in touch with the principal or superintendent. The co-worker then begins to commiserate that she knows what it's like. She tried for a week to get in touch with their daughter's teacher before they made contact. "Schools just don't care about parents," the co-worker concludes.

As the above example illustrates, there is no such thing as a simple message from one person to another. Communication is not static and does not stop with the receiver. Nor does internal organizational communication remain contained within the organization. All messages, no matter how simple and forthright, will be filtered through receivers' values and belief systems and will be interpreted and decoded by receivers in terms of their experiences.

Organization Culture

Organization culture is probably the most important element of a school system's internal social infrastructure because of its power to influence human attitudes, beliefs, and behavior. Organization culture ultimately defines the essence of a school system because it describes the "way things are done" in the district. People's actions and behaviors are based upon underlying beliefs and values that are shared among the persons who are working in a school district, even though these beliefs and values may not be explicitly expressed. The underlying values and beliefs of culture are often described in terms of assumptions and norms. Assumptions are ideas and concepts that are accepted as true and nonnegotiable. They are seldom discussed and inherently taken for granted. Norms are unwritten rules of behavior that arise from cultural assumptions.

School district culture is also reflective of the larger societal culture in which it exists. Goodlad (1984) and others (for example, Cuban, 1984; Rowan, 1995) found that there is routine sameness in classrooms across the country. Additionally, social issues that impact the larger, national culture are mirrored within the school setting, such as divisions or subcultures that arise based upon gender, ethnicity, or socioeconomic status.

Culture is closely tied to the history and traditions of a school system and those who enter a district are socialized to understand and agree to the district's values, beliefs, and norms. Such socialization is accomplished both through formal means, such as induction training, and through informal ways, such as informal mentoring, peer dialogue in the teachers' lounge, or modeling "normal and accepted" behavior at various school functions.

A school district's culture is influenced and impacted by other elements of the organization, including the facilities, structural organization, purpose, leadership, and subcultures within the organization; for example, a typical high school departmental organizational structure tends to separate teachers by disciplines where each department may form its own subculture. In large high schools, it is not uncommon for faculty in a particular department to have little opportunity to regularly interact with teachers in other departments. The same is true in elementary schools where one may hear such statements as "The primary teachers do things differently than we do in the intermediate grades." At the district level, high school administrators and teachers are often isolated from elementary principals and teachers, thus leading to disunity of purpose. Without opportunities to interact, the articulation of a district's instructional program may be lost and the district can become fragmented into disconnected elementary, middle, and high schools.

As stated earlier, the culture of a school district is defined by the shared values, social norms, and role expectations within the system. Shared values and beliefs may be manifested through the vision or mission of a school district or by the way in which a district conducts its daily business (Chance, 1992). In a broad sense, values, norms, and role expectations are evident in the way people behave in a school district.

All persons within a school system bring with them their own set of beliefs and values. These personal values and beliefs become enmeshed with the values and beliefs of a school system. Those who find their personal beliefs and values to be incompatible with the district's beliefs and values may become alienated or aggressive.

The importance of organization culture cannot be underestimated when thinking about strategic communication and public relations from a systems theory perspective, because as Kreps (1990) noted,

"Communication is irreversible [and] is bound to the context in which it occurs" (p. 26). If we accept the notion that the purpose of strategic communication and public relations is to develop mutual understanding among all stakeholders, then efforts to communicate to stakeholders must come in the form of building a spirit of community, promoting common understanding, and defining community values rather than reacting with defensive explanations of why or why not school systems are failing.

PUBLIC RELATIONS AS SYSTEMIC COMMUNICATION

Change leaders must do more than develop a "media package" when planning strategic communication and public relations. They must think in terms of organization systems, keeping in mind far-reaching consequences and effects of their communication on the educational mission and goals of the schools in their district. The following framework suggests possible strategies to communicate strategically, rather than reacting to external feedback.

Be Proactive and Think Systemically

Consider the inputs, conversion process, outputs, and feedback loops of the school system when communicating with stakeholders. Choose words carefully. Avoid educational jargon that may not hold common meaning for all receivers of the message. Provide opportunities for two-way communication. Encourage stakeholders to ask questions so that meaning can be clarified. Take the conversation to a level beyond rhetoric. Communicate in terms of community values and beliefs. Pay attention to the informal systems as well as the formal systems of communication. Determine if principals, teachers, and staff understand the intent of the message. Assess the degree to which they communicate messages to parents and other community members.

Consider the Power of Networks

Involve parents and other stakeholders in conversations about education, rather than issuing announcements. Discuss the community's values about education. Decide what students need to know and be able to do as adults twenty years from now. Determine the role that education should take in helping children become active, productive citizens. Identify the skills students will need to have for future work and for future participation in a global, information age. Help stakeholders think about new mental models of schools and their role in the educational process.

Engage Key Players

Identify liaisons, opinion leaders, and cosmopolites because these people can help increase the accuracy of communication—both messages fed out of the system and those received as input and feedback from the community. Remember that communication is contextually based and that perceptions, not intent, are what matter. By continuing to listen to and use feedback, especially from key players, misunderstandings can be more easily rectified.

THE ROLE OF COMMUNICATION IN TRANSFORMING SCHOOL SYSTEMS

More recent applications of systems theory represent thinking that is reflective of current large-scale shifts in human civilization and economic bases—from a second-wave industrial society to a third-wave information age. The information age is not necessarily changing the inherent nature of systems and organizations, but it is changing the way we see things. As Vaill (1996) observed, "Our own growth, education, increasing sophistication, and knowledge of other cultures and value systems may also be contributing to our feelings of uncertainty and confusion" (p. 16).

Vaill (1996) utilized the metaphor of permanent whitewater to describe a different perspective on systems theory and asserted that "the model of a smooth-running macrosystem and component parts is intrinsically invalid" (p. 8). Senge (1990) discussed this similar notion in terms of mental models, citing Einstein's observation that theories determine what we measure (p. 175). Senge contended that innovations fail to be implemented because "They conflict with deeply held internal images of how the world works, images that limit us to familiar ways of thinking and acting" (p. 174) (see chapter 8 for more information about unlearning and learning mental models).

Both Vaill's and Senge's observations about change are conceptually derived from a subset of systems theory known as chaos theory. Chaos theory, along with complexity theory and evolutionary theory, emanates from the biological sciences. These theories provide new metaphors and new ways of thinking about organizations as systems. In physics, chaos theory is actually a search for patterns at the subatomic, or quantum, level. This theory explains relationships between seemingly disparate and random events. Chaos theory also describes systems in terms of nonlinear dynamics (for example, for a plain-English description of this theory, see Reigeluth, 2004). Thus, within the context of chaos theory change is not simply the function of adjusting one (or more) variables. Rather, altering an element of a system affects the state of other system elements, which in turn alters the original element, which in turn affects the state of other elements, and so on. Furthermore, quantum physics teaches us that apparently random variations when plotted through various mathematical models form a recognizable pattern; however, the way in which changes are manifested at a specific time within a system is not predictable, and change, therefore, is perceived as chaotic.

Applied to school systems, concepts from chaos theory add to our understanding of districts as complex, open systems that are influenced by other systems in a district's external environment. Change leaders should note that major problems for their school systems often grow out of seemingly minor events in the external environment. Chaos theory refers to this as the butterfly effect, noting that systems are sensitive to slight changes in their external environment. In discussing studies of meteorological patterns, Lorenz (1979) introduced the often-cited aspect of chaos theory referred to as the butterfly effect in which he proposed that the flap of a butterfly's wings today in Brazil could set off a tornado in Texas next month. The butterfly effect serves to illustrate the notion that a tiny change to one system could result in far-reaching, unpredictable consequences in other systems.

Another example of how chaos theory is applied to organizations is found in Wheatley (1992). She proposed that new and different information from a system's external environment can act as a random shock to a district, creating so much internal disturbance and resulting in such disequilibrium that the system falls apart. While dissipation may not be the demise of a system, it can be a process by which a system lets go of its present form and reemerges in a new form. Viewed from a broad perspective, this explanation of system theory is analogous to Toffler's (1980) prediction that industrial-based systems will give way to organizations better suited to civilization's needs in the information age.

Perhaps the most significant shift in thinking provided by systems theory is the notion that the whole is larger than the sum of its parts. Again, using metaphors from the biological and physical sciences, systems theory as applied to organizations is evolving to help us understand both the complexities and contextual nature of systems. Thus, early theories of social systems that analyzed an organization's parts have evolved to explain organizations as sets of relationships, interconnections, and networking; for example, Capra (1996) noted that "what we call a part is merely a pattern in an inseparable web of relationships" (p. 37).

CONCLUSION

Fullan (1999) proposed that collaboration is an essential element for effecting organization change, which he illustrated through an example from zoology, contrasting the adaptation of two species of birds to new environmental conditions. Scientists concluded that birds that are social learn faster and thus increase their chances for survival and evolve more quickly. Others have also identified collaboration and attention to human relationships as essential leadership qualities for effecting organization change. Sarason (1990) asserted that current power relationships in schools prevent educational reform, suggesting that collaborative efforts are needed in order to effectively implement change in school systems. He further commented that "educational reformers have trouble understanding that change by legislative fiat or policy pronouncements from on high" (p. 101) do not result in change and that reformers often "confuse a change in policy with a change in practice" (p. 101). Wheatley (1992) wrote that "nothing exists independent of its relationship with something else" (p. 34) and that what is critical is the relationship between the person and the setting. These observations about collaboration, relationships, and adaptation also fit within the concept of contextuality discussed earlier.

Successful implementation of change depends upon the meaning attached to the change by those who must implement it (Evans, 1996). For the people working in a school district to accept change, the proposed changes must fit their worldviews. If the proposed changes conflict with those worldviews, then efforts will need to be taken to reconcile the differences. Part of this reconciliation effort must also focus on changing a school district's culture if it also conflicts with the proposed changes. In fact, Evans considered cultural change as requisite to organization change.

Finally, developing a powerful and compelling vision of a desirable future for a school system can provide a strong focus and sense of purpose for both the school system and its community. A vision shared by a school district and its community acts as a platform for facilitating school district improvement and guides education reform that complements, rather than clashes with, community values (Chance, 1992; Chance & Bjork, 2004). In essence, working together with stakeholders to develop a common district vision is a process that directly taps into the community's shared values and beliefs—its culture. This process for vision development will be described more fully in chapter 7.

REFERENCES

Allen, G. (2004, October). Follow media strategy checklist to get your NCLB message out. *No Child Left Behind Compliance Insider*, 1–3.

Barabasi, A. L. (2002). *Linked: The new science of networks.* Cambridge, MA: Perseus.

Buchanan, M. (2002). *Nexus: Small worlds and the groundbreaking science of networks.* New York: W. W. Norton.

Capra, F. (1996). *The web of life: A new scientific understanding of living systems.* New York: Anchor Books.

Chance, E. W. (1992). *Visionary leadership in schools: Successful strategies for developing and implementing an educational vision.* Springfield, IL: Charles C. Thomas.

Chance, P. L., & Bjork, L. G. (2004). The social dimensions of public relations (3rd ed.). In T. J. Kowalski (Ed.), *Public relations in schools* (pp. 126–150). Upper Saddle River, NJ: Pearson Prentice Hall.

Cuban, L. (1984). *How teachers taught: Constancy and change in American classrooms, 1880–1980.* New York: Longman.

Evans, R. (1996). *The human side of school change: Reform, resistance, and the real-life problems of innovation.* San Francisco: Jossey-Bass.

Fullan, M. (1999). *Change forces: The sequel.* Philadelphia: Falmer Press.

Getzels, J. W., & Guba, E. G. (1957). Social behavior and the administrative process. *School Review, 65,* 423–441.

Goodlad, J. (1984). *A place called school.* New York: McGraw-Hill.

Granovetter, M. (1973). The strength of weak ties: A network theory revisited. *Sociological Theory, 1,* 203–233.

Katz, D., & Kahn, R. (1966). *The social psychology of organizations.* New York: Wiley.

Kreps, G. L. (1990). *Organizational communication: Theory and practice* (2nd ed.). White Plains, NY: Longman.

Lorenz, E. N. (1979). Predictability: Does the flap of a butterfly's wings in Brazil set off a tornado in Texas? Paper presented at the annual meeting of the American Association for the Advancement of Science, Washington, D.C.

Milgram, S. (1967). The small-world problem. *Psychology Today, 1,* 60–67.

Public Relations Society of America. (n.d.). *The public relations profession.* Retrieved January 7, 2005, from http://www.prsa.org/_Resources/Profession/index.asp?ident=prof1

Reigeluth, C. M. (2004). Chaos theory and the sciences of complexity: Foundations for transforming education. Retrieved on April 9, 2006, from http://www.indiana.edu/~syschang/decatur/documents/chaos_reigeluth_s2004.pdf

Rogers, E. M., & Agarwala-Rogers, R. (1976). *Communication in organizations.* New York: Free Press.

Rowan, B. (1995). Institutional analysis of educational organizations: Lines of theory and directions for research. In R. T. Ogawa (Ed.), *Advances in research and theories of school management and educational policy,* Vol. 3 (pp. 1–20). Greenwich, CT: JAI Press.

Sarason, S. B. (1990). *The predictable failure of educational reform.* San Francisco: Jossey-Bass.

Senge, P. M. (1990). *The fifth discipline: The art and practice of the learning organization.* New York: Doubleday/Currency.

Toffler, A. (1980). *The third wave.* New York: Bantam Books.

Vaill, P. B. (1996). *Learning as a way of being: Strategies for survival in a world of permanent white water.* San Francisco: Jossey-Bass.

von Bertalanffy, L. (1975). *Perspectives on general system theory.* New York: George Braziller.

Wheatley, M. J. (1992). *Leadership and the new science: Learning about organization from an orderly universe.* San Francisco: Berrett-Koehler.

CHAPTER 6

Establishing Relationships and Building Trust to Facilitate School District Improvement

Pick up any major newspaper, listen to any daily news broadcast, or engage in neighborly conversation about current affairs in this country, and the "dismal" state of education is among the leading topics of discussion.

"Students aren't achieving."

"Schools are failing."

"Teachers can't teach."

"Principals can't lead."

"We need CEOs with 'real-world' leadership experience to reform our school systems."

There is apparent and overt mistrust in our public schools that is being fueled and reinforced by lawmakers and policymakers keen on solving the "educational crisis" through legislative mandates aimed at forcing schools to be "accountable" for student achievement. And, we wonder, "Why aren't schools getting any better?" "Why isn't student achievement improving?" "Why can't we attract and retain quality teachers?" Fingers begin pointing:

"It's the teachers' fault."

"It's the principal's fault."

"It's the superintendent's and school board's lack of leadership."

"Parents are absent in our schools."

"Kids can't speak English."

We seem to be spinning out of control through a litany of dialogue, educational "reforms," legislative mandates, and constant confusion and chaos. But when we are frazzled and in a frenzy of constant motion, we are not likely to see an obvious solution to our problems.

Wheatley (2002), an author and scholar of organizational theory for

113

30 years, recently wrote a book that she characterized as very different from anything she had written in the past. She began that book by saying, "I believe we can change the world if we start listening to one another again" (p. 3). Listening to one another requires trust. In this chapter, we will explore the concept of trust as a fundamental element of effective change leadership and strategic communication.

Effective transformational change must be built upon a foundation of positive relationships and trust. One cornerstone of this foundation is constructed on facts—the facts about the characteristics of effective schools and school systems. So, we begin this chapter with a summary of the research on effective schools as foundation for exploring the challenges of establishing relationships and building trust.

SCHOOL EFFECTIVENESS RESEARCH

Contemporary research on the characteristics of effective schools has its roots in the research of Edmonds, Lezotte, and Brookover in the late 1970s in which they studied schools that were successful in improving student achievement and were closing the achievement gap associated with poverty and ethnicity. Based upon this research, Edmonds (1982) identified five correlates that appeared to be associated with student achievement. These were:

- the principal's leadership and attention to the quality of instruction;
- a pervasive and broadly understood instructional focus;
- an orderly, safe climate conducive to teaching and learning;
- teacher behaviors that convey the expectation that all students are expected to obtain at least minimum mastery;
- the use of measures of pupil achievement as the basis for program evaluation (p. 4).

Lezotte (1991) provided a second generation of effective school correlates that included:

- instructional leadership,
- clear and focused mission,

- safe and orderly environment,
- climate of high expectations,
- frequent monitoring of student progress,
- positive home-school relations, and
- opportunity to learn and student time on task.

Brookover and Lezotte (1979) maintained that effective principals are more assertive in their leadership role and assume responsibility for the school's success. Edmonds (1982) corroborated earlier research by Brookover and Lezotte when he stated that the principal's leadership and attention to the quality of instruction was a major characteristic of effective schools.

More recently, Reeves (2000) presented case studies of high-achieving schools that were identified as 90/90/90 schools. These were schools where 90% of students were from low income families, 90% of the students were from ethnic minorities, and 90% of the students achieved high academic standards as measured by tests of academic achievement. In these schools, five common characteristics of high-achieving schools were identified as (1) focus on academic achievement, (2) clear curriculum choices, (3) frequent assessment of student progress and multiple opportunities for improvement, (4) an emphasis on nonfiction writing, and (5) collaborative scoring of student work.

When comparing research on school effectiveness over a 35-year period, Marzano (2003) discovered strikingly similar findings among this body of research, which he categorized into five school-level factors. These were: (1) guaranteed and viable curriculum, (2) challenging goals and effective feedback, (3) parental and community involvement, (4) safe and orderly climate, and (5) collegiality and professionalism.

While most of the research on school effectiveness has focused on individual schools, there have been some recent studies on district-level change that transformed low-performing school districts into high-performing districts. Cawelti (2003) reported on the results of a study of six school districts that served large numbers of students from low-income families where all or most of the schools in the districts showed substantial gains in student achievement over a 5-year period. He noted that these districts were similar in the following ways:

1. They restructured the school system in ways that clarified the roles of the school principals and staff for being accountable for improved results.
2. They focused on a limited number of standards considered important for student success.
3. They focused school-based staff development on the knowledge base for improving classroom instruction.

In discussing whole-district school improvement, Cawelti (2003) noted that "the leader's job is to see that . . . effective classroom instruction for all students remains at the forefront of *discussions* [emphasis added] about changes in the school or district" (p. 50). His use of the term "discussion" was not accidental but rather relates to the principle of restructuring for greater accountability where teams and school-level decision making are emphasized.

In the multitude of characteristics of effective schools, there are many statements regarding a common understanding among teachers, administrators, parents, and community members about the primary mission of their schools. These statements imply a common understanding among internal and external stakeholders about what is important in their school systems. Lezotte (1991) described this common understanding as "clear and focused of mission." Marzano's (2003) category of a "guaranteed, viable curriculum" suggests a similar common understanding. Reeves (2000, p. 188) described this common focus as "clear curricular choices" that emphasized core skills in reading, writing, and mathematics, which would lead to student success in a wide variety of other academic endeavors. Additionally, the research findings on school effectiveness suggest that a school system's focus on academics is something commonly understood by all stakeholders.

Marzano (2003) identified collegiality as one of the factors for school effectiveness. He specifically pointed out that effective leadership encourages teacher involvement in decision making and staff development. Such shared leadership is also implicit in early school effectiveness research, which indicated that teachers held common expectations for high student achievement and that school staffs were consistent in monitoring student success. Reeves (2000) also noted that the 90/90/90 schools continually assessed student performance through weekly classroom assessments, implying this was a practice throughout all classrooms and thus a cultural norm based on common values. He further noted that teachers collaborated in assessment, working toward uniform evaluation processes and consistency in expectations.

What is not clearly evident in all of the research on school effectiveness is the critical role of trusting relationships and effective strategic communication. However, when you peel away several layers of research findings about school effectiveness factors, you begin to see that trust and strong relationships form the bedrock upon which the foundation of an effective school system sits. None of the improvements touted in the effective schools research could have been realized without trusting and effective relationships. It is not surprising, therefore, that so much of the contemporary literature on effective schools and school systems focuses on using strategic communication to build effective, trusting relationships through professional collaboration and shared decision making, and by building teacher leadership capacity (for example, Blankstein, 2004; Fullan & Hargreaves, 1991; Schmoker, 2001).

BUILDING TRUSTING RELATIONSHIPS

Bryk and Schneider (2002) concluded from their study of the Chicago public school system that trust was a key factor that significantly influenced whether meaningful improvement efforts emerged within that district. In comparing low-achieving to high-achieving schools in that district, they found that trust among teachers, among teachers and principals, and among teachers and parents was strong or very strong in high-achieving schools in the district. Conversely, levels of trust were minimal or nonexistent in low-achieving schools within that district. They further noted that trust fostered districtwide conditions conducive to implementing and sustaining activities necessary for improvement. Specifically, trust reduced the sense of vulnerability experienced when taking on new and uncertain reform efforts. Furthermore, trust facilitated problem-solving within a school system and promoted the organizational norm of mutual support for sharing professional practices. Finally, trust promoted commitment to the district and common beliefs in its mission.

What is trust and how is it developed? Hoy and Tschannen-Moran (1999) identified five components of trust: (1) benevolence, (2) reliability, (3) competence, (4) honesty, and (5) openness. Coleman (1990), on the other hand, conceptualized three "systems of trust." He defined these three systems of trust in the context of a whole organization. The systems of trust are:

1. *Mutual trust.* This is where members of a community or organization are all engaged in an activity where all have similar interests in the outcomes of their system.
2. *Intermediaries in trust.* A second system of trust involves intermediaries. This form of trust exists in all aspects of people's lives. For example, a manager writes a letter of recommendation for a former employee. The acceptance of that recommendation by a new employer indicates that the employer places his or her trust in the judgment of the reference (i.e., in the intermediary) about the applicant.
3. *Third-party trust.* Third-party trust refers to a situation where two parties can trust each other, even if they don't know each other, based on a relationship each has with a mutual, trusted third party. In third party trust, one person or group acts to ensure the trustworthiness of the other two parties.

Finally, Coleman described the effect information can have on systems of trust. He noted three sources of information that could lead to an expansion or contraction of trust: (1) the actions of the trusted person or group; (2) the opinion of others who have similar reasons for trusting a person or group; and (3) the opinion of others who have different reasons for trusting a person or group. The extent of trust within the organization depends upon the mix of these three sources of information.

Bryk and Schneider (2002) expanded on Coleman's concept of systems of trust in their notion of relational trust as a system of trust that specifically applies to school districts. "Relational trust views the social exchanges of schooling as organized around a distinct set of role relationships: teachers with students, teachers with other teachers, teachers with parents and with their school principal" (p. 20). Bryk and Schneider noted that building trust in a school community involves establishing relations between groups of people who do not have equal power within the system, but at the same time, each group is dependent upon the other. For example, a principal has greater power by virtue of his assigned roles, but is dependent upon the support of teachers and parents to maintain his job and to sustain efforts to improve school conditions or reform educational practices. Groups with less power than others are also more vulnerable to the actions of those with more power. Thus, trust is developed through the conscious acts of those with more power by reaching out to those with less power.

IMPLICATIONS FOR CHANGE LEADERS

School district change leaders must take every opportunity to use strategic communication and school public relations tools to build trust and develop collaborative relationships with internal and external stakeholders. Districts in which teachers, administrators, parents, students, and other community members are comfortable with their schools, participate in open dialogue about their schools, and feel welcome to participate in school activities are districts that have, at the very least, set the stage for increasing student achievement and school district improvement. Marzano (2003) recommended three action steps to gain this kind of parental and community involvement in schools. These are

1. Establish vehicles for communication between schools, parents, and community members.
2. Establish multiple ways for parents and community members to be involved in the day-to-day operations of a school district and its schools.
3. Establish governance vehicles that allow for the involvement of parents and community members (p. 49–50).

Kochanek (2005) suggested fostering "low-risk exchanges" (p. 23) to build trust, such as social events or special projects that can involve all stakeholders. After these types of activities have become established, then more formal structures that involve a higher level of risk can be implemented. Others (for example, Blankstein, 2004; DuFour & Eaker, 1998; Fullan & Hargreaves, 1991; Schmoker, 2001) recommended the development of professional learning communities to engage teachers in a common focus and shared leadership toward school district renewal and continuous learning and improvement.

All of these recommendations involve either one-to-one relationships or collaboration among individuals within a team or group setting. These vehicles or approaches to collaboration help educators build trusting relationships.

Building Individual Relationships

A relationship between two individuals begins with two-way communication, which involves one person sending a message and another person receiving a message and then providing feedback to the sender. However, this apparently simple process (sender → receiver → feedback to sender) is, in reality, not so simple. For communication to be truly effective, and thus for relationships to be built, it is essential that the sender and receiver agree on the meaning of the sent message.

A message is an idea that a sender wants to transmit to a receiver. Messages, therefore, are essentially symbolic representations of ideas that involve encoding by the sender and decoding by the receiver. The sender encodes meaning using symbols that may use language, hand or facial gestures, body movements, or pictures. Receivers decode these symbols into meaning in the form of ideas, images, and thoughts. Meaning is assigned by both the sender and the receiver; thus, communication involves not so much the message itself but what is intended by the sender and what is perceived by the receiver. The receiver is the most important element in the communication process because it is the receiver's perception of the message that will define the effects of the communication process. Rogers and Agarwala-Rogers (1976) defined effective communication as "communication that results in those changes in receiver behavior that were intended by the source" (p. 13). Thus, effects are the changes in knowledge, attitude, or actions of the receiver that result from the message. Feedback is the receiver's response to the message, resulting in dynamic, two-way communication. Effective communication requires feedback (both positive and negative) and denotes the sender's concern for whether the receiver understands the intent of the message.

When communicating with others, whether as a sender or receiver of information, attention to some basic skills and strategies will lead to more effective communication. These skills and strategies are discussed below.

Actively listen. Active listening is demonstrated by showing another person that you hear and understand what he or she is saying. This may be achieved through eye contact, body proximity, and affirmations. In general, keeping eye contact with the person speaking lets the person know you are listening to them. Body proximity refers to establishing a comfortable position for communicating. Sitting side by side rather than across the desk from one another enhances communication because there are no physical barriers separating one from the other. Finally, silence may inhibit communication when the speaker is unsure whether or not he has been heard. When listening to another, give affirmations that lets the speaker know you are listening or that encourages her to continue speaking. Utterances such as "uh-huh," "mmm," "I understand," or "Tell me more" let the other person know you are attending to what she is saying.

Paraphrase, reflect, and summarize. Paraphrasing, reflecting, and summarizing are ways to check with the other person to make sure you have understood what he was saying. Paraphrasing means to rephrase what a person said without simply repeating his exact words. For instance, a parent says to you that his child was excited about the science lesson today. To paraphrase, the person listening might say, "Sounds as if your child learned something new and exciting in science today." The wonderful part about paraphrasing is that it gives the sender an opportunity to affirm or correct your understanding. Depending upon the intent of the sender, he may say, "Yes, it was a wonderful lesson about marine animals," or he might inform you that his child was excited about the fact that one of the boys in class threw a squid at a group of girls. Either way, you have a better understanding of what the parent was trying to tell you.

Reflecting is essentially the same thing as paraphrasing but places emotion in what is paraphrased. For example, a teacher comments to his colleague, "Boy, what a day! I'm exhausted." The colleague might reply, "Sounds like you had a frustrating day," which may or may not be correct. Perhaps the teacher is exhausted because it was a wonderful day. Again, this reflection gives the sender a chance to confirm or correct the listener's understanding of the message.

Summarizing accomplishes much the same thing as paraphrasing and reflection. By stating something like, "Let me summarize what I've heard you say so far" and then doing so, the receiver has an opportunity to correct your understanding of the intended message.

Pay attention to body language. Facial expressions, voice intonation, dress, body position, and gestures play an important part in the communication process. Receivers of messages look for these nonverbal cues to confirm the words being communicated; for instance, the principal who says to a teacher, "I want to hear about your concerns with Mary's progress," while looking out the window and glancing at the clock is sending an inconsistent message to the teacher. Her words say, "I care" but her actions say, "I don't." Mehrabian (1981) concluded that when verbal messages conflict with the vocal (intonation, projection, and resonance) and visual (facial and body expressions) elements accompanying the verbal message, people believe what is being communicated nonverbally. Vocal and visual elements work in tandem with the verbal message and confirm the sender's intent. For instance, the principal who tells a teacher, "I have confidence in your ability to lead the school improvement team" and places a hand on the teacher's shoulder or pats the teacher's back at the same time increases the effect of his message. In fact, Mehrabian (1981) found that only 7% of a message's effect comes from the verbal element, while 38% comes from the vocal and 55% from the visual elements.

Forming and Developing Groups and Teams

School district transformation requires change leaders to create a parallel organization (discussed near the end of chapter 4) composed of several change leadership teams. These teams should participate in structured team-building activities early in your district's transformation journey.

A district's transformation journey also requires forming coalitions of external stakeholders. When properly developed, these groups result in a level of expanded self-esteem for coalition members while building a strong degree of cooperation among various group members (Maeroff, 1993).

Change leaders who successfully build trusting relationships and collaboration among internal and external stakeholders are ones who are knowledgeable about group dynamics and skilled in facilitating communication among diverse populations. The following principles should be applied when forming groups of teachers, parents, and community members and facilitating their work toward achieving a district's transformation goals.

Consider diversity. Building change leadership teams within a school district and developing coaltions of external stakeholders involves bringing together people from diverse backgrounds and bridging multicultural boundaries. In discussing multicultural aspects of public relations, Banks (2000) proposed that public relations is cultural because it "communicates across cultural borders" and "it is a cultural practice itself" (p. 29). Moreover, Banks pointed out that cultural boundaries are determined by a group's cohesive and homogeneous understanding of particular practices. Thus, even though a school district's internal and external stakeholders may represent various cultures as defined by race, ethnicity, religion, gender, and so on, these groups may come together as one culture bound by their common understanding of and lived experience in a school district's community. Furthermore as groups and teams are formed to accomplish transformation tasks, it is necessary to have appropriate diversity represented within them. This creates a strong support foundation for transformation decisions. Diverse groups and teams may be more difficult to work with, but members will often have more useful aggregate knowledge and skills to accomplish their agenda.

Acknowledge and explain how groups and teams evolve. Groups and teams develop in a sequential, highly predictable manner. Groups and teams, like systems, have characteristics similar to living organisms. They come into being, evolve, change, and mature as a result of experience, opportunities, and knowledge. Tuckman and Jensen (1977) concluded that all groups evolve through five distinct stages. These stages are forming, storming, norming, performing, and adjourning. All five stages are best utilized by change leaders as they relate to the group's task and changes in interpersonal relationships. A brief summary of each stage is presented below.

- Forming is associated with the creation of a new group and the feeling of discomfort that can result from such a situation. This initial period of caution, apprehension, and uneasiness is followed by a period of storming.
- Storming occurs when the group members begin to focus on their individual perceptions of the task and when they vie for influence and power. Conflict can come in several forms and, in the extreme, can destroy group productivity before the group reaches the next stage.
- Norming is the stage where explicit and implicit norms are established. A sense of order is evidenced.
- Performing is characterized by the group's focus on the task. Group membership and individuals' roles are well defined, and group norms are entrenched. Productivity is high, and there is an increased sense of camaraderie among group members.
- Adjourning takes place after the group has accomplished its task. Groups should be disbanded after their task is complete.

Establish ground rules and identify the group's and team's tasks. Ground rules for effective group and team performance should include three basic tenets. First, all members will be recognized and heard. Second, ideas (not people) are critiqued. Third, members should be objective and honest in their discussions. A leader can facilitate the development of positive norms, which promote a group's effectiveness, through modeling desired communication strategies and interpersonal behaviors. If team coordination and facilitation is delegated to group members, the leader should provide training and direction to these individuals. The group's task should be clarified and expected outcomes delineated. Questions to be considered at this stage might include:

- What is the task?
- What standards or criteria must be applied to the problem?
- What are the group's boundaries or limitations, especially related to time, money, and information to be provided?

- What is the authority of the group? Will the group make recommendations to administration or will the group make final decisions that will be implemented? (Scholtes, 1988)

Be ready to facilitate individual roles within groups and teams. Not all groups and teams work as effectively as expected. Often that is because the group is unable to move past the storming stage. It may also be related to the roles that individual group members choose. Roles may reflect personality, the group task, or the level of individual commitment to the task. Some roles facilitate group performance and others hinder group productivity. Chance and Chance (2002) noted that leaders should foster the roles that assist with group output while discouraging roles that are negative.

Some roles that are supportive of a group task include:

- Encourager: Praises and supports others
- Compromiser: Willing to yield for the team's progress
- Summarizer: Brings the group's ideas into focus
- Elaborator: Builds on the ideas of others
- Harmonizer: Mediates disagreements and seeks common ground
- Procedural Expert: Understands rules and policies of the organization
- Energizer: Motivates and moves the group forward

Roles that disrupt a group include:

- Blocker: Disagrees for the sake of disagreement
- Aggressor: Attacks group members, not their ideas
- Dominator: Tries to control and manipulate the group
- Withdrawer: Fails to participate and blames the group for this failure
- Recognition Seeker: Wants to talk of himself or herself and be the center of attention
- Special Interest Pleader: Has a personal agenda for the group

Change leaders must facilitate the development of group and team roles that support their district's transformation journey.

CONCLUSION

Developing relationships is the first step in building trust and fostering community. It is a necessary prerequisite to moving your school district toward a desired future. The next move is to work with the school district's external stakeholders in examining common values and developing a shared vision for the community's school system. What does your community want for its children? What should students be learning and what do they want your school system and its schools to be? Answers to these and other questions can be discussed in structured large-group events like the Community Engagement Conference and System Engagement Conference that are part of the Step-Up-To-Excellence transformation protocol presented in chapter 4.

In the next chapter, you will explore the process of using strategic communication and trusting relationships with internal and external stakeholders to envision a desirable future for your school district.

REFERENCES

Banks, S. P. (2000). *Multicultural public relations: A social-interpersonal approach.* (2nd ed.). Ames: Iowa State University Press.

Blankstein, A. M. (2004). *Failure is not an option: Six principles that guide student achievement in high-performing schools.* Thousand Oaks, CA: Corwin Press.

Brookover, W. & Lezotte, L. (1979). Changes in school characteristics coincident with changes in student achievement, East Lansing: Michigan State University College of Urban Development.

Bryk, A. S., & Schneider, B. (2002). *Trust in schools: A core resource for improvement.* New York: Russell Sage Foundation.

Cawelti, G. (2003). The new effective schools. In W. A. Owings and L. S. Kaplan (Eds.), *Best practices, best thinking, and emerging issues in school leadership* (pp. 42–52). Thousand Oaks, CA: Corwin Press.

Chance, P. L., & Chance, E. W. (2002). *Introduction to educational leadership and organizational behavior: Theory into practice.* Larchmont, NY: Eye on Education.

Coleman, J. S. (1990). *Foundations of social theory.* Cambridge, MA: Belknap Press of Harvard University Press.

DuFour, R., & Eaker, R. (1998). *Professional learning communities at work:*

Best practices for enhancing student achievement. Bloomington, IN: National Education Service.

Edmonds, R. R. (1982). Programs of school improvement: An overview. *Educational Leadership, 40*(3), 4–11.

Fullan, M. G., & Hargreaves, A. (1991). *What's worth fight for? Working together for your school.* Andover, MA: Regional Laboratory for Educational Improvement of the Northeast and Islands.

Hoy, W. K., & Tschannen-Moran, M. (1999). Five faces of trust: An empirical confirmation in urban schools. *Journal of School Leadership, 9,* 184–208.

Kochanek, J. R. (2005). *Building trust for better schools: Research based practices.* Thousand Oaks, CA: Corwin Press.

Lezotte, L. W. (1991). Correlates of effective schools: The first and second generation. Okemos, MI: Effective Schools Products. Retrieved on March 1, 2006, from http://www.effectiveschools.com

Maeroff, G. I. (1993). Building teams to rebuild schools. *Phi Delta Kappan, 74*(7), 512–519.

Marzano, R. J. (2003). *What works in schools: Translating research into action.* Alexandria, VA: Association for Supervision and Curriculum Development.

Mehrabian, A. (1981). *Silent messages: Implicit communication of emotions and attitudes* (2nd ed.). Belmont, CA: Wadsworth.

Reeves, D. B. (2000). *Accountability in action: A blueprint for learning organizations.* (2nd ed.). Denver, CO: Advanced Learning Centers.

Rogers, E. M., & Agarwala-Rogers, R. (1976). *Communication in organizations.* New York: Free Press.

Schmoker, M. (2001). *The results fieldbook: Practical strategies from dramatically improved schools.* Alexandria, VA: Association for Supervision and Curriculum Development.

Scholtes, P. R. (1988). *The team-handbook: How to use teams to improve quality.* Madison, WI: Joiner Associates.

Tuckman, B., & Jensen, M. (1977). Stages of small group development. *Group and Organizational Studies, 2,* 419–427.

Wheatley, M. J. (2002). *Turning to one another: Simple conversations to restore hope to the future.* San Francisco: Berrett-Koehler.

CHAPTER 7

Creating School District Renewal Through a Shared Vision

The quality of education in American school systems has been and is a topic of political debate. Educators are barraged with mandates and "flavor of the month" change proposals intended to ensure higher accountability and bring about reform. Policies and ideas for change aimed at creating reform, however, have failed to live up to expectations and have failed to create sustained improvements in our nation's school systems. One reason for this failure at the policy level is found in a comment by Tyack and Cuban (1995) who pointed out that the "institutional structure [of schools] probably has more influence on the implementation of policy than policy has on institutional practice" (p. 134). An important factor contributing to failed ideas for change is that the multitude of reform ideas are often in conflict with each other—all competing for the minds, hearts, and dollars of communities who want their school systems to provide children with a quality education.

At the heart of the matter of failed policies and failed ideas for change is a simple question: What is the purpose of education?—a simple question without a simple answer. Everyone with an interest in education seems to have an answer to this question. But the real answers must come from a community if those ideas and policies are to succeed. Stakeholders in a school district's community and the faculty and staff who work in school districts must decide what they want from their school district. And these decisions must be shaped into a form commonly called a "vision"—a powerful and compelling picture of a desirable future for a community's school district.

VISION

Goodlad, Mantle-Bromley, and Goodlad (2004) suggested that educational renewal rather than educational reform is a more appropriate approach to education and schooling in a democratic society. The process of renewal is meant to "prevent present conditions from deteriorating and to address problems as they arrive" as well as "to effect changes and to sustain those changes that prove desirable" (p. 102). Others call for a total transformation of school systems (Duffy, 2004; Reigeluth, 1995) so that they become something quite different and significantly more effective than they are. Either way—renewal or transformation—the community members and school district employees must take part in a structured conversation about their school district's future. Through structured conversations, community members and school district employees must consider questions such as:

- What do we want schools in our district to accomplish?
- What should our schools look like?
- What should we expect from students, teachers, administrators, parents, and community members in relation to our schools?
- What is our vision for the schools in our community?

Vision provides a strong focus and sense of purpose for a school district, its schools and supporting work units, and its community. A shared school district–community vision acts as a platform for facilitating school district improvement and guiding education reform that complements, rather than clashes with, community values. A vision represents where people want their school system to be in the future. Visions are, without exception, future oriented in wording and concept.

A vision has been variously described as "the development, transmission, and implementation of a desirable future" (Manasse, 1985, p. 150) or as a "journey from the known to the unknown . . . creating a montage of facts, hopes, dreams . . . and opportunities" (Hickman & Silva, 1984, p. 151). Bennis and Nanus (1985) described vision as something compelling. At the core of all vision definitions is that a vision shapes an organization or an institution as it moves toward a better future (Chance, 1992; Rutherford, 1985; Shieve & Shoenheit, 1987). The transformation of vision from a concept to reality is the result of leadership.

Carter and Cunningham (1997) in their study of school superintendents indicated that "the superintendent must lead the schools in developing a clear vision of curriculum, instruction, and student achievement connections" (p. 189). They expanded on the importance of the role of the superintendent in leading the visioning process by concluding that "successful superintendents recognize that the power of a clear vision . . . can be more effective than the power of authority" (p. 189).

Even though a superintendent may have a vision for his school district, if it is imposed on the system the vision will undoubtedly fail to create significant change in the system. Any approach to developing a vision should adopt a philosophy of inclusiveness instead of exclusiveness. The vision development process should be viewed as a collaborative effort among internal and external stakeholders. The creation of a shared school district–community vision may be one of the most important activities in which a superintendent participates during a district's transformation journey. A vision developed collaboratively opens lines of communication, provides for constructive involvement of a broad base of representatives of the school district's stakeholders and constituents, and charts a path for the school district's future.

How is a collaborative school district–community vision developed? For certain, it does not happen spontaneously or serendipitously. Vision development is a planned event, requiring strong senior-level leadership committed to building coalitions among a school district's internal and external stakeholders. Chance (1992) devised a process for vision development that invites significant participation and collaboration. The most significant result of shared vision building is the tremendous community support that it generates for the school district. Through school district–community vision building, everyone comes together in mutual agreement about the direction in which the school district should be moving. The feeling of goodwill between those in the school district and those in the community even extends to issues such as school board elections, curriculum design, school discipline, and parent-teacher conversations. In essence, a collaborative approach to vision development promotes trust.

THE VISION DEVELOPMENT PROCESS

Below is an outline of Chance's (1992) five-step vision development process. This process can be built into the Pre-Launch Preparation phase of the change navigation protocol presented in chapter 4.

Step 1: Reflect on Personal Educational Visions

The first component of the five-step vision development process involves school district leaders' reflecting upon their personal visions for their district. Those participating in this first stage include, but are not limited to, the superintendent, other central office personnel, site administrators, board members, and lead teachers. This initial step in the process provides an opportunity for reflection by asking those involved to recognize their personal values and beliefs while examining their professional careers. Upon the completion of self-reflection, school district leaders are asked to think about the strengths and weaknesses of the school district. They are also asked to examine the school district's relationship with the external environment and reflect on how all the various interpersonal components of the school district work together in the educational process. Finally, they discuss with one another their concepts of an ideal school system and identify the types of learning-related activities that should occur. At this point, participants do not write or develop a vision; the initial step simply asks participants to reflect and share with one another. During this first stage, the leadership cadre forms a bond in preparation for leading other stakeholders through subsequent stages of the visioning process.

Step 2: Develop a Districtwide, Collaborative School District–Community Vision

This step begins by inviting a variety of individuals who represent the diversity of a school district and its community. Participants should include community leaders, parents and nonparents, teachers, staff members, board members, district administrators, students, representatives of minority or underrepresented groups, as well as those in the community who are critics of the school system. Depending on the size of a school district, the total number of participants can range from 40 to 300. It is important to be as inclusive as possible at this point. The Community Engagement Conference and the System Engagement Conference that are part of the Step-Up-To-Excellence change protocol described in chapter 4 are particularly useful for completing this step.

All of the people invited to help develop a new vision for a district participate in a multi-tiered effort that gradually moves from numerous small groups composed of five to seven members to a single large, democratically selected group of 10 to 15 members. The various small groups, which represent the diversity of a school district and its community, respond to questions related to school district strengths and weaknesses, community support, community concerns, and the focus of the school district for the future. A consensus-building process is used that allows group members to come to agreement on how to respond to questions and concerns that come to the groups.

Next, people from each small group are elected to move forward to create new groups composed of representatives from the other groups. These mixed groups go through the same consensus-building process that was used with the earlier groups. The process continues in a similar manner until a single group of 10 to 15 members is formed—one that represents the stakeholder groups participating in the vision-building process.

The primary outcome of the single group of stakeholders is a new vision for their school district. This shared school district–community vision represents input and agreement from the diverse stakeholders who were involved in the process. The result is a collaboratively formed school district–community vision statement that reflects everyone's appraisal of the school district and their ideas of what the school district should look like in the future. Secondary outcomes of this group are short- and long-term goals to support the vision.

Step 2 is a complex, time-consuming process, and it is important to allow sufficient time for participants to process their discussions. Group interaction and dialogue are as important as the product—the vision statement. The discussions that occur in this process allow people to work together in a positive way for the good of the school district. The sharing of ideas, concerns, and beliefs allows for a unification of school district and community forces and creates a greater sense of collaboration and cooperation among stakeholders.

Step 3: Communicate the Vision Along With Short- and Long-Term Goals to the School District's Community

Effectively communicating the vision is important. A strategic communication plan to disseminate the vision and to explain the district's strategies for achieving is crucial. Generally, a vision is best communicated using emotionally powerful metaphorical statements, symbols, or models. Pronouncements representative of the vision such as "Where Dreams Grow," "Excellence and Equity," and "Striving for Excellence" provide both impetus and direction for an organization. Communicating the vision is not an end in itself—the vision must be made real through deliberate action. A vision without action is just a dream. Action is represented by setting and achieving short- and long-term goals for moving a district toward its vision.

Step 4: Actualize the Vision by Implementing Short- and Long-Term Goals

Tactics to achieve short- and long-term goals are developed. In addition, measures for assessing the district's success in meeting these goals are determined. Without monitoring and evaluation, it will be difficult to determine success and failure. The establishment of vision-monitoring teams at each school site and support work unit within the district is a useful way to determine how the actualization process is proceeding. The On-Track Seminars that are part of the change navigation protocol presented in chapter 4 are particularly helpful for this kind of evaluation.

A periodic "vision audit" provided to the community is another way to maintain the focus on the district's vision while documenting to stakeholders what the district has accomplished. Appointing those who have been involved in the vision development process as "vision ambassadors" to the community is another good way to engender support for the school district. The saying "Those who create something will support it" certainly holds. Vision ambassadors who represent the diversity of the community become the "sales staff" for the school district's vision.

Step 5: Sustain the Vision

School districts and the schools within them are very busy places, and although they are often open to new ideas and approaches, following through on change initiatives can be challenging, especially as new, exciting ideas compete with current changes. This is why this final step is important. A sustained focus on a school district's vision is necessary if a district doesn't want to be drawn off course by "flavor of the month" ideas for change. Before anything new is adopted by a school district, one question must be answered: "Does this new idea help the district achieve its vision?" The same question should guide all decisions made during a transformation journey. There must be an ongoing opportunity by district and school-based leaders to reflect upon and analyze the direction of the school district and to make sure that all the changes being made are strategically aligned with the district's vision.

The creation of a collaborative school district–community vision is a powerful element of a district's strategic communication plan. The vision development process opens lines of communication across all ethnic, social, political, and economic barriers. It provides a positive image of the school to all internal and external stakeholders because there is a clear focus on where the school district is going and how it plans to get there. The use of internal and external vision ambassadors assists in institutionalizing the vision into the school district so that all subsequent decisions and programs are evaluated on their ability to achieve the school district's vision. The district's internal stakeholders and key external stakeholders share in the responsibility of ensuring the actualization of the vision. The processes of building, communicating, and sustaining vision are in essence public relations activities that result in a "win-win" situation for all stakeholders. And, of course, ultimately the real winners are the students who benefit from the collaboration of all stakeholders.

CONCLUSION

Vision development as outlined by Chance (1992) is a reflective process. It requires individuals to first engage in intrapersonal reflection and then to converse with one another about their values and beliefs relative to education. Through these conversations, consensus about the future of a school district is built among all stakeholders. Participants in the process reflect personally upon such questions as:

- What are the attributes of the most effective leaders you have known?
- What are the attributes of the least effective leaders you have known?
- How do you evaluate yourself in relationship to the above leaders you have described?
- What are your greatest strengths?
- What are your weaknesses?
- What are three things you value most in your professional life?
- What are the most important things you want to accomplish in your school district?
- What do you want to "prove" as an educator?
- How do you want to be remembered as an educator?

Through the period of consensus building, stakeholders discuss questions such as:

- What are the strengths of your school district?
- What are its weaknesses?
- What are external factors that hinder the proper functioning of your school district?
- What are the interpersonal strengths and weaknesses in your schools?
- How well do various components of the district function together?
- What does your ideal school (and school district) look like?

Stakeholders involved in the process of building a school district–community vision resolve their differences and find common ground, which results in a shared vision for their school district. Stakeholders become partners in the education of their community's children, and this education is the core purpose of all school systems in America.

REFERENCES

Bennis, W., & Nanus, B. (1985). *Leaders: The strategies for taking charge.* New York: Harper & Row.

Carter, G. R. & Cunningham, W. G. (1997). *The American school superintendent: Leading in an age of pressure.* San Francisco: Jossey-Bass.

Chance, E. W. (1992). *Visionary leadership in schools: Successful strategies for developing and implementing an educational vision.* Springfield, IL: Charles C. Thomas.

Duffy, F. M. (2004). *Moving upward together: Creating strategic alignment to sustain systemic school improvement.* No. 1, Leading Systemic School Improvement Series. Lanham, MD: Rowman & Littlefield Education.

Goodlad, J. I., Mantle-Bromley, C., & Goodlad, S. J. (2004). *Education for everyone: Agenda for education in a democracy.* San Francisco: Jossey-Bass.

Hickman, C. P., & Silva, M. (1984). *Creating excellence: Managing corporate culture, strategy and change in a new age.* New York: New American Library.

Manasse, A. L. (1985). Vision and leadership: Paying attention to intention. *Peabody Journal of Education, 63*(1), 150–173.

Reigeluth, C. M. (1995). A conversation on guidelines for the process of facilitating systemic change in education. *Systems Practice, 8*(3), 315–328.

Rutherford, W. L. (1985). School principals as effective leaders. *Phi Delta Kappan, 67*(1), 31–34.

Shieve, L. T., & Shoenheit, M. B. (1987). Vision and the work of educational leaders. In L. T. Shieve and M. B. Shoenheit (Eds.), *Leadership: Examining the elusive* (pp. 93–104). Washington, DC: Association for Supervision and Curriculum Development.

Tyack, D., & Cuban, L. (1995). *Tinkering toward utopia: A century of public school reform.* Cambridge, MA: Harvard University Press.

CHAPTER 8

Changing Minds and Hearts: A Challenge for Strategic Communication

A central leadership challenge for creating and sustaining whole-system change is the daunting task of reducing resistance to change while simultaneously maintaining support for change. Reducing resistance and maintaining support can be facilitated by helping individuals, teams, and systems unlearn old mental models and learn new ones. Unlearning and learning mental models is extraordinarily difficult, yet extraordinarily crucial to the success of any school district improvement effort. The strategic communication messages that are developed in support of whole-district change can be a critical tool for helping internal and external stakeholders change their minds and hearts so that instead of resisting whole-system change they support it. Change leaders, including school PR specialists, must also be willing to examine and unlearn their personal mental models because these models may stand in the way of whole-district improvement. In this chapter, aspects of this challenge are examined and tips for helping individuals, teams, and systems unlearn and learn mental models are provided.

MENTAL MODELS DEFINE REALITY

People construct cognitive representations of what they learn. These representations are commonly called "mental models" (for example, Johnson-Laird, 1983). The important influence of mental models on thinking and behaving is reflected in comments by Bradford (1995–1996) when she said,

> The way we think and receive stimuli are governed by unspoken assumptions and inherent modes of thought. If we can break free of these con-

fines, we can see patterns and combinations that previously were not apparent to us. How we see is important because it so strongly influences our attitudes and behaviors.

There are two kinds of mental models: personal and organizational (Duffy, 2003). Personal mental models are internal paradigms that help professionals know and understand their worlds. An organizational mental model is a collective representation of what an organization stands for and how it accomplishes its goals. An organizational mental model is embodied in its internal social "infrastructure" and in its relationships with the outside world and it is often captured by a district's strategic vision (see chapter 7 for more about vision). Both kinds of mental models are not easily described in words because some of what the mental model represents is at an intuitive level.

An example of a personal mental model for teachers is found in a teacher's response to the statement "Effective classroom teaching is . . ." Every teacher should have a personal mental model that defines effective classroom teaching. Elements of this mental model might include "communication skills," "classroom management," and "learning styles." A teacher's mental model of effective classroom teaching guides his work. When asked to describe his mental model for effective teaching, a teacher might not be able to provide a detailed description of that model and might focus instead on its general features. The more abstract and vague the mental model is, the less likely it is that the teacher's work will be effective.

An example of an organizational mental model for a school district is: "Our school district is a learning community." Elements of this mental model might include "collective decision making" and "teachers as stakeholders." When asked to describe in words their district's mental model, educators might not be able to provide a complete and accurate description of the details of that model and might focus instead on its general features. As with the personal models, the more abstract and vague the mental model is, the less likely it is that the mental model will be effective in guiding thought and action.

HOW MENTAL MODELS AFFECT YOUR CHANGE LEADERSHIP

When attempting to lead whole-system change, you will be faced with a set of intimidating insights to the limitations of your change leadership. Kegan and Lahey (2001), two developmental psychologists from Harvard University, identify these insights as:

- leading inevitably involves trying to effect significant changes;
- it is very hard to bring about significant changes in any human group without changes in individual behavior;
- it is very hard to sustain significant changes in behavior without significant changes in individuals' underlying meanings [their mental models] that may give rise to their behaviors; and,
- it is very hard to lead on behalf of other people's changes in their [mental models] without considering the possibility that [change leaders] must also change [their mental models]. (p. 3)

Most change leaders are not specifically aware of the above insights. Instead, these insights often manifest themselves as one big disappointing experience; that is, despite everything you do to lead change, often very little significant change actually occurs (Kegan & Leahy, 2001, p. 3).

According to Kegan and Leahy, people have a built-in, anti-change "immune system." This immune system is dynamic and provides us with powerful inclinations not to change. If this immune system can be unlocked and modified, people can then release new energy on behalf of new ways of seeing and being. New ways of seeing and being serve as the foundation for unlearning and learning mental models, and, therefore, exist at the critical core of leadership for whole-system change. According to Kegan and Leahy, our internal anti-change immune systems are powered by three significant forces: entropy, negentropy, and dynamic equilibrium. Each of these is highlighted below. Additional insights about these concepts were presented in chapters 2 and 3.

Entropy. Entropy is the process by which dynamic systems (such as people, organizations, mechanical systems, or solar systems) gradually fall apart. Entropy is motion toward increasing disorder, randomness, and dissipation of energy (Kegan & Lahey, 2001, p. 3).

Negentropy. Mechanical and natural systems cannot improve themselves. People and their organizations, however, do have the potential to improve by increasing complexity, becoming more ordered, concentrating and using greater energy, and creating extraordinary solutions to their problems. This increase in energy is the opposite of entropy and physicists call it negative entropy, or more commonly negentropy. Regarding negentropy, Kegan and Leahy (2001) said, "It is a distinguishing and heroic feature of living things that they participate not only in deteriorative processes of declining complexity, order, choice, concentration, and power but also in processes that lead to greater complexity, order, choice, concentration, and power" (pp. 4–5).

Balancing Equilibrium. One of the most powerful forces blocking your district's path toward high performance is balancing equilibrium. Balancing equilibrium is an invisible force that tends to keep things pretty much the way they are. It is more commonly called the *status quo* (e.g., see Kim & Anderson, 1998). The forces of balancing equilibrium play a large role in blocking change in individuals and organizations.

Balancing equilibrium is not about standing in place or lack of motion. Balancing equilibrium is about motion. But it is the motion of positive and negative forces working against each other, balancing each other out, and keeping everything basically locked in place. The consequences of balancing equilibrium are reflected in the French adage, "The more things change, the more they stay the same." As most of us have experienced in our lives, we produce change only to find ourselves reverting back to prechange conditions. We lose 10 pounds, and gain it back. We create a new vision for our school districts, and we march to the tune of the old vision. The competing forces for and against change balance each other out and keep us and our organizations in a relatively stable state of being.

Balancing equilibrium creates something in individuals and their school districts that functions like an immune system in our bodies. Just as bodily immune systems fight off foreign substances, the metaphorical anti-change immune system powered by balancing equilibrium holds people and their organizations in place and blocks change (Kegan & Lahey, 2001, p. 6). This "immune system" is difficult to change because people are captives of their systems; or as Kegan and Lahey said, "We do not have them; they have us" (p. 6).

CHANGING MENTAL MODELS

The performance of school districts is influenced by the forces of entropy and negentropy. Personal and organizational mental models are held in place by anti-change "immune systems" (both personal and systemic) that are powered by the forces of dynamic equilibrium. So, if change leaders want to change personal and organizational mental models; how in the world do they do that? Senge, Kleiner, Roberts, Ross, and Smith (1994) offered advice about how to do this. They said,

> Because mental models are usually tacit, existing below the level of awareness, they are often untested and unexamined. They are generally invisible to us—until we look for them. The core task [for changing them] is bringing mental models to the surface, to explore and talk about them with minimal defensiveness—to help us see the pane of glass, see its impact on our lives, and find ways to re-form the glass by creating new mental models that serve us better in the world. (p. 236)

Before people can learn a new mental model, they have to unlearn what they think they already know. In some way or fashion, they must realize that they can no longer rely on their current knowledge, beliefs, and methods (that is, their current mental models). So, how do people unlearn what they think they know?

What We Know Prevents Us From Seeing What We Don't Know

Unlearning begins when people can no longer rely on their current knowledge, beliefs, and methods. Current knowledge, beliefs, and methods influence perceptions and, as such, they blind people to other ways of interpreting events around them (Starbuck, 1996). People do not and will not cast aside their current mental models as long as these models *seem* to produce reasonable results (Kuhn, 1962). As Petroski (1992) put it, people "tend to hold onto their theories until incontrovertible evidence, usually in the form of failures, convinces them to accept new paradigms" (pp. 180–181). However, people are notorious for sticking with their current beliefs and methods despite very poor and even disastrous results. Even after abject failure, some people will attribute their failures to some external event or person instead of recognizing the inadequacies of their own personal mental models.

Starbuck (1996) observed that professionals are among the most resistant to new ideas and to evidence that contradicts their current mental models. This kind of resistance has several sources. Professionals must specialize, and their specialized niches can lock people in place (Beyer, 1981). Because professionals accrue social status in organizations and, in some cases, earn high incomes, they have much to lose if there are significant changes in their fields of expertise. This state of being "blinds" them from seeing opportunities to create change in their mental models (Armstrong, 1985).

An Organization's Social "Infrastructure" Blocks Unlearning

An organization's internal social "infrastructure" is that collection of policies, procedures, organization culture, organization design, climate, job descriptions, and communication patterns, among other things, that support life in an organization. People in organizations hold certain beliefs and values that are collectively built into that infrastructure. People then create and defend policies, procedures, decisions, and behaviors that support and reinforce their beliefs and values. Further, as people interact, all of these beliefs and values are woven together to create an organizational mental model that reflects what people *think* their organization stands for and how they *think* it should function as an organization. This organization-wide mental model then takes on a degree of rigidity that makes it very difficult for people to think and act in ways that don't fit that model. People, therefore, often find it difficult to accommodate new and innovative ideas and they find it challenging to change (which is one of the key reasons why people resist innovative, "outside-the-box" ideas, where the "box" is their organizational mental model).

Sometimes organizations change in spite of their internal social infrastructure. Tushman, Newman, and Romanelli (1986) commented on this phenomenon by observing that organizations develop over long periods of convergent, incremental change that are interrupted by brief periods of "frame-breaking change." They suggested that frame-breaking change occurs in response to or in anticipation of major changes in an organization's environment. Starbuck (1996), however, believes that frame-breaking change happens differently. He thinks that big changes happen when people and organizations unlearn their old mental models and then undertake breathtaking change to enact their new mental models (that is, change is in response to a dramatic and sudden internal paradigm shift).

Political Pressure Can Stimulate Unlearning

Unlearning by people in organizations is also influenced by political pressure. People and groups with power and political influence affect what people think about and how they act (Hedberg, 1981). The political influence of school administrators, building principals, supervisors, and teacher union leaders is especially potent because these people can either block or support actions proposed by faculty and staff. Having the political support of these people is absolutely crucial for helping teachers and support staff unlearn old and learn new mental models for teaching, learning, and school district improvement.

HELPING PEOPLE UNLEARN

Starbuck (1996) offered advice about helping people unlearn mental models that prevent them from seeing the opportunities before them. Although his insights focused on changing individual mental models, the ideas very easily apply to changing organizational mental models.

Starbuck suggested that the foundation for unlearning mental models is doubt. Any person, event, or information that raises doubt about current beliefs and methods can become a stimulus for unlearning. Starbuck (1996) identified several ways to raise doubt and use it to stimulate unlearning. Each one is summarized below.

It Isn't Good Enough

Dissatisfaction is probably the most common reason for doubting something. Dissatisfaction, however, takes a long time to work. Often, when someone fails or something doesn't work right, people come up with all kinds of reasons to explain their failures, but none of the reasons focus on a person's mental models. Their mental models are quite resistant to change and it takes a lot of painful failures to become dissatisfied with them.

It's Only an Experiment

If people believe a new method they are trying or a new idea they are considering is only an "experiment," they are more likely to allow themselves to act outside-the-box of their existing mental model. When they step outside their box, they find opportunities to be surprised. Because these new ways of acting and thinking are just "experiments," the risks associated with failure are substantially reduced. Because attendant risks are reduced, people become more willing and able to consider feedback with an open mind and they are more likely to evaluate results more objectively. Experimentation allows them to modify their mental models to allow new ways of seeing, understanding, and doing.

Surprises Should Be Question Marks

Unexpected events or results, both positive and negative, can stimulate unlearning. If people are in an experimental mode, the results of their experiments can be surprising. Faced with a surprise result or outcome, people can then question what happened and why it happened. Answers to these questions can help people unlearn their old mental models as their answers point to new ways of thinking and doing.

All Dissents and Warnings Have Some Validity

When bad news is announced or when warnings about impending failure are given, you have to take this information seriously. Of course not every person who disagrees with a course of action or a decision should be taken seriously. But, as Starbuck suggested, there are many sensible, well-intentioned people who see things going wrong and they will try to alert you about that. Therefore, it is usually a mistake to hastily reject bad news or innovative ideas that seem to oppose your current personal and organizational mental models.

An organization's internal social infrastructure can block dissenting messages and warnings. Porter and Roberts (1976) analyzed why people in hierarchies talk upward and listen upward. Their analysis indicated that people send more messages up the hierarchy than down, while paying more attention to information that comes down to them from their supervisors than from their subordinates or peers. They also try harder to establish positive working relationships with their supervisors rather than with their subordinates. The messages that do get passed-up to superiors tend to play up good news and minimize or hide bad news (Janis, 1972; Nystrom & Starbuck, 1984). This censoring is particularly problematic for superintendents and other senior administrators who receive "filtered" information that may or may not be valid. This filtering or censoring of information is a serious problem because bad news is much more likely to motivate people to change than good news (Hedberg, 1981), and when there is filtering going on, change leaders don't get the bad news they need to hear.

Collaborators Who Disagree Are Both Right

If you have qualified people working together who have different beliefs about the same issue, each set of beliefs is nearly always based in some degree of truth. The challenge in situations like this is not to prove one set of beliefs wrong, but to try to reconcile the differences to show that there are commonalities and complementarity. These efforts to illustrate common and complementary features can help people unlearn their mental models as they see that their current mental model can expand to accommodate different ways of thinking and doing.

What Does the "Outsider" Think Strange?

Many people cannot and do not accept the views of outsiders. It is so much easier to listen to and respect the views of people who work in the trenches with them; after all, they are familiar with the work that is done in the trenches. Because outsiders supposedly do not know the "trench-dwellers" or do not understand their "situation," their observations and suggestions may appear naive, foolish, impractical, or impossible (as in "Your idea will never work in this district. You are a professor. You don't understand what it's like to be a practitioner"). Yet outsiders often see things without the bias of insiders. Although an outsider may be less experienced in the reality of the battle-scarred insiders, they are also free of the biases and the dominant organizational mental models that shape behavior in organizations. Thus, the outsider may see opportunities and possibilities that insiders cannot see and, therefore, they may be able to offer breakthrough ideas or methodologies.

All Problems Have Multidirectional Causes and Effects

A structured way to analyze the causes and effects of problems is to use a systems dynamics model that illustrates multidirectional cause-and-effect relationships. This kind of analysis can help people challenge their tacit mental models as they begin to see multiple causes of the problems they are experiencing and the multiple effects of those problems. Identifying and then examining these multidirectional relationships can lead to some breakthrough thinking about how to change personal and organizational mental models as people see the multiple cause-and-effect relationships.

What You Know Is Not Optimal

Starbuck (1996) asserted that no one should be confident that his or her current mental models are uniquely optimal. One can count on the fact that if one's beliefs about a particular person, method, or event seem valid, there are other equally valid, but different, perceptions about that same person, method, or event. For example, if a person has a preferred method for school district improvement that is viewed as effective, others will have an equally excellent, but different, method. This can be counted on. The problem is that once an individual has a well-formed mental model about what works, she doesn't want to abandon it. She shuts herself off from outside-the-box (the box is a person's or district's mental model) thinking and doing. Thus, to break free of the constraints of current mental models, it is helpful to become skeptical about the effectiveness of one's personal and organizational mental models.

The above tips proposed by Starbuck are useful for helping people become skeptical about their personal and organizational mental models. "It isn't good enough" and "It's only an experiment" are mental tools change leaders can use to help themselves and their faculty and staff stay alert for opportunities to improve. Change leaders need to be open to new ways of thinking about and practicing school district improvement.

Personal and organizational mental models will always influence how educators think and feel about district, cluster, school, team, and individual performance. This means that, knowingly or unknowingly, their existing mental models will filter information they receive about that performance and the filtering will tend to select information supporting their existing personal and organizational mental models and reject data and information that contradict them. However, it is the contradictory data, the critic's voice, the warnings from afar, and the "outsider's" views that may offer astounding ways to improve the performance of a school district. Thus, when change leaders are surprised by what they see or hear about their district's performance, they should turn the surprises into question marks, respond to disagreements and warnings as if they have some validity, and act as if outsiders' ideas are as valid as their own.

LEARNING NEW MENTAL MODELS THROUGH KNOWLEDGE CREATION

Learning new mental models is greatly facilitated by using a knowledge-creation process that surfaces personal knowledge and mental models, makes that knowledge and those models explicit, and then converts the best of those into organization-wide knowledge and mental models (Nonaka & Takeuchi, 1995). Let's explore this idea a bit further.

Theories of knowledge creation, which are generally classified as "constructivist" theories, describe the psychological processes people use to build their own understanding of information. People begin to understand information as they reconcile what they already know and what they already believe with new information or with old information that is being reconsidered from a different perspective. Each person brings to her personal learning a unique combination of prior experiences and understanding, as well as a set of learning aptitudes and beliefs about learning. Thus, knowledge creation, to a large degree, is idiosyncratic. To what degree does the idiosyncratic nature of knowledge matter when it comes to developing professional knowledge and mental models in school systems?

All educators have a different understanding of the world around them. Thus, it can be argued that their knowledge of the world around them is subjective to some degree (for example, Bednar, 1995). The individual subjectivity of knowledge suggests, therefore, that educators have a wide range of idiosyncratic mental models that guide their work. If educators' personal mental models are at odds with how their school district wants to improve, it can be predicted that those educators will resist their district's transformation journey because their personal mental models are powerful and difficult to change (as in "I don't care what the district wants to do. I know I'm right and I'm not going to change").

The subjectivity of knowledge and educators' resistance to other mental models may not matter in some cases. In situations where there are no "right answers," it doesn't make much difference if people have different views, perspectives, or opinions. In fact, in these situations educators should be encouraged to develop unique ideas about what's right or what's effective; for example, some believe there is no one "right" way to teach effectively. These people believe teachers should develop their own personal understanding of effective teaching and then use that knowledge to teach what their district expects (however, many of these same people do not believe that teachers should have the same degree of autonomy in deciding *what* to teach).

There are situations, however, where it *is* important for everyone to be working from the same mental model; for example, many times there are right answers and correct procedures that teachers must teach. It is doubtful that parents would want their children learning geometry from a teacher who constructed his or her idiosyncratic theorems. In situations requiring right answers and correct procedures, a school district's goal must be to develop a certain degree of uniformity among teachers' mental models.

Situated Cognition and Learning

Professional knowledge and mental models must be developed within a meaningful context. When educators work with information that is devoid of context, what they try to learn can appear meaningless and may be difficult to learn. For example, imagine that a social studies teacher needs to become certified to teach mathematics. She knows nothing about the world of mathematics and as she studies the texts she can't make sense of what she is reading because she has no context to help her understand those new and strange mathematical concepts, principles, and formulae. Without the context, all that information is meaningless to her and she struggles to learn it. But, once she starts teaching mathematics, a context is created within which all those strange ideas start to make sense; that is, all of the mathematical concepts, principles, and formulae become "situated" and therefore meaningful and understandable. Context is powerful.

Theories of situated cognition (for example, Lave, 1988; Suchman, 1987) focus on the context within which particular knowledge is required. The theories also influence how that knowledge is used. Theories of situated learning (for example, Brown, Collins, & Duguid, 1989) suggest that people develop knowledge by connecting new information to what they already know, and they do this in ways that make the learning meaningful.

The Social Dimension of Learning

There are three factors comprising the social dimension of learning. The first factor is the social construction of knowledge itself. The second factor is the social nature of situated learning. And the third factor is composed of educators' beliefs about other educators and about themselves, and the reasons they use to explain their own and others' behavior. Each of these dimensions is discussed briefly below.

Organization-wide professional knowledge and mental models are constructed socially. Although educators construct personal and idiosyncratic knowledge and mental models, there has to be a shared or common understanding among educators so they can communicate with each other about what they know and what they are doing. In other words, there has to be systemwide learning (also known as organizational learning).

Meaning is shared and negotiated when people have common knowledge (Vygotsky, 1978). Within a school system, this common understanding can be developed through organized, districtwide conversations about what people know and what they can do so that insights and perspectives can be shared among all educators participating in those conversations. Reaching consensus about the meaning and value of new knowledge and mental models has the advantage of requiring educators to at least consider others' perspectives even if they disagree with them. Important side effects of these conversations are the ability to communicate with others about new knowledge and mental models, to cooperatively create a context for new knowledge (that is, to situate it), and to apply that knowledge for the benefit of a school district. Methods for developing this kind of districtwide professional knowledge and mental models include seminars, formal discussions, and informal interactions among teachers and others. Pava (1983) calls all these different kinds of learning places "forums."

Consistent with constructivist theory, educators construct meaning from information based on what they *think* the information means. Educators' professional knowledge and mental models, therefore, are influenced by their beliefs about the information they receive, about the people who provide that information, and about their own ability to deal with the information (Bandura, 1977, 1978; Salomon, 1982). In almost all cases, an educator's professional knowledge and mental models are influenced by his or her perceptions of the source of that information (for example, "I like this speaker. I think I'll use those ideas"), and perceptions of the medium used to deliver it (for example, "I really like role-playing. It helps me learn"). When information is perceived negatively, people can also construct meaning that is in total opposition to the presented information (for example, "I think that gal is wacko. I am going to do just the opposite of what she is advising us to do").

Educators not only make attributions about the value and completeness of information they receive, but they also make attributions about their own abilities to use that information. These kinds of attributions are collectively called "self-efficacy." Self-efficacy is a powerful determinant of how well educators learn new knowledge and whether they enjoy doing so. Low self-efficacy becomes a self-fulfilling prophecy (for example, the thought, "I'm not good at dealing with disruptive students" leads to poor performance in dealing with disruptive stu-

·dents); whereas unusually high self-efficacy results in reduced effort to succeed; for example, the thought, "I already know this stuff inside and out. They can't teach me anything I don't already know" leads to reduced effort to study and learn which leads to low performance in a training situation.

CONCLUSION

Mental models are powerful because they frame the way people perceive, understand, interpret, and act upon their world. However, mental models are frequently inaccurate and incomplete and, therefore, often ineffective. An additional problem for school districts is that sometimes personal mental models do not complement, or may even conflict with, a district's desired organizational mental model as represented in its vision and strategic direction.

Mental models can stand as serious roadblocks to whole-system change in school districts. Helping educators in your school system surface, examine, evaluate, and change their personal and your district's organizational mental models, therefore, is one of the key steps toward effective whole-system improvement. The best time to begin unlearning and learning mental models is *before* you launch a whole-district improvement effort (that is, during the Pre-Launch Preparation phase in the change navigation protocol described in chapter 4). Efforts to move a district toward higher levels of performance will most certainly fail if change leaders do not engage themselves, their faculty, and their staff in the process of unlearning and learning mental models before they launch a transformation journey for their school system.

REFERENCES

Armstrong, J. S. (1985). *Long-range forecasting: From crystal ball to computer* (2nd ed.). New York: Wiley-Interscience.
Bandura, A. (1977, March). Self-efficacy: Toward a unifying theory of behavioral change. *Psychological Review, 84*(2), 191–215. (ERIC Document Reproduction Service No. EJ161 632)
Bandura, A. (1978, summer). Social learning theory of aggression. *Journal of*

Communication, 28(3), 12–29. (ERIC Document Reproduction Service No. EJ195900)

Bednar, M. R (1995). Teachers' beliefs and practices: Dissonance or contextual reality? (ERIC Document Reproduction Service No. ED374397)

Beyer, J. M. (1981). Ideologies, values, and decision making in organizations. In P. C. Nystrom & W. H. Starbuck (Eds.), *Handbook of organizational design*, Vol. 2 (pp. 166–202). New York: Oxford University Press.

Bradford, A. (1995–1996, December/January). It's all in your frame of mind—Changing mental models. *Marketer*. Retrieved on September 11, 2005, from http://www.smps.org/mrc/chapters-html/frameofmind.htm

Brown, J. S., Collins, A., & Duguid, P. (1989). Situated cognition and the culture of learning. *Education Researcher, 18*(1), 32–42.

Duffy, F. M. (2003). I think, therefore I am resistant to change. *Journal of Staff Development, 24*(1), 30–36.

Hedberg, B. (1981). How organizations learn and unlearn. In P. C. Nystrom & W. H. Starbuck (Eds.), *Handbook of organizational design*, Vol. 1: *Adapting organizations to their environments* (pp. 3–27). New York: Oxford University Press.

Janis, I. L. (1972). *Victims of group-think*. Boston: Houghton-Mifflin.

Johnson-Laird, P. N. (1983). *Mental models: Towards a cognitive science of language, inference and consciousness*. Cambridge: Cambridge University Press.

Kegan, R., & Lahey, L. L. (2001). *How the way we talk can change the way we work*. San Francisco: Jossey-Bass.

Kim, D. H. & Anderson, V. (1998). *Systems archetype basics: From story to structure*. Waltham, MA: Pegasus Communications.

Kuhn, T. S. (1962). *The structure of scientific revolutions*. Chicago: University of Chicago Press.

Lave, J. (1988). *Cognition in practice: Mind, mathematics, and culture in everyday life*. New York: Cambridge University Press.

Nonaka, I., & Takeuchi, H. (1995). *The knowledge-creating company: How Japanese companies create the dynamics of innovation*. New York: Oxford University Press.

Nystrom, P. C., & Starbuck, W. H. (1984). To avoid organizational crises, unlearn. *Organizational Dynamics, 12*(4), 53–65.

Pava, C. H. P. (1983). *Managing new office technology: An organizational strategy*. New York: New Press.

Petroski, H. (1992). *To engineer is human*. New York: Vintage.

Porter, L. W., & Roberts, K. H. (1976). Communication in organizations. In

M. D. Dunnette (Ed.), *Handbook of industrial and organizational psychology* (pp. 1553–1589). Chicago: Rand McNally.

Senge, P. M., Kleiner, A., Roberts, C., Ross, R. B., & Smith, B. J. (1994). *The fifth discipline fieldbook: Strategies and tools for building a learning organization.* New York: Doubleday.

Salomon, G. (1982). *Communication and education: Social and psychological interactions.* Beverly Hills, CA: Sage.

Starbuck, W. H. (1996). Unlearning ineffective or obsolete technologies. *International Journal of Technology Management, 11,* 725–737.

Suchman, L. (1987). Common sense in interface design. *Techné, 1*(1), 38–40.

Tushman, M. L., Newman, W. H., & Romanelli, E. (1986). Convergence and upheaval: Managing the unsteady pace of organizational evolution. *California Management Review, 29*(1), 29–44.

Vygotsky, L. S. (1978). *Mind in society: The development of higher psychological processes.* Cambridge, MA: Harvard University Press.

CHAPTER 9

Power, Politics, and Ethics: Dynamic Leadership for Systemic Change in School Districts

The challenges, paradoxes, problems, and predicaments that change leaders face while planning and implementing strategic communication to support complex, systemwide change in school districts require them to possess the will and capacity to use power and political behavior in ethical and skillful ways. The skillful use of power and political behavior is the driving force behind effective strategic communication. Without political awareness and skill, change leaders and PR specialists will predictably become caught up in bureaucratic infighting, selfish politics, and destructive power struggles, which will significantly impede their district's transformation journey because they will be greatly constrained in their ability to build internal and external political support for that journey. And, if they use power and political skills in unethical ways, they will almost certainly damage their reputation and injure their school systems. This chapter offers some insights to how power, politics, and ethics can influence strategic communication.

THE CONTEXT FOR THE ETHICAL USE OF POWER AND POLITICAL SKILLS

The term *systemic change* has many definitions. Squire and Reigeluth (2000) identify four distinct meanings of the term:

Statewide policy systemic change. This meaning focuses on statewide changes in tests, curricular guidelines, teacher-certification requirements, textbook adoptions, funding policies, and so forth. These changes are supposed to be coordinated to support one another

(Smith & O'Day, 1990). This meaning is frequently used by policymakers when they talk about systemic change.

Districtwide systemic change. Educators subscribing to this meaning see systemic change as any change, including new programs, intended to spread across an entire school district. This is the meaning often held by preK–12th grade educators.

Schoolwide systemic change. Using this meaning, educators see systemic change happening inside single school buildings and it typically involves "a deeper (re)thinking of the purposes of schooling and the goals of education" (Squire & Reigeluth, 2000, p. 144). This is the meaning that seemed to inform the work of groups such as the New American Schools, Inc. and the Coalition of Essential Schools.

Ecological systemic change. This meaning sees systems as rich networks of interrelationships and interdependencies within a system and between a system and its "external environment" (the larger system of which it is a part). This perspective recognizes that a significant change in one part of a system requires changes in other parts of the system. It also recognizes the need for changes in three interconnected aspects of a system: its relationships with its environment, its core and supporting work processes, and its internal social infrastructure (Duffy, Rogerson, & Blick, 2000). This view of systemic change subsumes the other three meanings, and it is how "systems thinkers" view systemic change (for example, Ackoff, 1981; Banathy, 1996; Checkland, 1984; Emery & Purser, 1996; Senge, 1990).

So it is important to know right at the start that in this chapter, and throughout this book, the term *whole-system improvement* refers specifically to ecological systemic change—that is, transforming an entire school district and its relationship with its external environment. This kind of transformation requires effective strategic communication colored brightly by the ethical use of power and political skills.

DYNAMIC CHANGE LEADERSHIP

It is also important to define the term *dynamic leadership.* Dynamic leadership means leading with courage, passion, and vision. Dynamic leadership means doing the "right thing" even when the right thing is politically incorrect or unpopular. Dynamic leadership requires a change leader to step out in front of her colleagues and lead. Dynamic leadership is about influencing relationships between and among individuals, teams, schools, and clusters of schools within a school district. Dynamic leadership is partially a function of a change leader's ability to earn and maintain the trust and respect of his colleagues. Dynamic leadership is enacted with technical knowledge and skills for leading change and turbocharged by using power and political skills in ethical ways. Dynamic leadership means orchestrating change much like a conductor arranges and manages a symphony orchestra.

Yet, despite the significant need for dynamic leadership for systemic change in school districts and despite what we know is needed to provide dynamic leadership for that kind of change, there remains a leadership conundrum that blocks the emergence of effective dynamic change leadership. This conundrum can best be characterized as a failure of change leadership.

THE LEADERSHIP CONUNDRUM

We all know them. They are our colleagues who move into leadership positions and then become intoxicated with their new authority and power. What is it about a leadership position that inebriates practitioners with their newfound power? What is it about leaders drunken with their power that brings them to use negative political acts to hurt others and ultimately hurt their school systems? Where and when in their careers do some education leaders lose their moral compass—their personal code of ethics? Or, worse yet, did they ever have one? And what is it about leadership for change that magnifies these negative leadership dynamics? These questions, and others like them, present a leadership conundrum—a failure of change leadership. Let's see if we can unravel this mystery to understand why it exists.

One of the answers to the above questions lies in preparation programs for education leaders. Consider what Vander Ark (2002) said regarding the lack of appropriate change leadership preparation: "Changing the basic organizational strategy of an American urban school district may be the toughest assignment on Earth. Superintendents must be politically savvy, possess sophisticated consulting skills, and be adept managers of change. Most preparation programs are lacking in all three areas" (p. 6).

Further, the premise for the existence of these programs is that leadership can be taught. Cook (2000), Block (2003), Farson (1996), and others believe leadership *cannot* be taught. Leadership, they believe, is a matter of who a man or woman is as a person. Therefore, how a person behaves in a leadership role is more a function of *who she is* rather than a function of *what she knows.*

The "who, not what" conceptualization of leadership suggests that there is a set of qualities that is somewhat analogous to human personality. People are born with their core personalities in place. Over time, personality qualities are refined until the personality is relatively unchangeable. These personality qualities cannot be taught or trained, but they can be enhanced. Leadership qualities, like personality qualities, may not be trainable, but they can be enhanced. Therefore, leadership behavior emerges as leaders act in ways that are congruent with their core values and beliefs. They behave this way almost unconsciously. Therefore, the content and orientation of their core values and beliefs will define how they lead.

The answers to the above questions about the failure of change leadership must also include a variation of the adage, "Teachers teach the way they were taught." Education leaders probably lead the way they were led. Thus, another way to understand the leadership conundrum is to suggest that some education leaders were probably significantly influenced by negative role models for leadership in school districts.

A more cynical explanation of why an education leader might use power and political acts in negative ways is that this behavior works. It produces results. Ethical behavior, however, never gets applause because it's tacitly expected. Even though ethical behavior can positively affect one's reputation over the long run, short-term praise and rewards for being ethical are not forthcoming.

Since unethical behavior creates results, it is sometimes tolerated. It is only punished when it is unashamedly and unskillfully used. And, when tolerated unethical behavior produces valued results, it is rewarded with extended contracts, merit pay increases, and promotions. Experience shows, however, that unethical behavior only works for the short run. In the long run, there are negative consequences such as the destruction of trust, the decline of morale, and the withdrawal of commitment. A more personal side effect of the unethical use of power and political behavior is that the reputation of the unethical leader can be permanently damaged for the remainder of his career within a school district. When this happens, a "damaged" leader may quit or be fired, but then, quite disturbingly, he gets hired by another school district where he repeats his patterned unethical leadership behavior. (Do you ever wonder about how and why this happens?)

The organization design of school systems also contributes to the unethical use of power and political acts. The dominant organization design in school districts is a mechanistic hierarchy organized as a bureaucracy. Leadership in bureaucratic hierarchies aims to enforce rigid chains of command, to control resources tightly, and to exercise strict command and control. This kind of control is not necessarily a bad thing, but it can be if people in the power positions fall victim to its temptations—the temptations associated with power and ego gratification.

While rigid chains of command worked well in the past when organizations like school systems required stability and little change, this design seems not to work in organizations within complex, rapidly changing environments and staffed with highly educated, semi-autonomous workers. These kinds of organizations are called knowledge organizations (Duffy, 2003). In knowledge organizations, leaders need commitment from followers, not compliance.

Negative leadership dynamics are also magnified during times of great change. This may happen because education leaders sometimes do not know how to lead large-scale change. They learned old-fashioned, outdated change theories that no longer work. In fact, these old theories probably never worked consistently to produce desired outcomes. Then, as they are repeatedly frustrated in their efforts to lead change with nonexistent or outdated change leadership skills, they resort to the negative use of power and political acts to force change—which, of course, fails more often than not.

TRANSFORMING LEADER AND FOLLOWER ROLES

We are not suggesting that education leaders should avoid using power and political behavior. They should and they must. What we are suggesting is that power and political behavior must be used in ethical ways to create good outcomes for entire school systems.

Furthermore, we are not suggesting that leadership positions should be abolished and transformational change turned over to a leaderless "mob." The voice of leadership is needed and will continue to be needed to guide whole-school systems along three winding change-paths toward desirable new futures (refer to chapters 2 and 3 for more information about these change-paths). Instead, the roles of leaders and followers must also be transformed. This transformation will redefine leader and follower roles in ways that allow each to act differently toward the other as they collaborate to improve student, faculty and staff, and whole-system learning in their school districts.

The transformation of leader and follower roles will not automatically create desirable and effective behavior. A school system's reward system will also need to be retooled to reinforce desirable behavior. Thorndike (1966) taught us that behavior that is rewarded is repeated and behavior that is repeated is learned. This principle is reinforced by Farson (1996) who suggested that people do not learn from their failures—they learn from their successes (success is rewarded and therefore the behaviors that created success are repeated and learned). Unfortunately, this principle applies to bad behavior as well as good—so it is important to reinforce the right behaviors. The right behaviors will be those that support a district's code of ethics, its grand vision, and its strategic direction.

The reshaping of leader and follower roles must begin at the level of a school district's school board. Superintendents won't change their leadership behaviors unless their school boards change how superintendents are evaluated and rewarded. Central office staff won't change their follower behaviors unless their superintendents change how they evaluate and reward their staff. Principals won't change their leadership behaviors until their superiors change how they evaluate and reward the principals. Teachers won't change their follower behaviors until building principals change the way they evaluate and reward teachers.

Unlearning dysfunctional and ineffective leader and follower mental models must start at the top of a school system.

Changing school board members' behavior is difficult. Often, people in these positions have political aspirations beyond the school board meeting room. These aspiring politicians have goals that create short-term wins for them, sometimes at the expense of their school systems. In creating their short-term political wins, school board members of this class sometimes use their school districts and its leaders as scapegoats. In responding to or anticipating scapegoating, district leaders can fall into one of two response modes: they either become defensive or they take aggressive preemptive actions. In either mode, district leaders can easily find themselves using power and political skills in unethical ways—for example, using their language skills to spin mendacious webs to destroy or sully someone's reputation.

Another reason why changing school board behavior is difficult is finding a lever to motivate them to change. This lever is not easy to find. Who evaluates school board members? To whom are school board members accountable? For elected school boards, some would argue that voters hold them accountable by periodically going to polling booths. Despite the prospects of being voted out of office, experience shows that some school board members thumb their collective noses at the voters and their communities. They, too, are drunk with their power. We see this behavior in how they treat people who show up at public meetings. We see it in their arrogance and condescension. We see it in the controversial decisions they make in closed executive sessions. And then they are reelected—more often as the result of their election campaign rhetoric than of the outcomes of their work. Fortunately, this is not true for all school boards.

What about appointed school boards? Who holds them accountable? The person who appoints them? Political appointees hold their positions because they kowtow to their benefactors' political agenda. As long as appointed school board members are in good favor with their benefactors, they stay on the board regardless of the kind of leadership they provide.

Teacher unions are another reason why education leaders sometimes fall into using power and political acts in unethical ways. Good and decent leaders descend into frustration and desperation in the face of their failed attempts to convince teacher union leaders to collaborate for change. Out of frustration and desperation, education leaders can resort to using power and political acts in unethical ways. Some local chapters of the two teacher unions in the United States are infamous for their recalcitrance and negative political behavior (e.g., see Gil in Duffy, 2005). Instead of acting as partners for change, local teacher union leaders occasionally act as combative adversaries who put the union's interests above those of children and their school districts.

EVERY LEADERSHIP ACT IS A POLITICAL ACT

In the world of change leadership, every act is a political act. A political act is one that uses power to achieve some aim—either personal or for the benefit of an entire school system. Sometimes these political acts are ethical and sometimes they are not. To act in a political way that is also ethical means that change leaders strive to make sure people fit appropriately into the power structure of their school systems. Fitting people appropriately into the power structure means making sure that the right people are in the right positions, have the right amount of power to do their jobs well, and have the capacity to use their power effectively.

Speaking of capacity to use power effectively, the concept of empowerment is insufficient. It is not enough to empower people. People need to have the *opportunity* to use their newly bestowed power, the *capacity* (that is, they need the knowledge and skills) to use that power, and the *willingness* to use it. Therefore, people need to be enabled to use power, not just empowered.

Some leaders are reluctant to share their power because of the mental model in their heads about the nature of power. They think their power is like the money in their wallet. If they share some of that money with others, they have less money and the others have more—a win/lose relationship.

Power is more like the knowledge we have in our heads. When we share our knowledge with someone, that knowledge interacts with the other person's knowledge and the potential to improve both the quantity and quality of the shared knowledge increases. Power sharing works the same way as knowledge sharing. But this is a hard sell to some folks in managerial and leadership positions who hang on to the win/lose mental model as if it was their dying breath.

Although we all are familiar with power abusers who use their political skills negatively, the more pernicious power players are those warm-hearted, touchy-feely, fuzzy-wuzzy huggy bears and the "father knows best" types who are absolutely convinced that we do not know what's good for us, *but they do!* And, by God, they are going to lead you to their worldview with their warm smiles, their gentle hugs, and their granite-hard dogmatism. We also need protection from those good people who think they know what's good for us. As Paterson (1993) observed, "Most of the harm in the world is done by good people, and not by accident, lapse or omission." The quote is a searing indictment of those with a deep-seated Maslovian need to act "in the best interests" of others.

POWER AND POLITICAL BEHAVIORS ARE NEEDED TO REINFORCE DISEQUILIBRIUM

Discontent with one's current situation does not by itself stir a desire for change. In the language of systems theory, discontent creates disequilibrium. Disequilibrium is a necessary antecedent of change. Kurt Lewin (1951) referred to the creation of disequilibrium as "unfreezing." However, if disequilibrium caused by discontent were the only ingredient to motivate educators in school districts to change, there would be a lot more change. The disequilibrium must be increased to the point of chaos[1] by change leaders who are willing and able to use power and political behavior in ethical ways.

Change leaders who feel powerless and in a state of stupefaction about their situations cannot lead change, no matter how unhappy their colleagues are with the current state of their school systems. When change leaders feel powerless, when they feel as if they have no influence, they predictably persist with what they know. They establish routines and habits of the mind that wrap them in the comforting delusion of being in control of their situations and this perception of being in control is fed by their nearly obsessive need to manage the minor details of other people's work.

To create and sustain whole-system change, change leaders must believe as a matter of deep faith that they have the power to lead their school districts' transformation journeys. Then, they must use their power because power held unused is remarkably useless. Furthermore, the use of power necessitates political behavior. Political behavior can be negative and destructive or it can be positive and constructive. Thus, the intent of political behavior depends on the ethics of the power user. This dependency is analogous to a double-edge sword lying on a table. The sword is neutral—it is neither good nor bad. It is the ethics of the swordsman that will make the sword an instrument for good or one for evil. It is the ethics of the power user that will make her political behavior an instrument for good or one for evil.

Positive political behavior benefits individuals, groups, and whole-school systems. Destructive political behavior injures people, groups, and school systems and is intended to benefit the self-serving needs of the power users. Although destructive political behavior benefits the power user in the short term, in the long term he will suffer from the consequences of that famous circular Karmic dynamic that is so familiar to many of us: "What goes around, comes around."

CONCLUSION

Creating effective strategic communication to support whole-system transformation that improves student, faculty and staff, and whole-system learning requires focusing on a number of issues emerging from the interplay of power and politics. The way change leaders respond to these issues should be based on their personal and systemwide codes of ethics. The issues will have a direct and powerful influence on their efforts to create requisite changes in three key areas: their district's relationships with its external environment, its core and supporting work processes, and its internal social infrastructure. The way in which they resolve these issues will affect their system's overall performance in the three areas just listed. Examples of these issues include:

- Implementing transformational change when people want the system to maintain its status quo;

- Fostering innovative thinking and puzzle solving despite resistance to new ideas;
- Acquiring resources and political support from individuals and groups who may have a political agenda that opposes the district's transformation goals;
- Managing conflict with others whose help and cooperation are needed; and,
- Diagnosing power relationships to anticipate and countervail negative politics by others.

The key to successfully implementing transformational change in a school district and improving the long-term performance of that district undoubtedly rests upon dynamic leadership for whole-system change. This kind of change leadership requires the use of strategic communication that is framed using power and political behavior in ethical ways.

REFERENCES

Ackoff, R. L. (1981). *Creating the corporate future.* New York: John Wiley & Sons.

Banathy, B. H. (1996). *Designing social systems in a changing world.* New York: Plenum Press.

Block, P. (2003). *The answer to how is yes: Acting on what matters.* San Francisco: Berrett-Koehler.

Checkland, P. (1984). *Systems thinking, systems practice* (Reprinted with corrections February, 1984 ed.). New York: Wiley & Sons.

Cook, W. J., Jr. (2000). *Strategics: The art and science of holistic strategy.* Westport, CT: Quorum Books.

Duffy, F. M. (2003). *Step-Up-To-Excellence: An innovative approach to managing and rewarding performance in school systems.* Lanham, MD: ScarecrowEducation.

Duffy, F. M. (2004). *Courage, passion and vision: A guide to leading systemic school improvement.* Lanham, MD: ScarecrowEducation/American Association for School Administrators.

Duffy, F. M. (2005). Power, politics and ethics in school districts: Dynamic leadership for systemic change. Leading Systemic School Improvement #6. Lanham, MD: Rowman & Littlefield Education.

Duffy, F. M., Rogerson, L. G., & Blick, C. (2000). *Redesigning America's schools: A systems approach to improvement.* Norwood, MA: Christopher-Gordon.

Emery, M., & Purser, R. E. (1996). *The Search Conference: A powerful method for planning organizational change and community action.* San Francisco: Jossey-Bass.

Farson, R. (1996). *Management of the absurd.* New York: Simon & Schuster.

Lewin, K. (1951). *Field theory in social science.* New York: Harper & Row.

Paterson, I. (1993). *The god of the machine.* New Brunswick, NJ: Transaction. (Original work published in 1943)

Reigeluth, C. M. (2004). Chaos theory and the sciences of complexity: Foundations for transforming education. Retrieved on April 24, 2006, from http://www.indiana.edu~syschang/decatur/documents/chaos_reigeluth_s2004.pdf

Senge, P. M. (1990). *The fifth discipline: The art and practice of the learning organization.* New York: Doubleday.

Smith, M. S., & O'Day, J. (1990). Systemic school reform. In S. Fuhrman & B. Malen (Eds.), *The politics of curriculum and testing* (pp. 233–267). Philadelphia: Falmer Press.

Squire, K. D., & Reigeluth, C. M. (2000). The many faces of systemic change. *Educational Horizons, 78*(3), 143–152.

Thorndike, E. H. (1966). *Human learning.* Cambridge, MA: Massachusetts Institute of Technology Press.

Vander Ark, T. (2002, December). Toward success at scale. *Phi Delta Kappan, 84*(4). Retrieved on February 18, 2005, from http://www.pdkintl.org/kappan/k0212val.htm

ENDNOTES

1. In the field of change theory, chaos is necessary to create transformational change. Chaos in this context, however, has a special meaning. It means that recognizable patterns of organizational life are removed through purposeful change leadership. When recognizable patterns are removed, this creates a chaotic situation for people. The removal of these patterns then creates space for new patterns to emerge and take root, where the new patterns are the ideas for change that are being created through a change navigation process like the one described in chapter 4. Reigeluth (2004) offers excellent insights to the nature of chaos and systemic change.

SECTION 3

Voices from the Field

This section is a collection of five essays using strategic communication during times of great change. Each essay represents voices from the field of education in general and school public relations in particular.

Marilyn Saltzman's essay focuses on communicating with key stakeholders to enable strategic change. Ms. Saltzman is the retired manager of Communications Services for the Jefferson County Public Schools in Colorado.

Barbara Hunter's essay explores the characteristics of a special external stakeholders—the Influentials. She discusses the importance of identifying these people and offers some ideas about how to do that. Ms. Hunter is the Director of Communications for the National School Boards Association.

Anne Bryant's essay is about the role of a school board in communicating change. Dr. Bryant is the executive director of the National School Boards Association.

Sylvia Soholt's essay describes her views about bringing order out of chaos by using school public relations processes and tools. Ms. Soholt is a school public relations consultant in the state of Washington.

Ms. Sunni Lee and Dr. Charles Reigeluth write about how change leaders in the Metropolitan School District of Decatur Township, Indiana, are engaging community members in their district's current transformation journey. Dr. Reigeluth is facilitating that district's transformation in collaboration with several of his doctoral students, including Ms. Lee. Dr. Reigeluth is a professor in the Instructional Systems Technology Department at Indiana University, Bloomington. Ms. Lee is a doctoral student in the Instructional Systems Technology Department.

ESSAY 1

Communicating with Key Stakeholders to Enable Strategic Change

Marilyn Saltzman

This essay focuses on the communications processes that led to staff and community buy-in and ongoing commitment to the change process and strategic planning efforts that created a more focused and successful school district—the Jefferson County (Jeffco) Public Schools in Colorado.

THE NEED FOR WHOLE-SYSTEM CHANGE

With rising local, state, and federal pressure to increase student achievement and a lack of clear focus and resources to meet these demands, Jefferson County Public Schools was faced with both a challenge and an opportunity when the superintendent retired in 1997. The district—the largest in Colorado—was suffering from a lack of direction and insufficient resources. At the time, there was a divided school board, a string of failed operating fund elections, and changes in superintendents. Now was the time for systematic, whole-system change.

In April 1997, the district hired a research firm to conduct a random sample telephone survey of Jefferson County voters. Results showed that 48% believed the district was on the wrong track, while only 37% said it was moving in the right direction.

As follow-up research and part of the superintendent search, the district conducted numerous focus groups to learn what qualities the community wanted in a new leader. The message was loud and clear—the district needed someone who would "establish common vision, mission, and goals" and "maintain focus on student achievement." As they searched for a new superintendent, board members purposefully looked for someone who would bring a new sense of direction to the district. They wanted to develop a mission, goals, and a comprehensive planning process that would lead to improved student achievement. They hired Dr. Jane Hammond because of her reputation as a strategic thinker and planner.

DEVELOPING A STRATEGIC PLAN

Superintendent Hammond's first charge when she took the reins of Jeffco Public Schools in July 1997 was to develop a strategic plan. The culture in Jefferson County required a transparent, collaborative process. Both staff and community members expected meaningful involvement in any systemic change process. If the strategic plan was to be successful, proven communications strategies would have to be utilized to maximize employee and citizen participation.

With a community of 500,000 citizens, 11,000 employees, and 87,000 students, public engagement was a daunting task. While district leaders knew that shared decision-making would take time, planning, and effort, they believed it would result in a strong foundation of support (Meadows & Saltzman, 2000). The district's managers believed that involving a community this large in the change process would require more time up front, but it would save time in the implementation phase because more stakeholders would already have buy-in. This belief was strengthened by the guidance of Senge (1990), who said, "We both fear and seek change. People don't resist change, they resist being changed" (p. 155).

THE STRATEGIC COMMUNICATIONS MODEL

The strategic communications model the district staff created to support Superintendent Hammond's efforts to transform our school district can be outlined as follows:

- Conduct comprehensive research with internal and external stakeholders to determine what the community values and expects from its public schools.

- Develop a comprehensive internal and external communications effort to ensure maximum community involvement in the strategic planning process.
- Convene a broad-based Strategic Planning Committee, composed of staff and citizens, to oversee the strategic planning process.
- Review results of research studies.
- Develop a draft mission, vision, and goals based on the data.
- Conduct follow-up research with the internal and external audiences to solicit reactions to the draft mission, vision, and goals.
- Revise mission, vision, and goals based on input.
- Adopt mission, vision, and goals and develop annual work plan.
- Develop an ongoing communication plan to inform staff and community about the adoption and implementation of the strategic plan.
- Evaluate communication efforts and knowledge of the strategic plan through follow-up surveys of staff and community.

THE ROLE OF THE COMMUNICATIONS DEPARTMENT

To engage the staff and community in developing and implementing the strategic plan, Hammond depended heavily on the Communications Services Department. She supported the theory that school public relations staff play a key role in a two-way symmetrical communication model (Hunt & Grunig, 1994) to build relationships between the school district and its publics. During the strategic planning process, the Communications Services Department followed the credo that "Communicators act as eyes and ears of organizations, spanning organizational boundaries with one foot firmly planted inside their organizations and the other outside" (Dozier, Grunig, & Grunig, 1995, p. 39).

The first step in the development of the district's strategic plan was research, coordinated by the Planning Department and the Communications Services Department, to gather community input on the mission and vision of the school district. Involving a department like Communications Services in the strategic planning process is supported in the literature. For example, Dozier et al. state,

> The communications department needs expertise regarding strategic research . . . the ability to systematically collect reliable information about large and small publics that affect the organization, organize that information into a manageable form, and share that information with the dominant coalition to improve strategic decisions. (p. 42)

With the assistance of Freeman Public Relations, an external consulting firm, the Communications Services Department and the district's leadership initiated a comprehensive public relations campaign to ensure widespread community engagement in the strategic planning process. The target audiences were:

- Internal: 5,000 teachers; 400 administrators; 5,000 classified staff members; 88,000 students.
- External: The 500,000-member community at large; news media; parents; business leaders; legislators.

The key messages were:

- The district is beginning a new era with an increased focus on student learning.
- The district wants you to "Make Your Voice Heard" and encourages every citizen and student to participate in the strategic planning process.
- This is an unparalleled grassroots effort, perhaps the largest ever in the state.
- The community is invited to remain involved as the plan is implemented and evaluated.

The public relations efforts began with an internal communications campaign in September 1997. Communications Services developed a video and distributed it to principals, accompanied by a script, overheads, and packets of handouts to introduce the planning process to staff. Principals were also encouraged to share the information with their parent committees.

Also, in September the board of education established the Strategic Planning Budgeting Council made up of 35 citizens and the district's administrative leadership. The citizens included business representatives, parents, board of education members, and employee association representatives. The committee's charge was to oversee the strategic planning process as well as implementation and evaluation of the plan.

In October, the district developed surveys for students, staff, and parents that would guide the district in setting the mission and goals. The surveys asked questions about what the key stakeholders wanted and expected from their public schools, from core subjects to extracurricular activities.

The Communications Services Department also conducted surveys of key community groups, including Chambers of Commerce and the PTA, using electronic keypad technology. This process allowed data collection and instantaneous display of results at public meetings. While individual feedback is anonymous, participants can immediately view group results on a large screen. This technology was used throughout the strategic planning process.

A press conference to kick off the community component of the campaign was held in early November. The media were invited to visit classrooms where students were completing their surveys so they could learn more about the other components of the "Make Your Voice Heard" public relations campaign. Other communications channels included paid radio announcements, an article in the district's parent publication, information on the district's website, and news releases and fliers distributed throughout the community.

During November, the district conducted research through a variety of methods:

- Paper-and-pencil surveys were distributed to every student for completion at school.
- Written surveys for parents were sent home with every student along with a cover letter explaining the strategic planning process.
- Written surveys were sent to community leaders and were distributed at district and school meetings.
- Thirteen focus groups were held with approximately 100 students, parents, employees, and business and community members participating.

- A Web-based survey allowed staff and citizens to participate through the Internet.
- Short oral surveys were conducted at grocery stores, libraries, and community meetings.
- The district held four town meetings, attended by approximately 400 citizens, where keypad technology was used to gather input.

These comprehensive efforts resulted in the participation of over 100,000 students, staff members, parents, and community members. Throughout the survey administration period, the Communications Services Department continued its public relations efforts. Ongoing press releases, e-mail updates to principals, articles in the district's employee publications, and school newsletter articles kept key stakeholders informed and engaged in the process.

In early January, the Strategic Planning Council reviewed the feedback from the student, staff, and community surveys to develop the preliminary framework for the strategic plan: mission, beliefs, customer requirements, goal, objectives, performance indicators, and evaluation measures. The Communications Department widely publicized the council's work, using a variety of channels to ensure all key publics were informed about the plan's progress.

In late January, the Communications Services Department helped organize and publicize staff and community meetings that were held simultaneously at six locations around the school district using state-of-the-art technology to provide feedback on the council's initial proposal. The community meetings used real-time, interactive technology with Superintendent Hammond on live video-cast. She was able to explain the initial strategic plan components and provide opportunities for participants to make comments and ask questions. Keypad technology activities gave participants the opportunity to provide instant feedback on the proposed goals. The meetings garnered support for the goals from an audience of 610 community members and 1,570 staff members. Another 400 citizens provided written feedback to the board of education. The meetings helped determine what phrases in the mission and goals were important to the community and what they wanted to omit. For example, the consensus was that it was important to include "all children" in the mission. However, the participants did not want to include the phrase "global education" in the mission and goals.

Based on the Strategic Planning Council's work and the feedback of the staff and community, the board of education in February 1998 adopted the district mission as: "To provide a quality education that prepares all students for a successful future." The board also established two goals: (1) all students will reach high standards through quality instruction, curriculum, and assessments; and (2) all employees will be accountable for an efficient, high-performing, customer-oriented organization focused on increased student achievement.

The Strategic Plan became not only the focus for the district's work but also was used to allocate resources. After board adoption of the plan, the district held meetings with principals and "accountability chairs" from all 140 schools to determine budget priorities based on the plan. Central administrators—curriculum specialists, financial experts, human resource professionals—used goals designed by the community to establish measurable annual objectives. The Strategic Planning Committee also developed an annual planning and review cycle. The purpose of this cycle was to increase the flexibility of the strategic plan and to help the district respond quickly to unanticipated events in its external environment.

After the adoption of the plan, public relations efforts took on a different focus. The communications goal now was to make the strategic plan an integral part of the district and community culture through ongoing one-way and two-way communications channels. The strategic plan became the focus of all employee and community communications. Communications tactics included:

- regular updates in the weekly employee newsletter, *The Messenger*
- copies of the strategic plan sent to every staff member
- focus groups with principals to determine what tools they needed to enhance staff knowledge and support for the strategic plan
- regular press releases on progress of the strategic plan
- ongoing articles in the external newsletter, sent to 65,000 parents and community leaders, about the plan; in addition, each article in the newsletter was tied to a strategic plan goal or indicator
- updates in the district annual report

- annual meetings to report progress to the staff and community
- posters in all schools and departments with the mission and goals
- a speaker's bureau to present the plan and its progress at community meetings, service clubs, etc.
- staff and community videos about the plan
- regular updates on the district's Web page

An employee survey in fall 1998 provided baseline data on the staff's commitment to and knowledge of the strategic plan. The employees had an overall positive response to the statements, "I am committed to the strategic plan indicators" and "I feel accountable for the strategic plan." Slightly less positive, but still over 3.0 on a 5-point scale, were responses to the statements, "The goals and objectives of the strategic plan are clearly explained," "Implementing the strategic plan is increasing student achievement," and "The strategic plan gives us the focus we need to be successful in the future."

Based on the survey results, the district initiated additional communications measures to increase staff support and understanding of the plan. First, the Communications Services Department trained employees across all job roles, from custodians to bus drivers, from teachers to principals, to serve as study circle facilitators. The district then sponsored a series of study circles facilitated by peers (teacher to teacher, support staff to support staff).

The study circles explored issues of concern to employees and how the strategic plan had affected their work. The quantitative data gathered through the study circles enhanced what the district had learned through the written employee survey and provided direction for how to increase employee support of the strategic plan. For example, employees said they trusted and depended on their supervisor as a primary source of information. The leadership realized the power of the supervisor as a communicator and sense-maker in times of great change, so district managers sponsored a series of meetings with principals and supervisors to learn what they needed to communicate effectively about the strategic plan. As a result of supervisor input, the district established a number of public relations communications tools to ensure that all employees were informed:

- Cabinet-level managers visited with school staffs to discuss the strategic plan and their role in implementing it.
- Area administrators, each of whom supervised about 20 schools, developed common messages to share with their principals so that everyone was getting the same information no matter where they worked.
- Communications Services established a weekly online newsletter for management, *The Leadership Memo*. This concise, easy-to-read publication ensured that key district information was being shared with all managers who could then share the information with their staffs.
- Communications Services developed *Talking Points* on key issues, which principals and supervisors could use to make oral and written presentations to their staff members.

When the district surveyed employees in 2000, results indicated a higher commitment to the strategic plan and a higher rate of agreement that the strategic plan gave the district the focus needed to be successful in the future. In addition, there was a higher level of agreement that the goals and objectives of the strategic plan were clearly explained. According to a "key driver" analysis of 2000 employee survey results, the strategic plan was one of the factors with the most influence on employee perceptions of Jeffco Schools as a world-class education system. A follow-up survey in 2002 found that employees had even stronger beliefs that the district was achieving its mission.

How did the community respond to the district's new focus and direction? If the bottom-line measurement of school district support is voter approval of tax levies, then Jeffco succeeded in turning around community perception! In fall 1999, the district passed, for the first time in 16 years, a mill levy override to increase operating funds. Finally, voters were willing to support additional funding.

Community support has been sustained although Superintendent Hammond left the district in 2002. For example, in November 2004, with the advocacy of the business community and employee associations, voters in Jefferson County passed both a $323.8 million bond issue (with 57.21% in favor) and a $38.5 million mill levy—operating fund—override (60.18% voting in favor). It was the first time in the district's 54-year history that both a mill and bond passed in the same election.

Perhaps most important is that the strategic plan has served as a way to ensure the district stays focused on student achievement. Although government accountability mandates for public education have increased since the strategic plan's adoption, including the federal No Child Left Behind legislation, the plan is both comprehensive and flexible and continues to guide the work of the district.

Each year, the objectives and indicators for the plan are revised to reflect changing needs of the district. For example, the goals have been updated and now read:

- All students will graduate with meaningful choices for their future as a result of the quality instruction and rigorous curricula in Jeffco Schools.
- All employees will be efficient, welcoming, customer oriented, and accountable for a high-performing organization to ensure that all students graduate with meaningful choices.

While the strategic planning process was time consuming and labor intensive, the results showed that the efforts were worthwhile. Jeffco Schools is now a stronger school district with increased support from staff and community and most importantly, improved student achievement as measured by the Colorado Student Assessment Program. In 2003–2004, for example, Jeffco students increased achievement on 17 of 23 state assessments.

LESSONS LEARNED

What did the district learn about the change process and communications through the development and implementation of the strategic plan in Jeffco Public Schools? The process reaffirmed the district's belief in the necessity of using a wide variety of both one-way and two-way, ongoing communications channels to implement whole-system change in the school district's community. Jeffco Schools learned the power of involving large numbers of stakeholders in developing a strategic direction and continuing to engage the public as change is implemented. The district realized the importance of not only providing ongoing strategic communication with internal and external audiences but also regularly measuring the effectiveness of the communication efforts. By conducting quantitative and qualitative analyses of staff and community knowledge and attitudes, the district was able to modify its communications efforts to ensure maximum participation in the ongoing planning and implementation process.

The experience of Jeffco Schools supports Hunt and Grunig's (1994) observation that

> Although an organization with good public relations may have to incorporate the goals of strategic publics into its mission, in the long run it will choose better goals and will be able to pursue these revised goals more effectively than it would if it ignored or fought the goals of the publics. (p. 5)

POSTSCRIPT

The strategic planning process that the district employed and the strategic communication strategies that accompanied it have been proven successful through both longevity and results. The district has experienced success with both bond and operating levy elections, improved staff and community support, and increased student achievement. The district's strategic plan continues to guide the work of the district and the district's mission is widely known, understood, and accepted by internal and external stakeholders.

REFERENCES

Dozier, D. M., Grunig, L. A., & Grunig, J. E. (1995). *Manager's guide to excellence in public relations and communications management.* Mahwah, NJ: Lawrence Erlbaum.

Hunt, T., & Grunig, J. E. (1994). *Public relations techniques.* New York: Holt, Rinehart & Winston.

Meadows, B. J., & Saltzman, M. (2000). *Building school communities: strategies for leaders.* Golden, CO: Fulcrum Resources.

Senge, P. M. (1990). *The fifth discipline.* New York: Doubleday.

ABOUT THE AUTHOR

Marilyn Saltzman, APR, is a public relations consultant and the retired manager of communications services for the Jefferson County Schools, Colorado. She may be reached by phone or fax at (303) 838-6520 or by e-mail at msaltzman@evcohs.com.

ESSAY 2

Finding and Engaging the "Influentials": Effective School Public Relations During Times of Great Change

Barbara M. Hunter

Helping school leaders communicate effectively about whole-system change to a wide range of audiences is no easy task. Change, especially in school systems, often involves issues that are fraught with complexities. Experiencing change can be psychologically uncomfortable, even when change is welcome. While we would like to believe that many of us can dissect issues in a fair and balanced way, we generally don't have the time to examine fully all the complex matters that impact our lives, especially in this charged-up world where information comes at us at a million bytes per minute.

Instead, humans quite naturally construct realities around their own experience base, which can be sometimes broad and balanced, or in other cases, narrow and out of synchrony. Either way, perceptions—right or wrong, broad or narrow—form one's personalized version of reality—hence, the adage "perception is reality."

One of my favorite fables that I rely on to help me explain this concept to others, especially as it relates to communications, is the three blind men and the elephant. It goes like this:

> Once, three blind men lived in a village in India where they argued about a great beast they had heard so much about but never got to see for themselves. One day, a villager got tired of hearing them argue and decided to bring them to an elephant so they could touch the animal and finally see what it was.
>
> The first blind man reached and touched the side of the huge animal and declared, "An elephant is smooth and solid like a wall." The second

blind man put his hand on the elephant's limber trunk: "An elephant is like a giant snake," he said. The third blind man felt the elephant's pointed tusk and said, "I was right, this creature is as sharp and deadly as a spear."

In truth, each man was right as he described the reality that he had come into contact with. An elephant is all those things that they described. But what they missed was the complete picture, the whole beast, if you will.

There are lessons that we can glean from this fable and apply to those who are leading change in school systems. First, whole-system change can be likened to a beast that has many aspects, understood sometimes only by those who are touching them. Take, for example, a school superintendent who wants to change a school district's traditional calendar to a year-round schedule. All of a sudden, parents are unhappy about the loss of summer vacation, teachers are afraid of burnout, and students are excited about other learning experiences they can have during intersessions. What we see is that parents, teachers, and students all have a hold on a different part of the elephant, and their reality is based on whichever part they're experiencing.

The second lesson is that unless someone communicates what the whole elephant looks like, those different perceptions cannot be integrated into a common reality. And unless leaders create a common reality that everyone can embrace, there will be much energy lost to divisiveness and fighting as people get embroiled in convincing others to see their individual realities.

In fact, one of the tactics used by both harsh critics and ardent supporters of public education is to take advantage of the propensity of humans to boil down complex issues to a simplified version. Critics or supporters present only a piece of the picture, label it reality, and hammer it home.

School district leaders on the front lines of change would do well to consider a communications strategy to help key stakeholders understand the "elephant" in all of its complexity. School public relations practitioners are uniquely positioned to help others see the whole elephant and to craft and deliver key strategic communication messages about it.

A NEW OPPORTUNITY

Today, there are two reasons why I believe we are standing at a new opportunity to communicate about this elephant called public education and move public opinion to support the change necessary to transform whole school systems.

First, our capacity to communicate is at an all-time high and our trust of information sources is at an all-time low. The public is literally being bombarded with information. The New York firm Media Dynamics estimates that the average American is now exposed to 254 different commercial messages a day, up nearly 25% since the mid-1970s. There are millions of websites on the Internet, and cable systems routinely carry up to 900 channels of programming. Ninety-eight percent of homes have television sets. Everywhere we turn, we have more and more information that we have to analyze, synthesize, economize, and theorize about how all of this applies to our own world.

Compounded with this all-time high quantity of information, we have developed an all-time high level of distrust with the same people who deliver this information to us. For example, a study published by the Pew Research Center for the People and the Press (2005) indicated that the public's view of the news media is as low as it has ever been. Over the last 20 years, the public's believability of daily newspapers has declined 30 points from 84% in 1984 to 54% in 2004. Likewise, during the same time period, the public's believability of local television news and network television news programs has declined 23 points.

Interestingly, the authors of the Pew study suggested that the public is not rejecting the principles underlying traditional journalism, but rather the public suspects journalists are not living up to those principles. This is evidenced by the study's finding that more people than ever believe that the press plays favorites and is influenced by the power establishment.

Taking this one step further, I believe that the proliferation of new information sources is related to the decline of the public's trust of traditional sources of information. In other words, the more the public distrusts the information it's receiving, the more they want to seek out even more information to help them make a decision.

Google and other Internet search engines are prime examples of delivering information to people who need lots of sources to make what they feel is an informed decision. The dramatic rise in the number of Internet blogs is another clear indicator that people want to seek information outside the traditional sources. Clearly, technology plays a big role in helping the public access nontraditional sources of information.

The second reason we are looking at a new opportunity in helping the public to embrace change in public education builds on the first. Today, more than ever before, as we turn away from traditional sources of information due to our growing distrust, we are turning to individuals whom we consider credible and trustworthy. Berry and Keller (2003) believed that "The channel with the greatest influence in America is not traditional media, or advertising, or the Internet, but the human channel of individual, person-to-person, word-of-mouth communication."

THE INFLUENTIALS—NOT YOUR MOTHER'S KEY COMMUNICATORS

Berry and Keller's book, *The Influentials,* is a beautiful summary of 30 years of research carried out by the Roper Organization, a marketing research firm that studies trends in attitudes and behaviors. What they discovered is that a personal network of friends, family, and others is among the best sources for ideas and information. The bottom line? They believe that when Americans make decisions today—they make them through a conversation!

In addition to the rise of new technologies such as e-mail and cell phones that make communication easier, Berry and Keller laid out several other reasons for the shift toward personal communication. America is a vastly more educated nation than two or three decades ago. In their research, they found that with education comes confidence. They say that Americans may not be "smarter" than their parents or grandparents, but we do seem to be more adept at critical-thinking skills, such as challenging opinions, making calculations, and parrying with others—skills that serve people well in the kinds of conversation in which word-of-mouth influence is spread.

Finally, they say, age may not make people wiser, but it does make people more experienced and, like education, tends to make people more certain of themselves. More confident in themselves and more skeptical of "official" wisdom, Americans are more willing to seek out answers from other people.

Every school public relations professional worth his or her salt maintains a list of key communicators in his or her community: elected officials, civic leaders, current and former school board members, retired school employees, and others. These people are called "Influentials." They receive regular news about school system activities and events in the hope that they will spread the word in the larger community. But while some Influentials may be on the key communicator list, there are many more Influentials that school public relations folks may not have on their contact list. Berry and Keller put it this way:

> If word of mouth is like a radio signal broadcast over the country, Influentials are the strategically placed transmitters that amplify the signal, multiplying dramatically the number of people who hear it. The signal becomes stronger and stronger as it is beamed from Influential to Influential, and then broadcast to the nation as a whole.

Who are these Influentials and how do we identify them? Berry and Keller said they are one out of every ten people, male and female, middle-aged, middle/upper-middle class, college educated, married with children, homeowners, and employed at the executive or professional level. One of their hallmark characteristics is that they are activists. Often, they attend public meetings; write or call politicians; serve on committees of local organizations; are officers of clubs or organizations; attend political rallies, speeches, or organized protests; write letters to the editor; or work for a political party.

Berry and Keller said Influentials are connected to many communities at once; for example, they have connections to their neighborhood or town, religious or spiritual group, workplace, and alumni association. Most of all, Influentials are highly regarded for their advice and opinion in issues relating to government and politics, restaurants, health problems, handling children and teens, and career choices, to name a few.

School public relations professionals who want to rally their publics around their school district's transformation journey must think outside the key communicators' box to identify who in their community fits the Influential profile. Could it be the church choir leader, the high school alumni association president, or the director of the private preschool? Yes. Could it be the parent activist who testifies regularly at school board meetings or the chairman of the town's archeological commission? Yes.

How else can we identify Influentials beyond keen observations? One simple way is to ask them to identify themselves; for example, a school district website could have a link on the front page that invites visitors to sign up to receive regular updates about the schools in the district. A simple postal card inserted into the community newspaper that can be filled out and returned can serve as another way to connect Influentials to your school system and its schools. Another easy way to identify Influentials is to obtain a copy of the roster of speakers at school board or city council meetings.

The potential power of identifying and communicating with Influentials was borne out in a recent study conducted by Learning First Alliance (June, 2005), a collection of 12 national education associations. This survey, conducted by the Mellman Group, revealed that voters who indicated they received adequate information from their public school system were more likely to believe that an increase in school district funding would result in better education and not be wasted. Further, they went on to say that receiving more information would significantly increase their confidence in public schools.

What are we waiting for?

WAYS TO ENGAGE THE INFLUENTIALS

Once we've identified who they are, how can we engage the Influentials? As we have learned, this 10% of the population would not qualify as shrinking violets. They are, by nature, activists, and thus need activities in which to be authentically engaged.

School districts can consider hosting focus group discussions to gather ideas for helping students meet the rigors of higher standards or ways to connect nonparents to the schools in their district. Many challenges that school districts face as they work to transform their schools can be turned over to Influentials in facilitated discussion groups that allow full debate of the issues and that hopefully produce ideas for positive resolution.

To engage a larger number of Influentials, town hall meetings can be useful if they are not constructed as a one-way delivery of information. One local school district used this format successfully as it engaged Influentials on identifying what the city's new high school should look and feel like for its students and community. After a brief presentation on the construction plans, more than 150 Influentials worked in small groups for several hours to hammer out the goals for the school's smaller learning communities.

By engaging these Influentials in a meaningful way, both the school district and Influentials reaped benefits such as:

- School leaders heard fresh and innovative ideas that they hadn't considered before;
- The community gained a sense of ownership in the outcome for student learning at the new high school;
- A renewed respect and trust developed between the community and school leaders as they tackled challenges together.

But perhaps the most important benefit is that those Influentials who were engaged in this process returned to their workplaces, their community organizations, and their grocery stores and began to talk with others about the new opportunities for high schoolers and the openness of school district leaders to new ideas. That alone cast the school district in a positive light in many minds throughout the community.

OBSTACLES TO ENGAGING INFLUENTIALS

Superintendents and school board members often believe that they have to have all the answers to the challenges schools face. It generally doesn't take long at a school board meeting to begin hearing solutions floated into the air like balloons without any real reasoning tied to them. That sets up unrealistic expectations within the school system and throughout the community that the school board and superintendent will fix every problem the school system has. This phenomenon often fuels the "us versus them" mentality that can easily derail a change process. But by drawing more community members into the mix, school district leaders can signal that they don't have all the answers and can welcome new partners in the change process.

Clearly, drawing more community members into the change leadership mix is time consuming. It takes time to identify the Influentials and to set up authentic ways to engage them. Often, school district leaders don't perceive they have the time to engage a broader group of individuals. But as my grandmother used to say, haste makes waste and I would add that haste creates a lot of missed opportunities to shift public opinion in your community to support change in your school district.

THE SCHOOL PR CHALLENGE

A critical part of the school communicators' job is to understand what his or her school district's elephant—the common vision—looks like, then help school district leaders and the community reach the same understanding.

After reaching an understanding, school communicators need to help their superintendents and school board members craft simple and strong key messages to communicate about this common vision. Imagine the synergy that will emerge when all publics touched by a school district's transformation are able to understand and articulate the whole elephant. Consider, for example, the following fictitious vision for a school system:

> In 10 years, our school district will be transformed into a vibrant K–12 system in which our students will learn the skills and gain the knowledge to succeed in the workplaces and communities of their choice. How will we accomplish this? We will do this by (1) making sure our children come to school ready to learn having had experience in a quality preschool program; (2) working with parents so they understand how to fully support their children; (3) finding and keeping the best teachers

who know how to reach and teach each child; and (4) making sure we have adequate funds to keep the school district financially stable.

While just an example, the above vision statement differs from similar statements in other school districts' because of its simplicity. There are no words that are difficult to understand or jargon that only education insiders know. This kind of simplicity is important for communicating key messages to various publics. After understanding the vision and crafting key messages around it, school communicators then identify the Influentials in their community who are willing and able to spread the message about the future of their school system.

We have a responsibility as school communicators to engage our publics and to seize and reframe a message that will resonate strongly with our Influentials. When we craft a message that resonates so well, when we can define the elephant so articulately, the public itself will start to grab on to this message and embrace the change needed to transform their school systems.

REFERENCES

Berry, J., & Keller, E. (2003). *The influentials.* New York: Free Press.
Learning First Alliance (2005, June). *Values, vision and performance.* Washington, DC: Author.
Pew Research Center for the People and the Press (2005, June 26). Public more critical of press, but good will persists. Retrieved on April 10, 2006, from http://people-press.org/reports/display.php3?ReportID = 248

ABOUT THE AUTHOR

Barbara M. Hunter, APR, is the director of communications for the National School Boards Association in Alexandria, Virginia. Over the past 20 years, she has held public relations and communications positions including executive director of information and outreach for the Alexandria City Public Schools, Virginia; and editor of *The School Administrator* magazine published by the American Association of School Administrators.

Ms. Hunter holds a bachelor's degree in communications and management from Hood College in Frederick, Maryland, and a master's degree in public relations management from The American University in Washington, DC. She also holds accreditation in public relations from the Public Relations Society of America. She is a past president of the Chesapeake Chapter of the National School Public Relations Association and a member of Leadership Alexandria. She may be reached at bhunter@nsba.org or at 703-838-6153.

ESSAY 3

The Role of a School Board in Communicating Change in Front of and Behind the Camera[1]

Anne L. Bryant

Communicating change is one of the most difficult challenges facing districts. And the role of the school board in this process is critical. School board members are the elected "voice" of the community. Clearly, the superintendent and professional staff have vital roles in communicating with the public, but the school board is at the center with its job of setting the vision for the district. This essay highlights this important role for a school district and includes two real-life examples.

When it comes time to communicate change at the Hogwarts School of Witchcraft and Wizardry—like making sure no students accidentally open the chamber of secrets—all it usually takes is a wave of the wand. Before you know it, Professor Dumbledore has made his point and no one wanders the second floor, except for maybe Harry, Ron, and Hermione. There is no Hogwarts school board nor do the parents living near Privet Drive demand more of a say about how the changes are communicated.

But, alas, Privet Drive is only a fantasy. In the real world, the world that we live in, change is different and difficult. When school districts decide to implement changes, the result often can be confusion, anger, and even opposition from the community, parents, and school employees. This kind of reaction can happen with major change, such as school boundaries, or with small change, like the menu in the school cafeteria.

When you examine the community's reaction to minor changes, the importance of clear communication becomes even more apparent. A change in the bus schedule results in a barrage of phone calls to the superintendent's office, a hastily arranged early release day brings out hordes of complaining parents, and an abruptly changed policy about school closings due to inclement weather swamps the school board president's voice mail.

And, since the community can be as fickle as the weather, it is critically important for the school board to set policy and direction for communicating change. Having a clear strategic vision and clear goals helps make the communication process run more smoothly and also helps create a level of trust and confidence in the community.

Moreover, virtually every change that affects a district—from bringing in a new superintendent to changing curriculums to instituting new standardized tests—is driven by or involves to a great extent the school board. Each of these cases involves board decisions and should be explained and communicated to the public by the school board.

Communicating change is not about a new video sent home with students or about the star of the district's cable TV show or who is quoted in this week's *Gazette*. Successful change—and the communication to the community about that change—is all about vision, working together, accountability, funding, and ensuring continuous improvement. That is the role of the school board—and it may not always be seen on the evening news, but it is the most critical part of the process.

HOMETOWN CREDIBILITY

In communicating to the public about these changes, school board members also possess an important gift—hometown credibility. For the most part, school board members are longtime, even lifelong, members of the community. (At our conferences or my meetings with school board members, some tell me jokingly that a quick dash to the supermarket can quickly turn into a three-hour tour!)

But the school board cannot and should not perform this communication function alone or in a vacuum. The school board employs the superintendent and a professional staff to handle the day-to-day operations. This is the team that leads the school district and community through the process of change.

Developing an effective plan for communicating change is essential. The school board's role in this development is not generating the key ingredients of the strategy (that is, the who, what, and how). Rather, the school board's role is to set the vision for the district, focus on the mission at hand, and ensure that the mission is clear.

The school board builds relationships at the grassroots level. The board meets with business and civic leaders as well as with parents and employees to communicate the same message. Broad public support and alliances with business, faith communities, organizations representing minorities, and neighborhood associations are critical to the success of the school district's communications efforts.

The district's professional staff prepares answers to the questions, issues, and concerns of the community. They try to anticipate how the public will react to the change, the possible questions they will raise, and the issues that may result.

The school board, with input from the community, sets the vision for the district, sets standards and goals, creates a measurement and accountability system, develops a way to ensure the money and resources are being directed to meet the goals, collaborates with the community, and sets up a continuous improvement process. In essence, the school board's role is to oversee, set policy, and set direction. The National School Boards Association calls this framework for governance the key work of school boards.

However, this does not mean that the school board is absent from communicating to the public or must always leave the communication job to the superintendent or professional staff. Without question, board members give increased credibility to a school district's efforts to communicate change. School board members are entrepreneurs, accountants, and lawyers—the proverbial butcher, baker, and candlestick maker. What they are not, generally, are education professionals. To most people, school board members are more than just their elected representatives; they are neighbors and friends who are, to a degree, outside the inner education circle of teachers, principals, and superintendents.

A CASE IN POINT: FT. WAYNE COMMUNITY SCHOOL DISTRICT

In recent years, these school board/superintendent teams have been making a positive difference in the quality of their district's education through effective communication. I have worked closely with the American Association of School Administrators to help support this team concept. Our recent collaboration—*Team Leadership for Student Achievement*—is a publication that helps build mutual understanding and productive collaboration between the board and superintendent.

One good teamwork example that I have seen is the Ft. Wayne Community School District in Ft. Wayne, Indiana. Several years ago, the district, which is the second largest in the state, was facing a crisis of funding, an influx of students who spoke little or no English, and a sharp rise in the number of students qualifying for meal assistance.

Following the hiring of a new superintendent, the school board and the district faced an extraordinarily sensitive and divisive issue—redistricting. The way that the board, superintendent, and professional staff addressed this issue is almost a textbook study in communicating change.

One of the first steps in the communication process is for the school board to learn from each other and build a solid team. The Ft. Wayne school board held a series of retreats to forge a closer working relationship. A key feature of those retreats was the development of communications skills—skills that are critical for all board members when they tackle great change.

School board members must develop critical message points relating to the change, anticipate the tough questions that will come from the community and the media, learn that a "no comment" statement is often counterproductive, and most of all, they need to understand the importance of selecting the proper spokesperson when a reporter calls. They have to make a determination if a school board member or the professional staff should respond to the request.

The Ft. Wayne retreats also allowed school board members to discuss the value of unity and the value of explaining to the media the reasons they support the proposed change. Media coverage of school board meetings frequently focuses on the board member who is opposed to the plan, because that is usually the board member who speaks up and explains why he or she is against the idea. But school board members also need to explain their "yes" votes; for example, why they support a controversial recommendation such as redistricting. School board members need to listen and give their support to recommendations offered by superintendents and professional staff when it's merited, but they also need to understand the value of explaining that support to the school board's constituents in the community.

And that is exactly what the Ft. Wayne board did. The school board and superintendent worked with the community to change school attendance areas. The superintendent and staff held numerous community forums and board members attended sessions and continually exchanged ideas and feedback with the superintendent. Using this information, the district designed a redistricting plan—with unanimous school board approval—that totally addressed the community's needs.

The community overwhelmingly accepted the communication process used by the school board/superintendent/professional staff team. In fact, at all the meetings communicating the new attendance areas, not a single parent spoke against the plan. Equally important, the board and superintendent empowered the school-level staff in the new clusters to make more decisions locally and gave them more flexibility in the use of their funding.

A CASE IN CONTRAST—THE ANNE ARUNDEL PUBLIC SCHOOL DISTRICT

Contrast the climate in Ft. Wayne with a recent situation in Anne Arundel County Public Schools, Maryland—a 75,000-student school district on the Chesapeake Bay. The school board hired a new superintendent, calling him "a change agent" and the "educational equivalent of a number-one draft pick." During the year, the board and superintendent achieved a number of successes: a $10 million increase in county funding, higher reading scores, a new International Baccalaureate program, and an increase in the number of students taking advanced placement tests.

But frustration began to appear in the community at the start of a new school year. Teachers were upset, feeling unappreciated and underpaid; some parents said the changes were too fast, too soon. The superintendent, in a candid press interview, said he was disappointed that he was unable "to figure out a better way to manage the change process." Several school board members also concluded that the leadership team failed to properly communicate the new initiatives to parents, teachers, principals, and students. They believed, in looking back over the past year, that they did not focus enough attention on outreach to the community.

It's absolutely essential for the leadership team to create the right climate for schools, to provide an exciting, thriving learning environment for both teachers and students, and to develop a collaborative relationship with the community. With this kind of activity in place, communication is smoother and the odds of successful change increase dramatically.

COMPLEMENTARY ROLES AND COLLABORATION: SCHOOL BOARD AND SUPERINTENDENT LEADERSHIP

If a neighbor on the school board explains the value of the change and why it will benefit the children, the schools, and the community, the perception can be different than when an education professional explains the same concepts. At the same time, the community needs to see the school board as being more than just a witness to the change. The board needs to be both a real and perceived partner to major change, again not merely to provide community representation into the change process but also to provide community insight and involvement.

School boards and superintendents may have different roles in communicating with the public, but they act as a complete unit. Together, they focus on how they can complement each other. The superintendent is the chief executive officer who offers the critical perspective of a professional educator. The school board, which strategizes with the superintendent, is the body that engages and involves the community in setting a vision for the school district.

Moreover, one of the key communication roles of the school board is to develop a plan for roles and procedures for the school board and superintendent and how they complement one another. The professional staff is writing the talking points and the plan while the school board is engaging the community. The superintendent and professional staff are writing about the change in a language that people understand while the school board is meeting with business leaders, the faith community, organizations representing minorities, and neighborhood associations to ensure success of the initiatives.

The superintendent and professional staff are preparing newsletters, e-mails, the cable TV show, and mailing packets while the board is building relationships with external stakeholders and collaborating with key political leaders.

The superintendent is doing a television interview while school board members are using their vast political skills, including what some call "aggressive listening." When a major change is being recommended, board members must be actively seeking public reaction. This means being visible listeners at forums, board meetings, the grocery store, and even the movie theater (not during the film!). It means asking the right questions of the right people and listening to the answers.

School board members are, for the most part, elected officials and often receive more or as many votes as the city council members or even the mayor. This gives school board members the power and the skill to bring together the stakeholders (teachers, parents, students, and community members) into the decision-making process. These collaborative relationships take time and attention to cultivate and maintain. But these relationships also are critical to ensuring support for change.

CONCLUSION

The jury is still out on the Anne Arundel district's efforts to communicate change because the school board and superintendent are committed to the initiatives put in place to improve student achievement. However, it is clear from this example that effective communication is essential. School board members have to make a deliberate and significant effort to increase effective communication about the change. The normal, routine communication process most likely is not going to work. Without an upgrade to the quality and quantity of communication, discussion of the change may go unnoticed.

In addition, the Ft. Wayne and Anne Arundel circumstances show how important it is for school board members to understand that their role in a major change situation goes far beyond casting a vote. School board members must demonstrate that they have studied the issue, listened to people, talked about what they've heard, and explained the foundation for either support or opposition to the change. School board members must have the public relations skills to craft an effective message, to seek opportunities to deliver that message, to do so effectively, and most of all, to understand that their voices can be just as important to the change process as are their votes.

The role of the school board in communicating change is quite complicated. When we think of communication, we often think of the local TV news, the morning newspaper, or a local talk radio program. But the school board's role is more complicated because, although it may include an appearance on the TV news, it most definitely involves setting the vision for the school district. Board members have to be poised in front of the camera as well as behind the scenes.

Successfully communicating change involves knowing how to work with the news media, having properly trained spokespersons and a top-notch cable TV station. But even the most expensive media relations plan in the world will fail unless the school board has done its job. Setting a compelling vision for the district, ensuring that the resources are aligned to effect the change, establishing clearly defined standards and a way to measure them, assuming responsibility for the process, setting the right climate for change to work, building networks, promoting continuous improvement, and having the skill to do what is needed—that is the job of the school board.

In summary, the school board is the voice of the community and offers hometown credibility in discussion of major change. The board sets policy and direction and oversees the professional educators who craft the communications plan. Collaboration with the superintendent and other professional staff is critical for success, as is the ability of the school board to act in front of the cameras and behind the scenes.

A good school board does not run the district; rather it ensures that the district is run well.

ENDNOTES

1. Dr. Bryant's essay first appeared as Bryant, A. L. (2003). The role of a school board in communicating change in front of and behind the camera.

Journal of School Public Relations, 24(4), 231–240. Reprinted with permission.

ABOUT THE AUTHOR

Anne L. Bryant, Ph.D., is the executive director of the National School Boards Association. She may be reached at 1680 Duke Street, Alexandria, Virginia 22314, or at 703-838-6722 (phone) or 703-548-5516 (fax). Her e-mail address is abryant@nsba.org.

ESSAY 4

The Role of School Public Relations: Bringing Order Out of Chaos[1]

Sylvia Soholt

School districts attempting to institute whole-system change often serve as models of chaos instead. Their employees are overwhelmed by all the balls in the air, and their communities are bewildered by the noise being generated. Somewhere in the midst of this cacophony there must be a plan, they hope.

This essay describes the important role of school public relations for bringing order out of what may seem to be chaos by keeping communications consistently focused on the primary objectives of communicating in times of great change. These primary objectives are: increasing student achievement, developing strategies to involve stakeholders in doing the work of schooling, and describing progress so that everyone can see evidence of success.

Never mind communicating in times of great change; let us start from the premise that school districts have a hard time communicating even in normal times. The challenge lies on both sides of the communications equation, with the sender (educators) and with the receiver (that vast audience in a school district's community).

In my experience as a school public relations consultant working with school districts throughout the United States, educators often see communications as something that happens naturally, which means that it does not require planning, resources, or even particular skill. A corollary belief is that there is certainly no need for someone who has been trained in communications or its tawdry stepsister, public relations. The collective attitude that emerges from these beliefs is: "We'll be responsive to our stakeholders—if it's a friendly question; but if it's something important, we can hold a meeting. If it turns out we do need to communicate better about something, then we'll assign it to someone who likes people or hire someone who knows how to do a press release." This approach to school public relations can be summarized as "We'll communicate *to* you."

For their part, the intended receivers (external stakeholders) of school district communications often have limited interest in the topic of school district improvement because they may believe they already know how best to run schools in their district. They have been to school and, therefore, they know what schooling is and how it should be done.

External stakeholders also often do not spend much time reading about schools or getting involved in schools because they pretty much trust that educators have their children's best interests at heart and will do the right thing. Trust disappears, however, when change leaders start talking about topics like school redistricting that will move their children from one school to another (in which case they will join others at a standing-room-only meeting in the boardroom).

It is challenging to get stakeholders to pay attention to communications from a district, including communications about important topics like a bond election. It is even more difficult to communicate with them about systemic change. It is difficult to explain systemic change to a public accustomed to reading hyperbolic advertisements about the benefits of some product or service. In the face of hyperbole, people might respond with skepticism to the news that their district will be engaging in whole-system change that will "significantly improve teaching and learning." In fact, transformational change in school systems may not be entirely welcome. Research conducted by Educational Testing Service (2001) and studies compiled by Public Agenda (2003) identified public attitudes toward changing school systems. Apparently, Americans do not see school systems as failing or in a crisis, but they do believe school systems can do better.

Failure to communicate change can yield adverse effects such as increased confusion and cynicism. This occurs when systemic change is announced with great fanfare and a committee has thought long and hard about a significant title for the change that becomes a clever acronym in the best cases (Serious Transformation = Achieving Results becomes STAR) or worst case, an acronym that requires help to pronounce and has no meaning independent of the words it represents (for example, EALRs—Essential Academic Learning Requirements). Confusion builds when there is no mention of students or student achievement. The community gets stumped on figuring out how the new program is different from the status quo, tries to remember what the strategic plan of a previous superintendent was called, or looks in vain for a timeline that defines when they might see something different.

Systemic change requires public relations not to communicate *to* the public about it, but to *engage* the public in helping it to occur (e.g., Dozier, Grunig, & Grunig, 1995). This point is reinforced with a simple logic model. Systemic change requires public support. Public support requires that people understand what the change is and how it will affect them (Rogers, 1995). The development of understanding that leads to stakeholder support requires serious partnerships between the school district and its various publics. Through my experience as a school public relations consultant, I have learned that strong school-community partnerships are built using the tools of public relations: listening, communicating with stakeholders, engaging them in helping to make change and not just read about it, and reporting on progress so that stakeholders stay connected and invested.

USING THE TOOLS OF SCHOOL PUBLIC RELATIONS

Listening

Whether change leaders are ready to launch an effort to institute systemic change or if they are in the middle of what feels unhappily like the perfect storm, they should devise ways to hear from their stakeholders. If they are at the beginning stages of whole-district change, they need to be sure they understand the changes they are proposing and that they can describe how they intend to make those changes happen. They also have to be able to describe the *what* and the *how* with enough clarity that any 10th-grade student in their school system can understand what they are saying. They might even try delivering their message of change without using the words "systemic change."

Change leaders' communications about whole-system change can start small over a cup of coffee with the mayor and other influential people in the community, then move to conversations with small groups of staff and community members, and then on to more structured Community Engagement Conference (Duffy, 2003). When engaging stakeholders in conversations about change plans, change leaders can use a broad, open-ended question such as "What should we do to make sure that our students can realize their dreams when they graduate?" Next, they could introduce or test their personal answers to this question as part of the overall discussion.

Another communications strategy is to ask gathered stakeholders to respond to a bulleted list of themes for improving their district. In presenting the themes, change leaders would also highlight how they intend to go about making those improvements. Then, they would invite their audience to react to the themes and the implementation strategies. Before adjourning the Community Engagement Conference, they would seek answers to the following question, "What will your role be?"(that is, the role of the stakeholders).

If change leaders are in the middle of a whole-district change effort, their conversation with stakeholders could start with a reminder of what the district is doing to improve and a progress report on the current status of that effort. They could also segment their stakeholder group into smaller groups and then use surveys to probe their opinions and garner feedback for each change initiative that the district is pursuing. In communicating about ongoing improvements, they would also devote time to learning whether stakeholders see the connections among different initiatives and to identifying and communicating about how student achievement is impacted by the changes.

Communicating with Stakeholders

The defining attributes of communication focusing on systemic change should be focus and clarity. Short sermons on the need for focus and clarity show up so often in journal essays that readers might think those of us warbling about communication would sing another song. I would change my tune if I heard a new story in focus groups with parents and teachers, but the story line remains pretty much the same. A teacher looking for focus from her school district says, "There's not enough time to get good at something. We cannot say no to the newest new thing." A parent expecting more clarity says, "My challenge is the learning objectives and the grading system. I'm confused about what students are expected to achieve."

Keeping the focus on the outcomes of an improvement effort requires the brain-stretching skill of seeing how other aspects of a school system, particularly the changes that are being made, are affecting student achievement. This kind of thinking is one element of systems thinking. With good fortune, careful hiring, or deliberate practice, a school district will have a few educators who can visualize their system as a whole entity, see how the pieces fit together, and, better yet, describe the fit. In my experience as a school public relations consultant, this capability is either relatively rare or not used.

Experienced systems thinkers, capable of connecting the pieces of their school system in their minds, can envision endless new initiatives to improve their systems. But resources are finite, opportunities to communicate are precious, and attention spans are short. Therefore, change leaders need to communicate what their district's top priorities are so they can then invest their district's resources on those top priority improvements.

Investing district resources on top priority improvements, however, is easier said than done. Everyone in a school district believes that what he or she is doing counts; stakeholders want to see publicity for their program, their school, their employee of the month, their fund-raiser, their sports team, their honor roll, their grant, their neglected department, or their underappreciated staff. Change leaders can get hopelessly muddled trying to see that everyone gets what he or she needs and they can generate substantial undifferentiated "noise" as people complain about what they are not getting, or complain about what others are getting. Communicating effectively about the priorities, the limited resources, and about how those resources need to be invested to support a district's grand vision and strategic direction will help reduce this "noise."

It should not be that hard to write and speak in words the public can understand, but clearly it is a hurdle for some administrators. Taking a page from Ernest Boyer (in Jackson, 2002) who once described reading as unlocking "frozen thought," my experience tells me that the "frozen thought" is one reason for this hurdle. For example, some educators may not know enough about the changes their district is making and they ad lib their communication about those improvements. Other educators may know too much about the changes and they overwhelm their audience with details. Other educators may fear what might happen if they do communicate clearly about the changes, so they obfuscate by hiding the truth in big words or complex manifestos.

One of the easiest ways to ensure that communications about systemic change are clear is to provide some key administrator in a school district with the authority to keep saying, "I'm not sure what you mean." This role often falls to the official communicator who has less face to lose by such an admission.

Engaging Stakeholders in Making Change

Stakeholders' engagement in a district's improvement effort can be supplemented by newsletters, websites, occasional essays in a local paper, and presentations at a PTA meeting. These media are manageable and offer a tangible form of communication. Depending on the frequency and clarity of communication, these media (and other similar activities) can offer efficient ways to inform stakeholders about systemic change in their district. Informing stakeholders, however, does not guarantee their understanding, support, or even that they will read or listen carefully to the message. Stakeholders will *buy in* when they are *brought in*—into the conversation, into the planning, into the decision making, and into the implementation.

In my experience, engaging stakeholders in a district's systemic change process is one key to creating and sustaining improvement. The hard work here is not just identifying the opportunities for their involvement but coordinating the opportunities that are developed at the district and school levels. Teachers, parents, and community members want to know that their investment of time is well spent, and that they are not duplicating efforts elsewhere or worse, creating contradictions in the system. As one superintendent once told me, "The district is like a flotilla. The goal is to steam forward. Within the flotilla there are battle groups represented by schools and support services. We all want to arrive at the same place. We try to stay together in general formation, but if individual members have to take different paths to avoid submarines, that is okay. We know where we are headed and we will show up there."

If possible, change leaders should appoint someone in their district who is blessed with both "big-picture" capacity and the ability to attend to details to oversee their district's community engagement efforts. In the more likely event that no one person with both capabilities works in a district, change leaders can charter and train a team to map existing community engagement strategies, identify new areas for stakeholder involvement, and devise creative and effective ways to monitor the progress of their district's improvement effort.

Reporting Progress

I always appreciate the maps in airports and amusement parks that include the arrow and the message "You are here." I need that help in establishing my location in foreign territory. In a collaborative effort to improve a school system, what was once familiar and navigable terrain (e.g., our classrooms look like this, the report cards look like this, the calendar looks like this) may start to appear like foreign territory. An important tool of public relations, therefore, to help people navigate this unfamiliar ground is a progress report that lays out in a clear and detailed way information that can be categorized as "we were here, we have made it this far, this is where we need to go."

Progress reports take many forms: print, presentation, conversation, delivered in mailboxes, e-mail, regular meetings, and special meetings. Reports should be frequent enough that readers and listeners can remember the primary initiatives in the change process so that major change goals and objectives do not appear new every time they are presented. Another advantage of using progress reports is that when change leaders create and publicize a timeline for those reports, the timeline motivates people to get things done; for example, "We've got to get this done because we have to write about it for our annual report."

CONCLUSION

Using the tools of public relations will not make the life of a change leader any less challenging, but their communications will be more purposeful, and over time, more productive. The rewards of effective school public relations come at each step in a district's improvement process as educators move from "We get it" to "We want it" to "Look how we've changed!" And communicating effectively during times of great change can support the achievement of a district's ultimate improvement goal—that is, creating unparalleled opportunities to improve student, teacher, and system learning (Duffy, 2002).

REFERENCES

Dozier, D. M., Grunig, L., & Grunig, J. E. (1995). *A manager's guide to excellence in public relations and communications management.* Mahwah, NJ: Lawrence Erlbaum.

Duffy, F. M. (2002). *Step-Up-To-Excellence: An innovative approach to managing and rewarding performance in school systems.* Lanham, MD: ScarecrowEducation.

Duffy, F. M. (2003). *Courage, passion and vision: A guide to leading systemic school improvement.* Lanham, MD: ScarecrowEducation/American Association of School Administrators.

Educational Testing Service. (2001). A measured response: Americans speak on education reform. Retrieved on September 18, 2003, from http://www.ets.org/aboutets/americaspeaks/survey2001.html

Jackson, Y. (2002, December). Comprehension and discipline literacy: The key to high school achievement. Retrieved on September 25, 2003, from http://www.newhorizons.org/strategies/literacy/jackson.htm

Public Agenda. (2003). Where we are now: 12 things you need to know about public opinion and public schools. Retrieved on September 15, 2003, from http://www.publicagenda.org

Rogers, E. M. (1995). *The diffusion of innovations.* New York: Free Press.

ENDNOTES

1. Ms. Soholt's essay first appeared as Soholt, S. (2003). Bringing order out of chaos: The role of school public relations. *Journal of School Public Relations, 24*(4), 285–293. Reprinted with permission.

ABOUT THE AUTHOR

Sylvia Soholt, a consultant with KSA-Plus, works with schools, school districts, state departments of education, and educational foundations to build support for high-quality public schools. Her work in public engagement has been profiled in *Education Week,* the *Journal of Staff Development,* the *American School Board Journal,* and *Educational Leadership.* She may be reached at KSA-Plus Communications, Seattle, 10515 SW Cemetery Road, Vashon Island, WA 98070, or (phone) 206-463-5599 or (fax) 206-463-2096 or at sylvia@ksaplus.com.

ESSAY 5

Community Involvement in Decatur's Journey Toward Excellence[1]

Sunnie Lee
Charles M. Reigeluth

Community involvement is crucial for systemic change to be successful in school districts. Without community members' approval and dedication to change, change efforts in school districts are not likely to succeed. The community has a direct and ongoing influence on its schools, and is connected by high intensity interactions (Banathy, 1992). Hence, as Duffy, Rogerson, and Blick (2000) and Reigeluth (1993) point out, community involvement is crucial for generating grassroots political support for whole-system change among respected parents, business leaders, and other community leaders.

To understand the importance of community involvement and what it should be like, it is helpful to reflect on the nature of systemic change. The term "systemic change" is used with different meanings by different people. Using it in the sense of Squire and Reigeluth's (2000) "ecological systemic change," it is an alternative to piecemeal change, which is the dominant paradigm for improving schooling. Ecological systemic change, which views school districts as whole systems, also provides a means by which educators and community members can experience an evolution of their mental models for what constitutes a "quality education" for their school system. Further, ecological systemic change requires this kind of mind shift in many people, both within and outside a school district. If only a small group of change leaders in a community transcends the traditional mind-set about what constitutes a "real school" (Tyack & Cuban, 1995), the rest of the community may resist whole-system change. Only through broad community involvement can a "critical mass" of like-minded people evolve to support a fundamental change in a school district's paradigm for defining what a quality education means for that district. Therefore, we believe that changing mental models through broad community involvement is one of the fundamental requirements for systemic change efforts in school districts.

Despite the importance of engaging external stakeholders in redefining what a quality education means for their school system, there is not much evidence suggesting that they are involved as much as they should be in most school district change efforts. Community members are generally the least represented stakeholder group when districtwide change initiatives are planned, partly because of educators' attitudes resisting the involvement of outside people but also because of the challenges of recruiting and selecting community members.

However, in a number of whole-system change efforts that have taken place, we see that community involvement can be a powerful driving force for smooth and successful systemic change efforts. A small school district in Indianapolis, called the Metropolitan School District of Decatur Township, is a good example. This essay describes Decatur's systemic change effort and the community's involvement in it. In addition, the essay provides some reflections and recommendations that emerged from involving the community members in the change process.

THE METROPOLITAN SCHOOL DISTRICT OF DECATUR TOWNSHIP

The Metropolitan School District (MSD) of Decatur Township is one of 11 public school corporations in Marion County, Indiana, and is located in the southwest corner of Indianapolis. Decatur's roughly 5,600 students attend the school corporation's Early Childhood Center, four elementary schools, two intermediate schools, a middle school, and a high school. That total enrollment is served by approximately 380 full-time teachers, 35 administrators, and 270 nonteaching staff members. According to the National Center for Education Statistics, Decatur's percentage of students receiving free/reduced lunches and textbooks for the 2003–2004 school year was about 42 percent, eclipsing the state average.

The majority of the Decatur students are from the Camby, West Newton, Valley Mills, Mars Hill, and Seerly Creek neighborhoods. Along with these students, the school system's enrollment includes African American students from the Indianapolis neighborhood of Mapleton-Fall Creek. Its students are bused to and from Decatur Township under a federal court order intended to desegregate the Indianapolis Public School System, but the busing program is now being phased out. These Mapleton-Fall Creek students make up most of the school corporation's minority population. About 80% of Decatur's student body is white, 10% African American, 5% Hispanic, and 1% each Asian and Native American students.

The Decatur Township is a growing community. The school corporation has been working on a construction/renovation project to meet the needs of the burgeoning population. The project has built two new intermediate schools and has carried out extensive renovations at the elementary schools. The school corporation is currently working on another construction/renovation project for the high school, which is in need of remodeling and expansion.

DECATUR'S DISTRICTWIDE "JOURNEY TOWARD EXCELLENCE"

In addition to its building and renovation program, the school corporation is collaborating with facilitators at Indiana University to work on a districtwide systemic change effort, called the Journey Toward Excellence. This change effort strives to transform the schools to better meet each individual student's needs and help each individual student reach his or her potential. Community members have been actively involved in this effort from the very beginning.

The systemic change effort is well timed for the school district because Decatur Township is now far into evolving from a heavy concentration of farming and somewhat rural characteristics to being more of an industrial and commercial locale. Much of that transformation results from the development of AmeriPlex, the state's largest business park. Decatur's Journey Toward Excellence is intended to address the resulting new educational needs of the community and new needs of information-age learners. The purpose of this journey is to transform the schools in the district into learning communities where all stakeholders are empowered to achieve excellence.

The following is a brief introduction to the vision, ideal beliefs, and process principles of the Journey Toward Excellence. These were formed during a two-year period by a Leadership Team with input and suggestions of numerous community members and other stakeholder groups in the township who were gathered together during events described later in this essay.

The vision for the school system is:

- An information-age school corporation that is committed to being learner centered;
- A focus on learning and continuous personal growth is promoted in a safe, respectful, and caring environment characterized by high expectations;
- Learning communities are the means to fostering collaboration and empowerment; and,
- Assessments, interventions, and accommodations are used to meet the academic, social, emotional, physical, and developmental needs of all learners.

The ideal beliefs that support this vision are:

- *Learning:* We believe a focus on learning must be part of the culture of our school community because learning is a community responsibility;
- *Learning Environment:* We believe the school must provide a welcoming, safe, productive, learner-centered environment for learning to occur. This nurturing climate will foster trust and high expectations;
- *Assessment:* We believe assessment must be used to guide the learning process to meet individual student needs rather than to compare students;
- *The Learning Community:* We believe the relationship between the school and the larger community must be an interdependent one because students learn in both settings; and,

- *Professional Development:* We believe that professional development is important to provide all stakeholders with the skills to improve student learning.

Some of the most important process principles that underlie this journey include:

- As many stakeholders as possible should be involved (Banathy, 1991);
- The stakeholders collectively should have ownership over both the change process and the changes that are decided upon;
- The change process should focus on student learning and development—all changes should be designed with that in mind;
- The change process is first and foremost a process of helping people to evolve and deepen their thinking about education, to help them evolve their mental models about education (Senge, 2000) and to thereby evolve the culture of their schools (Fullan, 2001); and,
- The process should encourage all participants to think in the ideal, and to then develop a strategic plan for evolving as close as possible to that ideal (Ackoff, 1981).

The above underlying process principles for Decatur's Journey Toward Excellence show how the school district is dedicated to involving the community in its systemic change effort. There are three levels at which community members have participated in the change effort:

- *Level 1: One-way communication*—the first level of community involvement is one-way communication, where community members are mainly receiving information from the school district about how the change effort has been proceeding.
- *Level 2: Two-way communication*—the second level is two-way communication, where community members give input and feedback on the change process and the prospective changes, in addition to receiving information from the school district.
- *Level 3: Change-team member*—the third level is as a change-

team member, where community members participate as active team members on one of the many change teams (see Figure E5.1).

These three levels of community involvement are illustrated in the following section, which describes the major events in which community members are involved in Decatur's Journey Toward Excellence.

EVENTS WITH COMMUNITY INVOLVEMENT

There have been seven large "events" so far in the Journey Toward Excellence in which community members have participated actively. These events in chronological order are:

- the Starter Team effort
- community forums on educational needs
- the Leadership Team effort
- a community meeting on the Framework
- community forums on the Framework
- the Ownership Committee effort, and
- the School Assessment Team effort

Along with the above seven events which have already occurred, an eighth event will be taking place very soon and will also involve com-

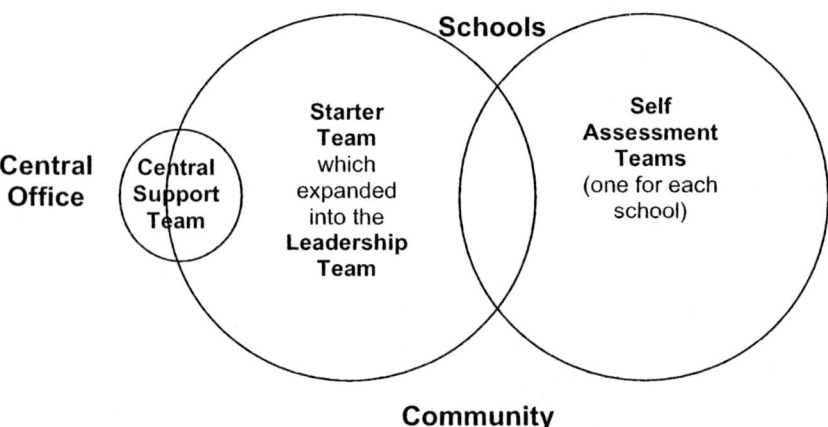

Figure E5.1. View of teams in the Journey Toward Excellence

munity members in the Journey Toward Excellence. This event is the "Design Team Work" event.

In this section, we describe each of the above seven events using four criteria: (1) level of community involvement, (2) how the community members became involved, (3) how community members were prepared and trained to participate, and (4) what kind of role community members played. The three levels of community member involvement are also highlighted.

The Starter-Team Effort

The five-member Starter Team was created at the beginning of the Journey Toward Excellence. Its purpose was to create an organization culture to support systemic change and to develop the system's capacity for that kind of change. Changing the culture in this way and developing capacity for systemic change helped lay the foundation for the Leadership Team that was formed later in the journey. A community member was recruited to serve as one of the five members of the Starter Team.

- *Community member's level of involvement:* Level 3, participating as a change-team member.
- *Recruitment.* The community member on the Starter Team was selected from among the PTA/PTO leaders. The other members of the Starter Team included the superintendent, a board member, a principal, and the head of the teachers association.
- *Preparation and training.* The Starter Team participated in many 2-hour meetings and several 1- and 2-day retreats to understand information-age educational needs, systems thinking, developmental leadership, the systemic change process, and how to work as a learning community. The notion of an ongoing learning community was especially emphasized so that the Starter Team could evolve later into the Leadership Team.
- *Role of community member.* The role of the community member on the Starter Team was the same as for all other members of that team—that is, to contribute ideas about the district's vision and to identify needs for the various schools within the system. The

community member was also expected to contribute to the development of the Starter Team's culture by helping the team become a learning community that understood information-age educational needs, systems thinking, developmental leadership, and the change process. The Starter Team members communicated their progress with other members of their respective stakeholder groups and continually worked to prepare for their evolution into a Leadership Team.

Community Forums on Educational Needs

To get many stakeholders involved in the Journey Toward Excellence, the Starter Team held six widely publicized meetings at different schools between January and April 2002. These were among the biggest and most influential events designed to engage community members in the district's Journey Toward Excellence. The purpose of these community meetings was to begin building broader stakeholder understanding of the need for and nature of systemic change and to broaden stakeholder participation in and commitment to the change process. This was done by asking forum participants to identify the current (information-age) educational needs of the Decatur Township students and community and see how they had changed over the past 25 years or so.

- *Community member's level of involvement:* Level 2, two-way communication.
- *Recruitment.* Open invitations were sent to all students' homes and flyers were distributed to encourage other community members' involvement. Approximately 20 participants attended each community forum (one forum in each school).
- *Preparation and training.* The community members were not prepared or trained in any way for these forums.
- *Role of community member.* The community members who attended the community forums first received some information on societal change (the transition from the industrial age to the information age). Then, they were asked to discuss four issues—not to reach consensus on them, but to understand why others believed

what they did so that they could become more receptive to others' thinking. The issues included: (1) how society and Decatur Township in particular have changed, (2) how the community should change, (3) what skills and personal qualities students must acquire to succeed in the future, and (4) how Decatur Township schools are doing now in providing those important skills and qualities. Community members provided valuable input that was reported in a newspaper article and the school district newsletter. This input was used later by the Leadership Team. The following is a summary of the community members' contributions during the meetings.

The participants agreed that the workplace had changed by having more service-related jobs that require more teamwork and more use of information technology. Participants also talked about longer commutes, greater workload, more job stress, and less job security. In terms of family, they concluded that the family has changed by having more single-parent households and two-working-parent homes, less family time, and that more parents want to be friends to their children instead of parents. Participants also identified the skills and personal qualities that their children will need to be successful members of their community; these included problem-solving, time-management, teamwork, conflict resolution, communication, and computer skills. Personal qualities included integrity; work ethic; responsibility; creativity; desire to balance family, faith, and work; respect for differences in others; passion for something positive; desire to learn; and service orientation.

The Leadership Team Effort

The Leadership Team was formed in February 2003. It is a large team (25–30 members) of opinion leaders representing the school system's stakeholder groups. Its primary purpose is to provide political support for the systemic change process and the resulting systemic changes. Therefore, consensus building and evolution of members' mind-sets were paramount. The first task of the Leadership Team was to develop, with input from many stakeholders, a districtwide "Framework of Vision, Mission, and Ideal Beliefs" about education. Beyond that, this team shepherds the systemic change process, builds broader ownership of the Framework, builds central office capacity to support systemic change in the district's schools, helps the schools to enhance their stakeholders' readiness for systemic change, and helps the schools engage in redesigning and transforming themselves.

- *Community member's level of involvement:* Level 3, participating as a change-team member.
- *Recruitment.* When the Starter Team expanded into the Leadership Team in February 2003, the community member on the Starter Team automatically became a member of the Leadership Team. Recognizing the importance of community involvement, the Starter Team then decided that half the Leadership Team members should be community members (who were not also working for the school district). Table E5.1 shows the community stakeholder groups identified by the Starter Team and the number of members they decided to recruit from each of those groups. Starter Team members recruited parent and other community leaders they knew might be interested in serving on the Leadership Team. While selection criteria were offered by the Indiana University facilitators and adapted by the Starter Team, there was little opportunity to use the selection criteria in a systematic way for community prospects because the challenge was to find anyone willing to devote sufficient time to the effort.

Periodically, a member would leave the Leadership Team, due mostly to competing demands on his or her time. New members were recruited in a fairly haphazard way. After a while, the Leadership Team established a formal process for recruiting and selecting new members, including new community members. The revised

Table E5.1. Number of community members by stakeholder group

Parents	4
Business	2
Clergy	2
Public Official	1
Fire Department	1
Lions Club, Civic Counsel, Senior Citizens	2
Youth Programs, Athletics, Boy/Girl Scouts	2
Dollars for Scholars	1

process calls for the Leadership Team to periodically monitor its membership to see if any stakeholder groups are underrepresented. Then, they reach consensus on how many members to add for each stakeholder group. The Leadership Team prepares a list with about three times more people than are needed. The selection criteria they use include: respected by peers, open-minded, flexible, and the lack of strong interpersonal conflicts. The Leadership Team discusses the candidates using their selection criteria to reach consensus on whom to invite to join the team. A Leadership Team member meets personally with each person invited. The purpose of this meeting is to encourage the invited community members to join the Leadership Team.

- *Preparation and training.* In lieu of a 2-day retreat, the Leadership Team devoted most of its first five 2-hour meetings to train on topics such as: (1) team-building activities, (2) guiding principles for the systemic change process (for example, developmental leadership, stakeholder empowerment, collaboration, consensus building, trust, disclosure, team learning), (3) what systemic change is and why it is needed, (4) the differences between the information age and the industrial age, and the educational implications of those differences, (5) the learning-focused paradigm of education and how it differs from the sorting-focused paradigm, (6) Decatur's systemic change process (the Journey Toward Excellence), and (7) systems thinking and the four other disciplines of a learning organization (Senge, 2000). As new members are brought on, they go through a 1-day workshop to catch them up on these topics. Furthermore, a retreat is held every summer to further the team's knowledge and capacity to lead the Journey Toward Excellence.

- *Role of community member.* The role of community members on the Leadership Team is identical to that of all other members. Community members have contributed equally to all the tasks of the team, such as developing the districtwide "Framework of Vision, Mission, and Beliefs," building broad ownership of the beliefs, planning to form a Central Support Team (central office administrators who will support the schools in their attempts to redesign themselves), and planning to form a School Assessment

Team in each school. They also periodically identify and invite new members to the team and constantly endeavor to work effectively as a learning community.

Community Meeting on the Framework

The Leadership Team conducted a community meeting in October 2004 to obtain broader community input on and ownership of the first draft of the districtwide "Framework of Vision, Mission, and Beliefs" that the Leadership Team had been developing for about a year. A brief presentation was given on the Framework, followed by small-group discussions of the Framework facilitated by a Leadership Team member. Important changes were made to the Framework as a result of this meeting.

- *Community member's level of involvement:* Level 2, two-way communication.
- *Recruitment.* The Leadership Team sent out invitations to all community members, school faculty, and staff through flyers and the township newsletter. Approximately 70 participants attended, about one-quarter of whom were community members who were not employed by the school district.
- *Preparation and training.* The community members were not prepared or trained in any way for this meeting.
- *Role of community member.* The community members played the same role as all other participants in the meeting. They received information on the Framework; discussed the vision, mission, and ideal beliefs in small, heterogeneous groups with members of other stakeholder groups; and contributed their thoughts, feedback, and suggestions on the Framework. Some community members participated as recorders who reported out to the large group on the results of their discussions.

Community Forums on the Framework

After the Leadership Team finalized the Framework, community forums were held to publicize and build community ownership of the

Framework. Forums were first held in each of the schools for teachers, administrators, and staff because they felt it was important for these people to be informed about the Framework before the parents were. Then other forums were held for community members in various schools throughout the district and at the local Lions Club. These forums were scheduled during fall 2005 and in February 2006.

- *Community member's level of involvement:* Level 2, two-way communication.
- *Recruitment.* The Leadership Team and each of the schools publicized these forums. Open invitations were sent to all students' homes and flyers were distributed widely for other community members' involvement.
- *Preparation and training.* The community members were not prepared or trained in any way for these forums.
- *Role of community members.* The community members who attended the forums received information on the ideal beliefs that the Leadership Team had finalized earlier in the process. Community members were asked if they agreed with these statements and were asked to support the beliefs.

The Ownership Committee Effort

The Leadership Team formed several subcommittees in January 2005 to work on different aspects of the systemic change process. The Ownership Committee worked on promoting ownership of the Framework and the change effort throughout the Decatur schools and community.

- *Community member's level of involvement:* Level 1, one-way communication, and Level 2, two-way communication.
- *Recruitment.* To increase stakeholder involvement and support from the community, the Ownership Committee printed flyers and posters for schools and classrooms and sent these out to the community through school newspapers, newsletters, and lunch notes. In addition, the Ownership Committee is currently organizing more community forums to publicize the district's beliefs. They

held one forum in the Mapleton-Fall Creek community in August 2005 and two districtwide community forums in late March 2006. Additional school-based community forums are being planned. For these forums, open invitations are issued to all community members through notes, newsletter, newspaper announcements, and personal invitations.
- *Preparation and training.* The community members were not prepared or trained in any way for these one- and two-way communications.
- *Role of community members.* Through the fliers, newsletters, and lunch notes, the community members received some information on the districtwide Framework and thoughts on the new paradigm of education and the systemic change process. The Ownership Committee provided a short glossary along with the fliers on the Framework to help community members easily understand the Framework. Community members were invited to contact the school district with any input they had to offer. The presentations made at the community forums are always accompanied by small-group discussions and input is taken back to the Ownership Committee and the Leadership Team. In general, the participants were pleased that the schools were changing and expressed that they wanted to be a part of it.

The School Assessment Team Effort

The Leadership Team charged the Central Support Team, which is made up of all the central office administrators, with the formation and preparation of the School Assessment Teams. These teams are responsible for assessing and enhancing the readiness of their respective schools to transform them to conform to the district's learner-centered paradigm of education. Later, each of those teams will guide the formation of a Design Team for its school to design, implement, and improve its learner-centered paradigm. Each School Assessment Team has at least four members: the principal, a teacher, a staff member, and a parent. These teams are currently collecting and analyzing data about their respective schools' readiness.

- *Community member's level of involvement:* Level 3, team member, and Level 2, two-way communication.
- *Recruitment.* Because community readiness for systemic change is an important part of school readiness for change, community member involvement on each School Assessment Team is particularly important. Each school's PTA or PTO was asked to find someone to serve on its school's assessment team. Furthermore, the assessment teams asked parents and community members to participate through online surveys and paper surveys that were sent home.
- *Preparation and training.* The Central Support Team held workshops for the School Assessment Teams. At the first workshop, five topics were addressed: (1) education in the information-age and the learner-centered paradigm of education, (2) the systemic change process, (3) the districtwide Framework of Vision, Mission, and Ideal Beliefs for the Journey Toward Excellence, (4) team formation and group process, and (5) data-collection planning. The second workshop will address criteria for readiness and planning to enhance readiness.
- *Role of community members.* All community members on a School Assessment Team have the same role—that is, helping to plan and conduct the assessment of their school's readiness for systemic change and to help plan and conduct any readiness enhancement activities that are warranted. Other community members provide input through the survey and through community forums and conversations that will take place.

Design Team Work (This Will Begin in the Near Future)

The next major event in which community members will be involved will be the design of a new paradigm of education in each school within the district and which must be aligned with the broad parameters of the districtwide Framework. There will likely be two community members on each Design Team, each with about 10 members. All members will have equal voice and similar roles. Furthermore, much input will be sought from other community members and all other stakeholders.

REFLECTIONS ON COMMUNITY INVOLVEMENT

In this section, we reflect on the many experiences with community involvement in the systemic change journey described above. What were some of the challenges? What were the strengths that we observed? And what could have been done better? These reflections are based on discussions in the Decatur Support Team (which is composed of the university-based facilitators) at Indiana University, which meets weekly to review what happened that week in the district, figure out how it might have been done better, and plan advice about next steps for the Leadership Team's consideration.

Challenges

We observed various challenges in having community involvement in systemic change. Perhaps the most fundamental challenge was helping community members to change their mind-sets about being involved. Community members were reluctant to participate in the change effort because they thought they did not know enough or that their opinions did not matter and would not be taken seriously. They needed to be convinced that their voices would be taken seriously and that their input would be valuable for the school corporation to move forward toward a more effective and humane system.

A related challenge for community involvement was the difficulty of recruiting and selecting members from the community. There was not much communication between the schools in the district, and community members and parents were typically not very involved in their schools' activities and decision making. A major reason for this appeared to be lack of time rather than lack of interest. This made the recruitment and selection of community members difficult. Furthermore, if a child is close to graduating from one school and will soon move into another school, parents are less likely to get involved on a leadership team for the school they are leaving. Also, since the intermediate schools and the middle school are all 2-year schools (grades 5–6 and 7–8, respectively), parents are likely to leave a school team before it finishes its work. The training and preparation of community members was also a challenge primarily because of competing demands on their time.

Strengths

However, in spite of the above challenges, the Indiana University facilitators (the Decatur Support Team) and the most active change leaders in the district felt that the community members who participated in the journey activities were more invested than many of the staff, administrators, and teachers on the teams. Community members' ability to use systems thinking, to honor the guiding principles of the change process, and to think "outside the box" (that is, to transcend their current paradigm of education) was generally impressive. They frequently set a good example for the other team members. This may be because staff, administrators, and teachers participated in the journey because it was part of their work responsibilities, while the community members participated because of their dedication to the goals of the transformation journey. It is also often easier for an outsider to think outside the box. Finally, community members may have been exposed to systems thinking in their workplace, which may have made it easier for them to participate effectively in journey activities.

How the Change Process Can Be Improved

Decatur's experiences with community involvement also show that several things could be improved in Decatur's Journey Toward Excellence or in other school district change efforts. One improvement is to ensure that each leadership team is transformed into a "learning community." While to date little time has been devoted to developing the teams into learning communities, the community members on the teams showed they were willing to learn new ideas, school culture, and language in order to move the change process forward. The major obstacle to their participation was their lack of time. A promising approach might be for a team's learning activities to be organized around the tasks in which the team is engaged using the just-in-time training philosophy.

Second, community involvement could be broadened by creating additional tasks for which community members could volunteer. This could also generate more learning communities. Such grassroots involvement could be enhanced through broader dissemination of information to community members about the systemic change effort. However, all this would require more management and coordination of the change process, and time is again an obstacle. External funding to buy some of the participant's time from their employers would be a big help for overcoming this obstacle.

A third area for improvement is learning how to increase word-of-mouth commentary about the success of the transformation journey. It is important to recognize the power of community members going back to their neighborhoods and talking to other people about the changes they are helping to create. Sharing new ideas, visions, and future directions for a school district's community is a powerful part of systemic change. Community members should be encouraged to acknowledge this responsibility and share their thinking and progress with others more often. Encouraging, nurturing, and educating others may also enhance the sustainability of community involvement over the long period of the systemic change process.

CONCLUSION

In summary, this essay described the many forms of community involvement in the systemic change effort in the Metropolitan School District of Decatur Township, Indiana. In addition, the essay provided some reflections and recommendations that emerged from the process of involving selected community members. Community members are usually the least represented stakeholder group in educational change efforts. Yet, in order to succeed in fundamentally changing in school systems, it is vital to build grassroots community support for these changes. Our experience in the Decatur Township school system showed that it is important to harness the power of building stakeholder ownership and helping community members to engage in learning communities.

REFERENCES

Ackoff, R. L. (1981). *Creating the corporate future.* New York: John Wiley & Sons.

Banathy, B. H. (1991). *Systems design of education: A journey to create the future.* Englewood Cliffs, NJ: Educational Technology.

Banathy, B. H. (1992). The prime imperative: Building a design culture. *Educational Technology, 32*(6), 33–35.

Duffy, F. M., Rogerson, L. G., & Blick, C. (2000). *Redesigning America's schools: A systems approach to improvement.* Norwood, MA: Christopher-Gordon.

Fullan, M. (2001). *Leading in a culture of change.* San Francisco: Jossey-Bass.

Reigeluth, C. M. (1993). Principles of educational systems design. *International Journal of Educational Research, 19*(2), 117–131.

Senge, P. M. (2000). *Schools that learn: A fifth discipline fieldbook for educators, parents, and everyone who cares about education.* New York: Doubleday.

Squire, K. D., & Reigeluth, C. M. (2000). The many faces of systemic change. *Educational Horizons, 78*(3), 145–154.

Tyack, D. B., & Cuban, L. (1995). *Tinkering toward utopia: A century of public school reform.* Cambridge, MA: Harvard University Press.

ENDNOTES

1. We are grateful to Kurt Richter, a co-facilitator for Decatur's systemic change effort, for his input on this essay.

ABOUT THE AUTHORS

Sunnie Lee has a bachelor's degree in educational technology from Ewha Womans University and a master's degree in instructional systems technology from Indiana University. She is currently a doctoral student at Indiana University pursuing research in systemic change in education and instructional design. She has done instructional design for such companies as McDonald's, Walgreens, and Accenture as a contractor with WisdomTools, Inc. She was an instructional designer for Solvit Media, Inc. prior to coming to Indiana University. She was also a high school teacher of English in Seoul, South Korea.

Charles M. Reigeluth has a B.A. in economics from Harvard University and a Ph.D. in instructional psychology from Brigham Young University. He taught high school science for three years. He has been a professor in the Instructional Systems Technology Department at Indiana University since 1988, and was chairman of the department for three years. He cofounded the Division for Systemic Change in the Association for Educational Communication and Technology (AECT) and founded the Restructuring Support Service at Indiana University. He has worked with several school districts to facilitate their change efforts. He served on the Indiana Department of Education Restructuring Task Force and proposal review team, and he advised several of the six pilot schools on how to conduct systemic change. He has been facilitating a systemic change effort in a small school district in Indianapolis since January 2001, and is using that as an opportunity to advance knowledge about how to help public school districts transform themselves into a learner-centered paradigm of education.

Epilogue: Communicating in Times of Great Change

Strategic communication is like glue—it can hold things together; the lack of strategic communication is like solvent—it can dissolve the connections between and among people. Transformational change in school districts needs glue, not solvent, because when change leaders work to transform their entire school district they need ways to bind people together in support of their district's new grand vision and strategic direction.

The people that need to be bound together in support of a district's new vision and strategic direction are not just the folks who work in the district. People in the community need to coalesce in support of a district's change efforts too. These people, often called external stakeholders in the literature on change, need to be involved in setting a course for their community's school district in ways that are authentic, valued, and meaningful.

The traditional tools of school public relations, of course, are useful for building political support for change, both inside and outside a school district (see chapter 9 for more about power, politics, and ethics in school districts). Some of these traditional tools include media kits, press releases, focus groups, and "town hall" gatherings. Advocacy kits, offered by organizations such as the Association for Supervision and Curriculum Development, offer advice and guidance on how to influence external stakeholders to support change efforts. None of these tools, however, should be considered as a succedaneum for strategic communication with stakeholders.

Strategic communication, as you learned in chapter 1, connects a school district's vision, mission, and strategic goals to the needs and aspirations of its community for educating children; this, in turn, creates significant support for the work that educators do in their school districts. Strategic communication also helps school systems and the people who work in those systems negotiate their roles in a community. They do this as they engage in authentic conversations about themselves and with external stakeholders about the meaning and value of education in our 21st-century society (see essays 1, 2, and 5 for more about engaging stakeholders). Strategic communication relies on responsible behavior on the part of change leaders and PR specialists in school districts to establish two-way communication so that the district can influence the opinions and behavior of key publics (employees, consumers, government, community, media), as well as to respond and adapt to the needs and aspirations of those publics.

Given the above definition of strategic communication, there are some innovative tools that change leaders can use to engage stakeholders as suggested above and as discussed in some of the essays in section 3 of this book. Although these tools were not originally designed as strategic communication tools, they are extraordinarily effective in producing desirable outcomes when engaging external and internal stakeholders in conversations about large-scale, whole-system improvement. These tools are the Community Engagement Conference, the System Engagement Conference, the Cluster Engagement Conference, and the Redesign Workshop, which are part of the change navigation protocol that was presented in chapter 4.

THE CHALLENGE OF WHOLE-DISTRICT TRANSFORMATION

In chapters 2 and 3, you learned that whole-district transformation is a complex but not impossible process. The Chugach School District in Anchorage, Alaska, one of the first two Baldrige Quality Award winners in education, stands as an example of successful transformation. Another successful example is the Franklin Special School District in Franklin, Tennessee. Another district currently engaged in whole-system change is the Metropolitan School District of Decatur Township in Indiana (see essay 5). Several other school districts that engaged in whole-system change were profiled in a study by the Learning First

Alliance titled "Beyond Islands of Excellence: What Districts Can Do to Improve Instruction and Achievement in All Schools" (Togneri & Anderson, 2003). These districts were the Aldine Independent School District, Texas; Chula Vista Elementary School District, California; Kent County Public Schools, Maryland; Minneapolis Public Schools, Minnesota; Providence Public Schools, Rhode Island; and San Diego Public Schools, California.

Of course, each of these districts has had different levels of success with its transformation; nevertheless, change leaders in each district had the courage, passion, and vision to engage their districts in whole-system change and to wrestle with the complex challenges of leading that kind of change. Several of the key challenges that all change leaders face are summarized below. These challenges expand upon the basic systems change concepts described in chapters 2 and 3.

ASSESSING THE EXTERNAL ENVIRONMENT

A school district, like other organizations, is an open system. As an open system, the quality and effectiveness of a district's relationship with its external environment is critical to the district's overall success and effectiveness. This vital relationship is even more central to a district's success during times of great change, because without the support of external stakeholders and without positive ways of responding to demanding societal pressures, the overall effectiveness of whole-system change is diminished at best and destroyed at worst.

The field of organization theory and design (for example, Daft, 2003) offers insights to the importance of improving an organization's relationships with its external environment. In chapters 2 and 3, we provided information about how systems function and why it's important to improve a school district as a whole system. An important element of a whole-system approach to improvement is to identify the characteristics of your district's external environment. So let's quickly examine some of the major characteristics of external environments and determine how these affect a school system.

There are four broad categories of external environments (Daft, 2003). These four categories are created by the intersection of two dimensions. The first dimension considers the relative stability of your district's environment. An external environment can be relatively stable (very little pressure for change) or relatively unstable (a lot of pressure for change). The second dimension identifies the relative complexity of your district's environment. An external environment can be relatively simple (a few key stakeholders, not a lot of professional issues or concerns) or it can be relatively complex (many key stakeholders, many professional issues or concerns). The intersection of these two dimensions creates four kinds of external environments: stable-simple, stable-complex, unstable-simple, and unstable-complex. The more complex and unstable the environment is, the higher the level of environmental uncertainty. Epilogue Figure 1.1 illustrates how these two dimensions create those four kinds of external environments.

When an organization exists inside a simple-stable (which has a low level of environmental uncertainty) or complex-stable environment (which has a low to moderate level of uncertainty), a mechanistic organization design is appropriate. A mechanistic design is characterized by hierarchy, bureaucracy, a centralized approach to management, and a lot of vertical strategic communication (that is, communicating up and down the chain of command). If an organization exists inside an simple-unstable (which has a moderate to high level of uncertainty) or an complex-unstable environment (which has a high level of uncertainty), it requires a different kind of organization design characterized as organic. An organic design requires less bureaucracy, more participation on the part of employees, a decentralized approach to management, and a lot of horizontal strategic communication (that is,

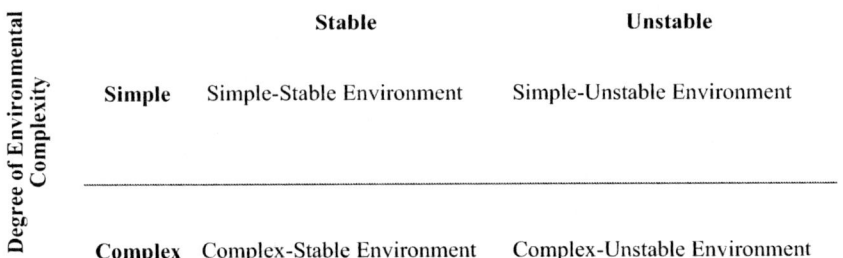

Epilogue, Figure 1.1. External environments

communication between and among teams, departments, and with external stakeholders).

In our opinion, many school systems throughout the United States exist within complex-unstable external environments. If you believe your district has this kind of external environment, your transformation effort must reconstruct your district's organization design to fit the requirements and demands of a complex-unstable external environment. The organization design of your school system is restructured, if necessary, during Step 1 of the change navigation protocol described in chapter 4. One of the key changes that needs to be made to improve the fit between your district's organization design and a complex-unstable environment must focus on reducing, but not eliminating, vertical strategic communication and increasing horizontal strategic communication.

VERTICAL AND HORIZONTAL STRATEGIC COMMUNICATION

Epilogue Figure 1.2 illustrates the flow of vertical and horizontal strategic communication in a school system. Because a child's educational experience is the cumulative effect of his or her interaction with all aspects of your district—curriculum and instruction, cafeteria services, bus services, administration and supervision, guidance counselors, and so on—every aspect of your school system must be vertically aligned to move your whole-school system toward its grand vision and strategic direction. In addition to being aligned with the district's grand vision, all these various pieces must be aligned to support each other (which is called horizontal alignment). It is ineffective and inefficient to have one element of your district working against another element of your district. Vertical and horizontal alignment requires improved vertical strategic communication and increased horizontal strategic communication.

Components of Effective Vertical Strategic Communication

Effective vertical strategic communication during times of great change has several components, each of which is essential. These are summarized below.

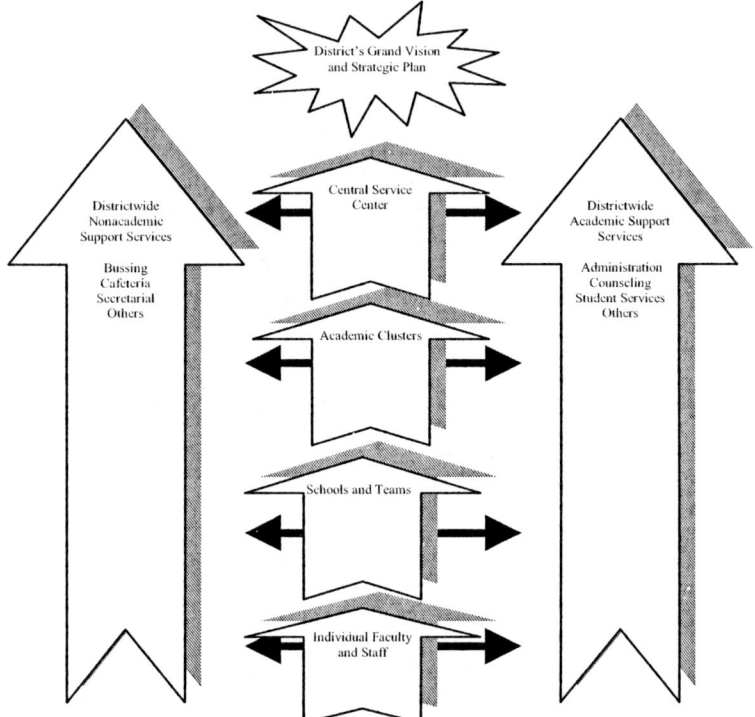

Epilogue, Figure 1.2. Vertical and horizontal strategic communication

Vision and mission. At the end of the Pre-Launch Preparation phase of the Step-Up-To-Excellence change protocol highlighted in chapter 4, your district's core purpose, mission, values, and goals are redefined. These strategic beacons become your district's North Star, guiding you along the three change paths identified in chapters 3 and 4: Path 1—improve a district's relationship with its external environment, Path 2—improve its core and supporting work processes, and Path 3—improve its internal social infrastructure. The strategic goals and objectives created to guide your district's journey toward its vision also serve as trail markers to ensure that everyone is headed in the same direction. The mission and vision provide the broad context for defining and appraising individual and team performance. Chapter 7 described a process for creating a shared vision of a desirable future for a school system.

Strategic plan. A strategic plan defines and communicates how your district's mission and vision will be achieved over time and thus provides direction to individual and team performance. Although a strategic plan is needed to set a course, please remember that whole-system change, as you learned in chapters 2 and 3, is not a sequential, linear process. In fact, it's quite nonlinear and chaotic—so do not assume that your strategic plan by itself will take you to your desired future.

Operating plans. Each school and supporting work unit in your district needs to create an operational plan that connects its work to the district's strategic framework that was developed in the System Engagement Conference at the end of the Pre-Launch Preparation phase of the change navigation protocol described in chapter 4. These plans need to be monitored so that the district creates strategic alignment.

A basic principle of strategic alignment is that the work of individuals must be aligned with the goals of their teams, the work of teams must be aligned with the goals of their schools, the work of schools must be aligned with the goals of their clusters, and the work of the clusters must be aligned with the district's vision and strategic goals. Team and individual planning is where these people align themselves with higher-level goals.

Team performance plans. All teams develop measurable performance objectives with their team leader and their building principals. These plans must be aligned with their work unit's goals. The information found in the individual performance plans, described next, is also found in the team plans, but modified to reflect team goals and performance expectations.

Individual performance plans. Each employee, working collaboratively with his or her team leader, principal, or supervisor, develops specific and measurable performance objectives that are aligned with his or her work unit's goals. These objectives define what results are to be achieved, how these results are to be achieved, what resources are needed to perform effectively, how the resources will be used, and how their performance is of service to internal and external customers.

Both vertical and horizontal communication require two-way communication channels because one-way communication is notoriously ineffective.

Two-way strategic communication programs. One of the key improvements made to your district during Step 1 of the Step-Up-To-Excellence change protocol described in chapter 4 is the redesign of your district's internal social infrastructure. You'll recall that social infrastructure refers to organization culture, climate, organization design, communication policies and procedures, informal norms, reward systems, and so on. One of the changes to your internal social infrastructure is the creation of a network of teams. A network of teams is especially important if your district has an external environment that is characterized as complex-unstable.

To make a network of teams effective, it is important to establish norms and procedures for two-way strategic communication. Your entire district, including the clusters, schools, and teams, should have a plan for two-way strategic communication with all of your employees about the district's direction, philosophy, values, policies and procedures, and performance. The strategic communication program should rely on multimedia approaches to communicating—for example, written memoranda, audiovisual presentations using media such as videotapes and PowerPoint presentations, and live, stand-up presentations by change leaders.

Feedback systems. Everyone, including administrators and supervisors, must receive regular performance feedback. Informal one-on-one sessions and team reviews provide for frequent two-way conversations about employee or team performance. Another element of vertical and horizontal strategic communication is your district's performance appraisal process, accountability requirements, and reward system. These elements of your district's internal social infrastructure have a significant effect on your district's overall performance, on individual and team motivation, and on job satisfaction.

Performance appraisals. Your district must have a system for fairly and consistently evaluating performance to determine how individuals and teams are aligning their work efforts to school, cluster, and district goals. Self-evaluation and peer evaluation should be part of this appraisal process.

Accountability measures. When you redesign your district's internal social infrastructure you want to create a web of accountabilities where everyone in the web is held accountable for aligning his or her work with established strategic goals. Positive consequences for creating and sustaining alignment should be embedded within your newly retooled reward system.

Reward systems. Your district retools its reward system during Step 1 of Step-Up-To-Excellence, described in chapter 4. Redesigning your reward system is one of the most important tasks for improving performance (Burke, 1982, p. 105). Your administrators, supervisors, and team leaders need systematic and effective ways of recognizing superior performance that is aligned with your district's vision and strategic framework. Then, effective value-added performance is rewarded using principles of intrinsic and extrinsic motivation.

Components of Effective Horizontal Strategic Communication

Daft (2001) describes the intent of horizontal communication. He said, "Horizontal communication overcomes barriers between departments and provides opportunities for coordination among employees to achieve unity of effort and organizational objectives. Horizontal linkage refers to the amount of communication and coordination horizontally across organizational departments" (p. 89).

Cross-functional information systems. One significant way to establish or improve horizontal strategic communication is to create a computerized information system that connects all of your district's clusters, schools, teams, and individuals. Sometimes this kind of system is called an "Intranet" because it works like the Internet, but it is designed for people working within an organization.

Face-to-face contact. Real-time contact with a person is a very powerful way to create and sustain horizontal strategic communication. Although this sounds like a reasonable idea in today's e-mail-driven world, it is often difficult for people to leave their computer and walk down the hall to talk face-to-face with someone. It is so much easier to tap out an e-mail and press the "send" button.

One formal and structured way that you can initiate face-to-face contact is for each cluster, school, and team in your district to designate one of their members as a formal liaison. Then, these liaisons make face-to-face contact with each other as required.

ASSESSING THE QUALITY OF DISCONTENT

The quality of discontent in a school system is a diagnostic clue indicating the relative success of the system's transformation. In less healthy organizations, people suffer from logorrhea about little things—low-order grumbles. These gripes are manifestations of what Maslow (in Farson, 1996, p. 93) called deficiency needs. In healthier organizations, people have high-order gripes that focus on more altruistic concerns. In very healthy organizations, people engage in metagripes—complaints about their need for self-actualization. When you start hearing metagripes, you know your system is moving in the right direction.

Low-order discontent does not invariably create a desire for change. Other factors have to be present. One of these is the willingness to use power and political skills in ethical ways (see chapter 9 for more about power, politics, and ethics in school districts). Those who stand in powerless awe of their situations do not think of change, no matter how miserable they are. When people believe they have no control over their work lives, they will tend to anchor themselves to their present situation, no matter how terrible it is. When stuck in situations like this, people establish routines that create the illusion that they have tamed the unpredictable.

Effective strategic communication during times of great change will tap into the discontent—the grumbles—in your school district. Assessing the quality of these grumbles will help you assess the progress of your transformation effort. This assessment starts during the Pre-Launch Preparation phase of the change navigation protocol described in chapter 4 and continues throughout the transformation journey.

INCREASING FACULTY AND STAFF PARTICIPATION

It's a fact: People tend to support that which they help create. Successful transformation will require, therefore, the significant and authentic participation of your faculty and staff. If you want to increase participation, you have to establish ground rules that reduce the fear of interacting within that democratic context. One example of a ground rule to reduce fear is found in Farson (1996, p. 78). He called it "conservation of resources." Here's how it works:

- Ask people in groups to identify their most valuable human resources.
- Once identified, discuss how to protect, enhance, and conserve those resources.
- This conversation reduces fear and creates a foundation for discussing more substantive issues related to the transformation of your district.
- Don't start talking about change until you lay down this foundation.

Although increased participation is important, to be effective it must be done correctly. For participation to be done correctly, people need to participate at the right time and in the right way using the right processes that will stimulate their creativity, motivation, and commitment. Most organizations, including school systems, overcommunicate through a mind-numbing series of meetings, memoranda, and e-mail. People suffer from mental overload when bombarded with too much communication. The first response to overload is to selectively ignore information perceived as unimportant or irrelevant. Subsequent responses to communication overload cause people literally to insulate themselves from all efforts to communicate with them.

While participation is important and needed and since too much communication can overload people's minds and stimulate dysfunctional responses to information, the Step-Up-To-Excellence methodology described in chapter 4 uses several change leadership teams to manage strategic communication. The teams are the Strategic Leadership Team, Cluster Improvement Teams, and Site Improvement Teams. These teams become communication filters; that is, they sort out what is important to consider and what is unimportant, and then they communicate important information to external and internal stakeholders. These teams are also the primary sources of strategic communication during a district's transformation journey.

In addition to the special leadership teams, Step-Up-To-Excellence also uses specially designed processes for involving internal and external stakeholders in your transformation process. These specially designed processes are the Community Engagement Conference, System Engagement Conference, Cluster Engagement Conference, Redesign Workshops, On-Track Seminars, and Organization Learning Networks, each of which was described in chapter 4.

A PARTING REFLECTION

In closing, please reflect on the words of Olive Schreiner (1883). Schreiner was a South African peace and antiapartheid activist. She lived from 1855–1920, and she wrote a book titled *The Story of a South African Farm*.

In the story, there is a character called "The Hunter." The hunter has spent his entire life on a quest to find the "white bird of absolute truth." As part of his quest, he built a stone stair into the sky in search of the "white bird."

There's a point in the story where the hunter is old, tired, and ready to abandon his quest and he says these words:

> My strength is gone. Where I lie down worn out, others will stand, young and fresh. By the steps that I have cut they will climb; by the stairs that I have built, they will mount. They will never know the name of the man who made them. At the clumsy work they will laugh; when the stones roll they will curse me. But they will mount, and on my work; they will climb, and by my stair!

That stair was the hunter's legacy. Your legacy as change leaders—your stair—will be a transformed school system. But building that stair will require your personal courage, passion, and vision. Your courage will help you stand your ground in the face of adversity; your passion will give you the emotional energy you need to persevere; your vision will be your district's North Star, guiding you toward a bright future.

If you are serious about leading the transformation of your school system, here's what you should do: On your first day back at work after reading this book, identify one person—just one—whom you think will be a superior ally. Call or e-mail that person and schedule a 15-minute meeting to talk about the idea of transforming your system.

During that meeting, make a commitment to each other to get the transformation journey underway. Identify others whom you would like to involve right away. Then, get started. Lead with courage, passion, and vision—and go build that "stair"!

REFERENCES

Association for Supervision and Curriculum Development. (n.d.). Advocacy Kit. Retrieved on April 12, 2005, from http://www.ascd.org/advocacykit/references.html

Burke, W. W. (1982). *Organization development: Principles and practices.* Boston: Little, Brown.

Daft, R. L. (2001). *Organization theory and design* (7th ed.). Cincinnati, OH: South-Western College Publishing.

Daft, R. L. (2003). *Organization theory and design* (8th ed.). Cincinnati, OH: South-Western College Publishing.

Farson, R. (1996). *Management of the absurd.* New York: Simon & Schuster.

Schreiner, O. (1883). *The story of a South African farm.* Retrieved on November 1, 2005, from http://www.zetetics.com/indfem/afrii2.htm

Togneri, W., & Anderson, S. E. (2003). *Beyond islands of excellence: What districts can do to improve instruction and achievement in all schools.* Washington, DC: Learning First Alliance.

About the Authors

Francis M. Duffy is a professor of change leadership in education at Gallaudet University in Washington, DC, where he coordinates an education specialist degree program in change leadership and teaches in a doctoral program in education leadership. He is also currently serving as a member of the Educational Leadership Constituent Council (ELCC), and he is the founding editor of Rowman & Littlefield Education's Leading Systemic School Improvement Series.

Dr. Duffy was a 2002–2003 Education Policy Fellow with the Institute for Educational Leadership. He also held an honorary postdoctoral faculty position in the Harvard Graduate School of Education that was sponsored by Professor Chris Argyris, and he served as a member of the board of directors for the Association for Supervision and Curriculum Development, as well as serving as the president of the Council of Professors of Instructional Supervision (COPIS). His experience includes service as a special education teacher in Pennsylvania where he is also certified as a special education supervisor, supervisor of instruction (K–12), and as an assistant executive director of an intermediate unit.

His bachelor of science degree is in special education from Mansfield University in Pennsylvania and his master's and doctor of philosophy degrees are in curriculum and supervision from the University of Pittsburgh. He also has a second master's degree in business administration from The Johns Hopkins University.

His books include *Power, Politics and Ethics in School Districts: Dynamic Leadership for Systemic Change; Moving Upward Together: Creating Strategic Alignment to Sustain Systemic School Improvement;* and *Courage, Passion and Vision: A Guide to Leading Systemic School Improvement.* He may be contacted at 301-854-9800 or at duffy@the fmduffygroup.com.

Patti L Chance is an associate professor in the Department of Educational Leadership and program coordinator for PK–12 Education Leadership at the University of Nevada, Las Vegas. She has served as a building-level principal, assistant principal, and as a coordinator for K–12 gifted education programs, and she has taught at the elementary, middle school, and high school levels. Dr. Chance serves as the editor of *The Rural Educator,* a national, refereed journal. In addition, she serves on editorial boards for several other national journals devoted to educational leadership and has published articles and chapters related to instructional supervision, educational administration preparation programs, and the application of organizational and leadership theory to the practice of education leadership. She is coauthor of *An Introduction to Educational Leadership and Organizational Behavior: Theory Into Practice,* an introductory text for educational administration.

Her Bachelor of Arts degree is in political science from the University of Oklahoma. She earned her Masters of Education in educational administration from South Dakota State University and her Ph.D. in educational administration, curriculum, and supervision from the University of Oklahoma.

She may be reached at patti.chance@UNLV.edu.

Strikes, xxii, 9, 15–16, 24, 57–58, 60, 79–80, 326, 381, 382; commercial, 73, 103n.8; hunger, 87; Israeli Arab sympathy, 344–45, 349. *See also* Sit-ins
Students, 12, 17, 55–56, 87; in 1936–39 uprising, 21
Student unions, 82, 83
Suez Canal, 312
Sumud, 19
Sununu, John, 257
Surani, Jamal, 357
Survey of American Jewish Leaders (SAJL), 221
Syria, xviii, 188n.150; vs. Arafat, 58, 100, 193, 205–10, 214; and Camp David accords, 115; and Chinese missilery, 150; defeat of in 1967, 38; Egypt and, 149, 208; Fatah support by, 38; and Intifada, 191, 192, 205–10, 214, 215; and Iraq, 149, 184n.52, 208; vs. Israeli Lebanon invasion, 52; and Jordan, 198, 206; and Lebanon, 52, 53, 76; and new Palestinian state, 196; and Palestine, 46; and Palestinian Arab accommodation of Israel, 28; and Palestinian Arabs, 19, 133; and PLO, 47, 50, 53, 76, 149, 205–10; religious extremism in, 69n.40; Shevardnadze in, 158–60; and Shultz Plan, 142; and Soviet Union, 149–50, 158–60, 177, 180, 184nn.51, 54. *See also* Assad, al-Hafiz; Golan Heights; Saiqa

Taba, 297
Talas, Mustapha, 184n.50
Tamari, Salim, 357
Tamil-Nadu, 68n.40
Tamils, 68n.40
Tamir, Avraham, 327
Tarasov, Genadi, 147, 158, 173, 174
Tarifi, Jamil, 92
Tartus (Syria), Soviet navy in, 150
Taxes, Israeli, 372
Tehiya, 271, 303, 329; birth of, 307
Tel Aviv: Arabs attacked in, 48; violence near, 229, 258
Temple Mount, violence on, 258
Terrorism: against airliners/terminals, 261n.28; Arafat's renunciation of, xi, 30, 90, 116, 136, 235, 242, 247, 248, 282n.6; Gorbachev's view of, 138–39; by Israeli Arabs, xxi, 345, 361; Israeli citizens' attitudes toward, 279; in occupied territories, 39, 39n., 48, 49, 247; PLO, 40, 65n.6, 183n.25, 185n.62; "rejectionist," 50; on Tel Aviv beachfront, 258; transnational, 49–50
Tibi, Ahmad, 362
Tourism: Europe to Israel, 378; Intifada and Israeli, xii, xxii, 370, 377–78; Israeli to Soviet Union, 164; Lebanon war and Israeli, 377; Soviets and Israeli, xvii; terrorism and, 261n.28, 377; U.S. to Europe, 261n.28; U.S., to Israel, 229–30, 261n.28, 378
Tourists: murder of Israeli, 258; Soviet Jews as Israeli, 145, 175, 183n.28
Trade, Soviet-Israeli, 175, 177–78, 179
Trade unions: as element in Intifada, 12, 55, 81–82; in 1936–39 uprising, 21; PFLP, 82
Transjordan, 19. *See also* Abdallah ibn-Hussein
Trans-Siberian Railway, crash on, 164, 180
Triangle, the: effects of partition on, 358; PLO flags in, 349; strikes in, 344
Tripoli (Lebanon), Arafat driven from, 206
Tubi, Tawfiq, 366n.21
Tunisia, Arafat retreat to, 53, 56
Turkey: Israel laborers from, 380. *See also* Ottoman Empire
Tzomet, 303, 329

UAHC. *See* Union of American Hebrew Congregations
UJA. *See* United Jewish Appeal
Ukrainian Soviet Socialist Republic, 188n.129
Ulamas, 22–23
Umm al-Fahm, xxi, 354
Unemployment: Israeli, 336, 372, 379–80; among Palestinians, xiv, 5
Unified Command. *See* Unified National Leadership of the Uprising
Unified National Leadership of the Uprising (UNLU), v, 21, 31, 56–60, 72–76, 81, 84, 91, 198, 350; founding of, 72; and HAMAS contrasted, 79–80; and Islamic Jihad, 78, and Israeli Arabs, 357; makeup of, 75, 98; PLO and, 57–60; power of, 93; religious front vs., 59–60,

Unified National Leadership of the Uprising (*continued*)
64; Shamir plan rejected by, 212. *See also* Democratic Front for the Liberation of Palestine; Fatah; Jordan, West Bank renounced by; Palestine Communist Party; Popular Front for the Liberation of Palestine
Union of American Hebrew Congregations (UAHC), 254
Unions. *See* Trade unions
United Arab Emirates, financial aid to PLO from, 195
United Jewish Appeal (UJA), 222, 224, 225, 226–27; "Passage to Freedom" campaign of, 261n.18; Shamir before, 251
United Kingdom. *See* Britain
United Nations: Arafat before, 117, 156, 245, 329–30, 360; depoliticization of, 189n.155; double standard of, 258; Israel condemned by, 140, 258; lobbied by Arafat, 13; and Palestinian question, 14, 90, 144, 152–53; PLO status in, 171–72, 181, 360; proposed ouster of Israel from General Assembly of, 178; relief agencies of, 346; and Zionism/racism equation, 169, 171–72, 178, 189n.155
United Nations Relief and Works Agency (UNRWA), 346
United States: and aid to Israel, 126, 127, 133, 150, 195, 227–30, 256, 257, 372; Arafat/PLO and, 14; Egypt and, xviii, 210, 212–14; and Intifada, xi, xvi, 109–35; Israel and, 27, 145 (*see also* U.S., and aid to Israel); Jews of (*see* American Jews); and Lebanon, 110–11; 1987 stock market crash in, 260n.11; and Palestinian question, 29–30; and PLO, xvi, xix, 14, 16, 26, 87, 90, 102, 116–17, 120–21, 124, 128, 145, 155–56, 162, 180–81, 189n.154, 235, 242–45, 259, 264n.72, 282n.6, 330; PLO public image in, 241, 244–45; pre-Intifada policies of, 110–13; and proposed territorial elections, 331; Soviet Jews as immigrants to, 165, 167, 169, 172, 178; and Soviet Union, 111, 137, 140, 141–43, 163, 169–72, 189n.154; and UN condemnation of Israel, 258. *See also* American Jews; Baker, James; Bush, George; Dole, Robert; Reagan, Ronald; Shultz, George
United States Interreligious Committee for Peace in the Middle East, 234
Universities, Palestinian, 55
UNLU. *See* Unified National Leadership of the Uprising
UNRWA. *See* United Nations Relief and Works Agency
USSR. *See* Soviet Union
U.S. Trade Representative, (USTR), 382–83

Venice Declaration, 14
Vietnam, as PLO inspiration, 40, 41, 63n.7, 89
Village Leagues, 93–94
Vilner, Meir, 349
Vocational schools, Palestinian, 55
Voice of Palestine, 72–73
Vorontsov, Yuli, 170, 173, 181
Vorspan, Max, 265n.96

Wadi Ara highway, blockading of, 345
al-Watan, 350
Water, Israeli restrictions on Arab use of, 55
al-Wazir, Khalil, 72, 77, 82–83, 101, 198; assassination of, 145–46, 206–7, 327
Weizman, Ezer, 166, 299, 300, 306, 328, 338; as Labor party force among Arabs, 354; and Peres, 340n.16; PLO meeting with, 362; and Rabin, 340n.16; Shamir vs., 175; Shevardnadze and, 175; WWII record of, 190n.177
Weizmann, Chaim, 32n.5
West Bank, xi, 15, 17, 84, 144; annexation of, 311–14; Bush calls for Israeli withdrawal from, 212; business restrictions in, 55; charitable organizations of, 83; Christian population of, 77; communism in, 81, 348; construction workers from, 376; economy of, xxii, 31, 370–71, 373–74, 380–85; elections proposed in, 121, 128, 174 (*see also* Shamir, Yitzhak, election proposals of); ethnic makeup of, 42; exports/imports of, 373; as "inherently Israeli," 311; Islamic millennialism in, 77; Israeli administration of, 19; Israeli conciliatory efforts in, xiv; and Israeli security, 294; Jordan-paid civil servants of, 202, 217n.32, 327, 382;

labor unions of, 81–82; land seizures in, 55; Likud position on, 51; religious life of, 354; renounced by Jordan, 26, 115–16, 151, 152, 180, 192, 197, 200, 215, 294, 330, 337; represented in Jordan's parliament, 198; Russian immigrants to, 173; school closings in, 80; schools of, 74; Shultz on, 243; strikes in, 79–80, 326; water restrictions in, 55; women's groups of, 81; youth movement in, 53–55. *See also* Palestinian Arabs
West Bank Data Project, 55
Western Wall, violence at, 258
West Germany, and Israeli reparations, 316
WFTU. *See* World Federation of Trade Unions
White Paper (1939), 15, 26
Wirshubsky, Mordecai, 328
Women: Israeli, 273–74, 277; in 1936–39 uprising, 21; of occupied territories, 12, 17, 81, 82, 83
World Congress of Jewish Studies, Soviet scholars at, 165

World Federation of Trade Unions (WFTU), 140

Yahad, 328
Yanai, Nathan, xiii, xx–xxi
Yarrow, Peter, 265n.96
Yasin, Ahmed, xv, 79, 80–81, 100, 355, 356
Al-Yawm al-Sabi', 89
Yom Kippur War, 293, 300; American Jewish financial support of, 225
Yoseph, Ovadia, 305
Young, Ronald, 234
Young Men's Muslim Associations, 21
Youth groups, 57, 83. *See also* Students

Zionism: alleged cooperation with Nazism, 190n.177; as "racism," 169, 171–72, 178, 189n.155; as Soviet bugbear, 139
Zionists: Hashemite courting of, 7; Palestinian Arabs vs., 5–36, 39–42; "Revisionist," 9
Ziyyad, Tawfiq, 349, 350, 359, 366n.21
Zotov, Alexander, 146